Highways and Heartaches

ALSO BY MICHAEL STREISSGUTH

HIGHWAYS
AND
HEARTACHES

How Ricky Skaggs, Marty Stuart, and
Children of the New South Saved
the Soul of Country Music

MICHAEL
STREISSGUTH

New York

Hachette Books
Hachette Book Group
1290 Avenue of the Americas
New York, NY 10104
HachetteBooks.com
Twitter.com/HachetteBooks
Instagram.com/HachetteBooks

First Edition: August 2023

Published by Hachette Books, an imprint of Hachette Book Group, Inc. The Hachette Books name and logo are trademarks of Hachette Book Group, Inc.

The Hachette Speakers Bureau provides a wide range of authors for speaking events.

To find out more, go to www.hachettespeakersbureau.com or call (866) 376-6591.

Books by Hachette Books may be purchased in bulk for business, educational, or promotional use. For information, please contact your local bookseller or Hachette Book Group Special Markets Department at special.markets@hbgusa.com.

The publisher is not responsible for websites (or their content) that are not owned by the publisher.

Print book interior design by Jeff Williams.

Library of Congress Cataloging-in-Publication Data
Names: Streissguth, Michael, author.
Title: Highways and heartaches : how Ricky Skaggs, Marty Stuart, and children of the
    New South saved the soul of country music / Michael Streissguth.
Description: First edition. | New York : Hachette Books, 2023. | Includes bibliographical
    references and index.
Identifiers: LCCN 2022061400 | ISBN 9780306826108 (hardcover) | ISBN 9780306826122
    (ebook)
Subjects: LCSH: Bluegrass music–History and criticism. | Country music–History and
    criticism. | Skaggs, Ricky. | Stuart, Marty. | New South (Musical group) | Southern
    States–Civilization–20th century.
Classification: LCC ML3520 .S68 2023 | DDC 781.64209–dc23/eng/20221227
LC record available at https://lccn.loc.gov/2022061400

ISBNs: 9780306826108 (hardcover); 9780306826122 (ebook)

Printed in the United States of America

LSC-C

Printing 1, 2023

*Dedicated to participants in this book
who passed before publication*

J. D. CROWE
(1937–2021)

BILL EMERSON
(1938–2021)

ROLAND WHITE
(1938–2022)

CONTENTS

PROLOGUE

CAMPER VANS AND station wagons from as far away as Washington, DC, to the east and San Francisco to the west rumbled along the green highways of Brown County in southern Indiana to the Bean Blossom Festival, one of the nation's marquee gatherings of bluegrass music talent. It was late spring of 1971, the fourth anniversary of the festival, and the travelers anticipated performances by young innovators such as the Bluegrass Alliance from Louisville, Kentucky, and the popular banjoist and songwriter John Hartford, along with stars from the so-called golden era such as Jim and Jesse McReynolds and the Goins Brothers, who emerged in the early 1950s. "If the audience seemed geographically diverse, the stylistic array of artists at the fifth festival was truly stunning," wrote Bean Blossom biographer Thomas A. Adler.

Entering a wonderland of mesmerizing jam sessions and Technicolor tour buses owned by the legends of bluegrass, the fans rushed to the main stage set in a grove of straight and tall trees, looking out for fellow music lovers from previous visits, many of them bluegrass aficionados who contributed essays to fan publications and maintained discographies of old-time music.

Pilgrims with Nixon bumper stickers and those who identified with the ethos of Woodstock and the counterculture bonded over their love of organically grown music and the sovereign of bluegrass, Bill Monroe, who owned the festival. Born in Rosine,

Kentucky, in 1911, Monroe and his band the Blue Grass Boys had first come to this area outside of Indianapolis in 1951 to play the Brown County Jamboree, a family-owned music park. So enamored was Monroe of the Jamboree grounds and the dedicated fans who flocked there that he bought the venue in 1952, staging his first Bean Blossom Festival in 1967.

With the help of his older brother Birch and his son James, musicians in their own right, he cared for the festival grounds with single-mindedness, cleaning up debris from the previous winter's storms and repairing various buildings on the campus in preparation for the festival season. Proud like a grandfather, Monroe welcomed Bean Blossom visitors, many of whom had come expressly to see him. He engaged them in conversation and, to the lucky few, showed off the farm animals he raised on the property. Only the Blue Grass Boys felt the sting that he was better known for inside the country music industry, as they were pressed into service at the festival grounds to cut back brush and stock the concession stand when they converged on southern Indiana.

Monroe kept draft horses at Bean Blossom that were like children to him, recalls mandolinist Ron Thomason, who served in Ralph Stanley's Clinch Mountain Boys for a year starting in the spring of 1970. "When one of the horses died, the old man wept," he says, "and he was determined that that horse wasn't going to go to his grave in a front loader on a tractor. He and Birch and Ralph and me, maybe forty of us together that day, managed to dig a grave for that horse. Monroe insisted on dragging it over to the grave. It wasn't far, maybe twenty feet. This was probably a fifteen-hundred-pound horse, and it was amazing how he felt about it."

A suspicious man, treated like an outsider in his own family during childhood, Monroe wandered the eastern half of the nation in the early days of commercial country music, first with his brother Charlie as the Monroe Brothers and then with his band of underpaid musicians, many of whom cycled through his employ like drivers at a busy toll booth, especially during the lean years of the late 1950s when rock and roll nearly killed country music. "In 1958, I went with Bill Monroe, and I almost starved to death," says banjoist Eddie Adcock. "The biggest amount of money I got from him was seventeen dollars. So needless to say, I could not make it, so I didn't stay with him very long." Monroe toured at a scorching pace, playing the *Grand Ole Opry* in his home base of Nashville on Saturday nights before speeding off to weekday engagements hundreds of miles away.

Home to Monroe was an abstraction. In the early days, parents of his musicians who happened to live on his meandering concert circuit waited with home-cooked dinners to create a temporary sense of domestic life, and for long stretches he traveled with a road wife—bassist Bessie Lee Mauldin—who stood in for his lawful wife, Carolyn, at home near Nashville with his children. Brown County, too, was a nest where he could preside over a sprawling community drawn to an art form that owed its very existence to him.

IN ADDITION TO Hartford, Jim and Jesse, and other performers, the Bean Blossom Festival of 1971 advertised the appearance of Lester Flatt and his band the Nashville Grass, igniting furious speculation about whether Monroe and Flatt himself—famously enemies at this point—might reunite onstage. By this time, Flatt had done as much to popularize the bluegrass tradition in country music as Monroe himself, having been part of a one-two punch with banjo innovator Earl Scruggs in Monroe's band during the 1940s that further developed the sound that later became known as bluegrass. But Flatt and Scruggs had left the band in 1948 and soon formed their own group, which roiled Monroe yet finally took bluegrass music into the heart of popular culture. Prone to resentment, Monroe saw their departure as the ultimate betrayal. For years, he prevented his former friends from joining the *Grand Ole Opry*, and when Flatt and Scruggs finally did join the cast of the radio jamboree in 1955, he routinely snubbed them.

However, by 1971 Monroe had mellowed, at least where Flatt was concerned, and through diplomatic channels worthy of the Vietnam War peace negotiations in Paris, he persuaded his old guitarist and lead vocalist to come to Bean Blossom. Flatt performed with his Nashville Grass throughout the festival, but on closing day Monroe, in his familiar western-cut suit, addressed what his biographer Richard D. Smith called the "unbearable anticipation." He invited Flatt to join him onstage, and they sang "Little Cabin Home on the Hill," lifted by Monroe's high tenor, while Flatt revealed his just-folks grin.

THE MUSICIANS WEDGED into Ralph Stanley's bus on the way to Bean Blossom after a festival date in Canada could have been fooled into thinking they were in Kentucky horse country, the land in Brown County was so green and undulating in contrast to the flat terrain more typical of Indiana. But most of them had traveled this way before, bemusedly noting the signs pointing to the nearby village with the familiar name of Nashville.

Perched in the front passenger seat, Stanley—the dean of mountain music—had carried on the legacy of the Stanley Brothers for five years since the death of his brother, Carter, whose golden vocals had driven their prosperous act. Alone, Ralph perfected a keening tenor style to accentuate the gothic overtones of his music. He rarely failed to hush his audience. But to please the ever-present Stanley Brothers fans, he had taken to traveling with two Kentucky-born teenagers—Ricky Skaggs and Keith Whitley—who capably reproduced the Stanley Brothers' familiar vocal blend. Skaggs's high tenor and Whitley's earnest lead singing transported audiences back to the standards: "I Long to See the Old Folks," "Don't Cheat in Our Hometown," "The Lonesome River," and others.

The boys—Skaggs from the community of Brushy Creek in Lawrence County and Whitley from tiny Sandy Hook in Ellicott County—had struck up a friendship barely a year earlier over their mutual love of Carter and Ralph, honing their heroes' sound in Whitley's garage and in high school talent shows. Stanley had encountered Skaggs—a child prodigy—on one of his frequent jaunts through eastern Kentucky where people craved the mountain ballads, and when he ran across Skaggs and Whitley at a country music park in Ohio, he invited them to the stage. But a later meeting in Fort Gay, West Virginia, sealed their collective fate. The boys had come with Skaggs's father to see Stanley and the Clinch Mountain Boys play a beer joint, but car troubles delayed the headliner, so Ricky and Keith unpacked their instruments and gave the audience a credible tour of the Stanley Brothers' greatest hits. When Stanley walked in like a wary outlaw, he could only take a seat while the music transported him.

On the bus to Bean Blossom in 1971, the seemingly preordained moment in West Virginia was still a recent memory. School had closed for the year, freeing the lads to travel with Stanley, although both would soon abandon formal education altogether. Long bus rides at this point still represented adventure, so they chirped about the festival, knowing Monroe was bound to be walking his grounds, greeting fans out among the tents and fireside guitar pulls.

In Stanley's employ, sixteen-year-old Skaggs crossed paths with Monroe at festivals and other venues every few weeks and witnessed up close the idiosyncrasies of the legend whom he had first encountered a decade earlier. When Skaggs was six years old, his father, Hobert, never shy about insinuating his talented youngster on big-time bluegrass talent, took the kid to a Monroe show in Martha, Kentucky, and suggested the skeptical artist give his son a turn on the stage. When the local audience began calling the child's name, Monroe hoisted him up among his musicians and tenderly adjusted the strap of his own mandolin before draping it over the boy's shoulder. Skaggs recalls singing "Ruby," his party piece, the standard associated with Cousin Emmy and, later, the Osborne Brothers. The crowd whooped and hollered, pleased to see one of their own in the spotlight, as Monroe guided him down from the stage. Undoubtedly, Skaggs touched the torch that day. But he also experienced the master's tender side.

WHILE STANLEY AND the Clinch Mountain Boys bounced into southern Indiana in that spring of 1971, a young musician named Marty Stuart traveled up from the Deep South, shoe-horned into a late-model station wagon among a host of genuine central Mississippi characters: his father, John, a steady supporter of his boy's talent, and a gospel trio known as the Page Family. They planned to rendezvous with the teenage banjo and guitar wizard Carl Jackson, who hailed from their part of the state and would be playing Bean Blossom with Jim and Jesse and the Virginia Boys.

Stuart—a mandolinist, though he could handle most any stringed instrument—had, like Skaggs, experienced Bill Monroe early in life, but indirectly. At home in Philadelphia, Mississippi, he had ambled into Frank Tank's discount store near downtown and left with the bluegrass king's "Wicked Path of Sin" on Columbia Records—the very first gospel number Monroe ever wrote.

Later in life, Stuart's fellow musicians noticed how he reacted obsessively to a new musical stimulus, chasing it down, owning it. And this is what happened when he discovered bluegrass in the late 1960s. He picked up the mandolin and, for a while, rested his guitar, filing away the Johnny Cash records scattered around his bedroom and searching for more music by Monroe and Flatt and Scruggs. "I wanted to know more about this stuff that Bill Monroe was playing," he says. "I just liked it, so I started hunting around for anybody to talk about bluegrass with."

Which was a challenge in the birth state of the blues. Some people knew about Carl Sauceman and the Green Valley Boys who barnstormed through Alabama, Mississippi, and Louisiana and starred in a syndicated television show that aired in local markets.

But few would give up their tickets to a semipro baseball game to see them. A sparse number of disc jockeys in the region spun Flatt and Scruggs and the Osborne Brothers. Yet, says Stuart, "You could have filled one car in the state of Mississippi with people that professed to like bluegrass music at that point in time."

Fortunately, Stuart found himself in that one car, snaking up north through Tennessee and on into Kentucky via the new US interstates. He was twelve years old.

In the vehicle, the Page Family—featuring Marzell and his wife, Audean, and daughter Kathy—lived close to Stuart's home, and on his way to school, he often noted the Pages' old tour bus, purchased from Jim and Jesse, who had bought it from Flatt and Scruggs, though the bus didn't run and weeds climbed up to the windows. The boy could discern the faint lettering of the original owners' names under Jim and Jesse's more recent paint job, but as far as anyone could tell, the Pages neither added their name nor drove it very much.

The Page Family had made records produced by Carl Jackson's father, Lethal, who also promoted live shows, hosted a bluegrass radio program, and played country music himself. "I would go to their house," says Stuart, "and spend two or three days at a time after I bought a mandolin from his dad. They were really patient and really kind and showed me how to play, and Carl and I loved talking about baseball and girls and dreaming. And he was already working on the *Grand Ole Opry* and on TV with *Grand Ole Opry* acts. So he was like a superstar to me."

From the backseat, Marty longed to see the many Bean Blossom giants in one place: Lester Flatt, Bill Monroe, Jimmy Martin. Fantasizing about playing on the stage, he carried his mandolin, but he was destined only to ogle the tour buses with famous names emblazoned on the side and help sell Jim and Jesse albums with Carl Jackson.

"The first two people I laid eyes on were Keith Whitley and Ricky Skaggs getting off Ralph Stanley's bus in those tuxedo coats," he recalls. "I thought, 'Wow, there's young people. Who are those boys?' Ralph Stanley was like somebody from the Old Testament to me, and here's these young guys with him. And over the weekend I heard them play, and I said, 'I don't know where these guys are from, but they're the real deal, absolutely.'"

Throughout Stuart's childhood, the future appeared unrelentingly, powerfully in concerts, country music television shows, and the long touring buses splattered with mud barreling past his house on their way to Jackson or Meridian. In Bean Blossom, a compelling, perhaps urgent, notion of the future appeared again, this time in the body of Skaggs and Whitley, young unknowns traveling with one of the top names on the southeastern bluegrass circuit and beyond.

Incredibly, Stuart would join Lester Flatt's traveling bluegrass band little more than a year later.

SKAGGS AND STUART at Bean Blossom were heirs to a bluegrass tradition transmitted to them early in life. One part mountain soul and another African American–influenced blues, the music they received would be alternately celebrated and neglected in the more than fifty years after the two met in 1971, but it has never stopped evolving and influencing the wider American culture thanks to the prodigies of Bean Blossom and other actors in this book, such as Jerry Douglas, Tony Rice, Keith Whitley, and Emmylou Harris.

Molded by forces in postwar southern culture such as racial conflict, economic and political ferment, evangelicalism, growing federal government influence, and stubborn patterns of Appalachian living and thinking, Skaggs and Stuart injected the spirit of bluegrass into their hard-wrought experiments in mainstream country music later in life, fueling the profitability and, more important, the credibility of the fabled genre. Skaggs's new traditionalism of the 1980s, integrating mountain instruments with elements of contemporary country music, created a new sound for the masses and placed him in the vanguard of Nashville's recording artists. When new traditionalism as a marketing label faded in the 1990s, Skaggs returned to bluegrass, while Stuart—frustrated by his own experiences in the mainstream—embraced seminal influences and attitudes from the riches of American culture to produce, starting in 2005, a line of significant recordings, including *Badlands: Ballads of the Lakota,* an album containing some of the sharpest social commentary anywhere in popular music.

Skaggs and Stuart formed a friendship that jelled only in recent years, but their similar pathways reveal a shared dedication to the soul of country music and highlight the curious day-to-day experiences of two lads growing up on the demanding rural route in bluegrass culture. Their journeys—populated by grizzled mentors, fearsome undertows, and cultural upheaval—influenced their artistic creations and, ultimately, cut life-giving tributaries in the ungainly, eternal story of country music.

1

Get the Music Out

IN THE LATE 1950s, when John Marty Stuart was born, residents in central Mississippi and beyond converged on the city of Philadelphia once a year for the weeklong Neshoba County Fair, known from Horn Lake to Hattiesburg as the state's "Giant Houseparty." An exclusive colony of shabby summer houses on the fairgrounds buzzed on weekends throughout the season, reaching fever pitch during fair week's carnival amusements, harness races, and political campaigning. Musicians from as far away as Nashville came, too—stars Skeeter Davis and Jean Shepard and Shepard's husband, Hawkshaw Hawkins, performed in the summer of 1959, sharing the bill with local rock and rhythm bands such as Andy Anderson and the Dawn Busters. The gospel-singing LeFevres from Georgia rousted the crowds, too, their purring message of Christian love in stark contrast to the antigovernment, anti-Black rants of politicians that had been a mainstay at the fair since its founding in the late nineteenth century.

As the civil rights movement gathered momentum in the late 1950s and early 1960s, white candidates for state office in Mississippi competed for the white crowd's loyalty with loud invective, fearful of being branded a "moderate," particularly on the subject of race relations. "Either you believe in states' rights, or you believe in turning over this state to a black minority," shouted Lieutenant

1

Governor Paul B. Johnson in his 1963 address, which was laced with epithets in common circulation in white Philadelphia. His audience roared in approval, "chuckl[ing] at the anti-Negro obscenities," reported a visiting journalist.

When the fair dispersed and rabid politicians moved on to other parts of the state, Philadelphia could seem quintessentially suburban—charitable, mindful of image—for a town set in the middle of endless pine forests, offering middle-class white citizens a golf club, public swimming pools, Cub Scout packs, twirling contests, and at least three grocery stores. The VFW hosted chicken dinners, while the Chamber of Commerce sponsored Christmas decorating contests and spearheaded support for a new hospital. In rural parts of the county, where Marty Stuart's parents had grown up and courted, farmers bonded over church suppers and home demonstration clubs. And with every new year in the 1950s and 1960s, that binding wire of middle-American life, the telephone, appeared in more and more homes, forecasting what seemed to be greater prosperity.

Such optimism was not unfounded even as rural families in the county abandoned the farms and lumber mills to join common migration patterns to cities and towns outside the South. Along with recreational amenities, Neshoba County boasted manufacturing companies that produced gloves and furniture, minimizing the flow of citizens relocating to St. Louis and Chicago. Stuart's father had found work in the brand-new US Motors plant that, according to the company, "employed 400 people who turned out 10,000 motors and components per month." His mother, Hilda, tapping into the thriving service sector, worked in a bank.

The young couple had married in 1952 and relocated to central New Jersey, where John was stationed in the army. Their first time living outside Neshoba County, they merged into a culture more tolerant of racial mixing than in their segregated hometown and explored sites and cities throughout the region, Hilda all the while snapping photos of the people and places they encountered. Hilda recalls their Italian landlords who treated them like family, and nobody blinked when she took a job in an airplane factory. Riveting photos from Hilda's portfolio reveal a couple coming alive while exploring the world together.

Hilda's photography, shaped by her work at uncle George Day's prosperous portrait studio in downtown Philadelphia, revealed an artist's soul. A trained eye could appreciate in every new image her attention to composition, depth of field, and the personality, if not the spirit, of her subject. Her framing of baptisms and family reunions in Neshoba County would not have been out of place in the archives of the Library of Congress with the work of photo documentarians Walker Evans and Dorothea Lange. Closer to ground, Hilda made sure her children—Marty born in 1958 and daughter Jennifer in 1960—were amply portrayed in her photo albums.

Set against the assigned roles of women during the 1950s and 1960s, rigorously defined in Mississippi, Hilda's photography communicated a certain modernism. Her choice to work outside the home and delay starting a family until six years into her marriage implied the same. When John was discharged from the army in 1953, they headed back to Neshoba County, where Hilda would prove to be the family's most reliable breadwinner and, in her son's eyes, a reasonable adjudicator of childish controversies and a sound font of advice. "I think Mama was my ally because Daddy was busy. It seemed like work always took him away, and when it came to important decisions that mattered, she was readily available and would hear me out and consider it and not just cave in and give me my way. There were some stern 'no's' along the way, but it was always halfway reasonable. I could always count on Mom to consider it."

The couple rented a small house at 407 Choctaw Gardens, and John went to work as a runner in George Day's studio, and then a brick mason, before landing at the US Motors manufacturing plant.

Stuart paints a picture of an obliging father, amicably following his son wherever the music took him and prone to innocent missteps recounted around café tables for years and years, like when John's brother accidently shot him with John's own gun on a deer hunt. And he was frequently kind, says Stuart.

> I remember Daddy coming in and waking me up one morning, and his sister's husband, Charles, was down in southern Mississippi working on a construction job. Somehow, the boys were out having fun in a café and a remark was passed to a deputy's girlfriend. Bottom line, they wound up in jail, and one thing led to another, and Charles was shot and killed. I remember when Daddy was telling me he had tears in his eyes. Until he got old, I never saw him cry hardly ever. Daddy was not a hard-hearted person. Like a lot of guys during those days, he ran his mouth a lot as an overlooked southern man probably still does, but I didn't see any malice in his heart.

In 1961 Hilda and John purchased a new brick rambler on Kosciusko Road and hired a Black woman named Jimmie Richmond to watch the kids during the workweek. In the new home, they were close to their friends Jane and Norford Hodgins, who had served in the army with them in New Jersey. "We would get together on Sundays after church at Marty's house because Hilda had a piano," remembers Butch Hodgins, Jane and Norford's eldest son. "A lady named Lillian Killen would play the piano, and we would gather around the piano and sing old gospel hymns out of the church songbook, like a quartet." While coffee and cake were passed around, Hilda, Jane, and Lillian would break out into their church trio to practice for the following week's services. Sacred songs recorded by the Chuck Wagon Gang and the Singing Rambos, beloved throughout the South, rated among the favorites of all living-room warblers.

Sharing in his family's prosperity, Stuart had received an acoustic guitar by 1967, when Johnny Cash and Buck Owens had sunk into his brain, and he then graduated to a Japanese-made Teisco

Del Ray electric guitar, which clung to his body as he wandered throughout his house. Still marveling at the memory, Hilda Stuart recalls the day her son sat down in the kitchen just picking and singing while she cooked dinner. When he finished, he glanced up and predicted he'd play the *Grand Ole Opry* in Nashville. "It made me stop and think, 'Well that was a dead serious statement. I better listen.'"

Like Elvis Presley, born a generation earlier in Tupelo, Mississippi, who loved the sacred melodies of church and the blues in the Black houses around his house, young Stuart gravitated to the religious and secular songs permeating Philadelphia. A neighbor who owned a dry-cleaning business downtown used to perch Marty on his front counter and let him flail away on a guitar made of cardboard, and when the boy finished there, he scampered down the street to a Black-owned luncheonette and barbershop called the Busy Bee Cafe. Hanging on the joint's screen door, often with sister Jennifer, he perked up at the jukebox's alluring rhythm. "We'd be looking in," recalls Jennifer, "and it was all Black people and they'd get so tickled at us. But they always had good music, and they always had the best-smelling food ever."

By the late 1960s, Stuart formed a little trio with Jane and Norford's boys, Butch and Ricky, which evolved into another group of five or six young people, including his sister and a kid who played the trombone. Now brandishing a Fender Mustang electric guitar, Marty called the band the Country Kids. "Marty and I were also in a talent contest at the Neshoba County Fair," says Jennifer. "It was just he and I. He played guitar. But we lost to a baton twirler."

The local postmaster, Bobby Barrett, often showed up at the Stuarts' house for country music jam sessions and helped Stuart and the Hodgins boys and the rest of the Country Kids to score gigs at the Rotary Club and the Lion's Club, in addition to Cub Scout meetings and birthday parties, where they played Johnny Cash, Merle Haggard, and Buck Owens. "We thought we were great," says Butch Hodgins. "All of us played the guitar, and we'd be arguing over who was going to take the lead on 'Folsom Prison

Blues,' that break that Luther Perkins played. I guess whoever was singing ended up taking it."

On Kosciusko Road, Stuart was an unusual playmate. He organized football games in his family's backyard, only to retreat inside with his guitar to observe the competition from the window. And there were very few male schoolmates interested in fashion, but he and Jennifer took note of the flashy visual motif of *The Porter Wagoner Show*, especially Wagoner's trademark costumes that shimmered like a Las Vegas casino. "Doc" and "Sis," their nicknames for each other, sketched out designs for stage costumes while Jennifer patched them together on her grandmother's old sewing machine. Early pictures of the children bear witness to their adventurous tastes, Marty in bell bottoms when they came into style, with a scarf tied carefully around his neck.

IN ONE INTERPRETATION of Stuart's suburban-like childhood, children played freely, adults swam and golfed in public facilities, and fathers and mothers raised families with a sense of unlimited possibility. But no such scenarios were accessible to the Black citizens of Philadelphia who were often denied the simple freedom to walk the streets without fear of harassment.

In Neshoba County, the most dangerous threat to Black people was the Sheriff's Department. Nominally concerned with busting moonshine production on the nearby Choctaw Indian reservation, the department's side hustles were skimming from annual tax payments and terrorizing Black people. Deputy Lawrence Rainey was the worst offender. For no apparent reason, while serving on the city police force in 1959, he had shot dead a Black man named Luther Jackson, born in Philadelphia and back in town visiting from Chicago. When a Black woman named Frances Culbertson, who had witnessed the senseless murder, complained to Deputy Cecil Price—a member of the Ku Klux Klan (KKK)— Rainey arrested her, threw her in jail, and beat her.

Having moved to the Sheriff's Department in 1961, Rainey answered a call from a Black family whose son was apparently in the grips of an epileptic seizure. Rainey drove out and picked up the twenty-seven-year-old to bring him to a state mental hospital. His father tried to come along, but Rainey rebuffed him, leaving unwitnessed what happened next. When the son lashed out on the ride, Rainey shot him like a dog, and the court ruled it "justifiable homicide."

While accommodating Rainey, most of the Philadelphia community also tolerated citizen brigades on the streets of downtown, their guns in plain sight, and regular cross burnings by the KKK. On an ominous night in 1964, twelve crosses burned simultaneously in Neshoba County, half of them in Philadelphia proper. Commented a federal investigator probing racial violence there, "In spirit, everyone belonged to the Klan. And as far as what we were hoping to get at, there proved to be no difference between a real Klansman and someone who was not a member but whose friends and neighbors were. Even if they themselves had declined to join the klavern, they identified totally with those who had."

Local customs freed white lawmen and white hate groups to kill or maim Black people, destroy their property, and unlawfully jail them. Any admission of Black humanity or civil rights would be an affront to the white way of life. The murder of Emmett Till in Money, Mississippi, and the assassination of Medgar Evers in Jackson were but two of the outrageous warnings white Mississippians issued to Black people who might be inspired by the liberation message of Martin Luther King Jr. Hundreds of Black people in the Deep South who somehow affronted the established order had met their deaths out of the public eye, their bodies dumped in hidden swamps or burned like tree stumps in the dark woods.

But change was rustling the branches of Neshoba County's loblolly pines. By the early 1960s, intensive voter registration and education projects planned by groups such as the Congress of Racial Equality and the Student Nonviolent Coordinating Committee had stirred the hopes of Black citizens across Mississippi, inspiring many to shed their fears of retribution and assist reform efforts in their cities and towns. Members of the Mount Zion Methodist Church in the Longdale community of Neshoba County were one such group of citizens embracing an attitude of assertiveness. They offered their building to young volunteers, many from the North, who were organizing freedom schools where individual rights as outlined in the US Constitution and voter registration would be discussed, a crucial task as not one Black person had been registered to vote in the county since 1955. The training would take place during the Mississippi Freedom Project in the hot months of 1964, known familiarly as "Freedom Summer."

Among the corps of young people participating in Freedom Summer were James Chaney, from nearby Meridian, and Michael "Mickey" Schwerner and Andrew Goodman, both from the New York City area. Chaney and Schwerner had worked together since the spring of 1964, teaching poor Black children in Meridian and recruiting disenfranchised people to register to vote. They had also met a number of times with the members of Mount Zion Church in Longdale, their visits not unnoticed by allied civil authorities and hate groups.

On the evening of Tuesday, June 16, masked night riders in search of Schwerner attacked members as they emerged from a meeting in the church sanctuary, and then they torched the building. The *Neshoba [County] Democrat* newspaper refused to report on the arson and beatings, but even when the story finally broke in an out-of-state news outlet, few in the white community cared.

Although the marauders missed Schwerner—he'd been in Meridian that night—they remained on alert, and five days after the arson, June 21, less than forty-eight hours after the Civil Rights Act had passed in the US Senate in Washington, they spied him on the Mount Zion grounds with James Chaney and Andrew Goodman, who had arrived in Meridian only the day before.

The events that ensued over the next six weeks would count as one of the bleakest chapters in the struggle for civil rights in

America. Following an elaborate plan devised by Edgar Ray Killen, a prominent Neshoba County resident who called himself a preacher and had received the honorific "colonel" from the governor of Mississippi, and with the assistance of others, including a former high sheriff named Ethel Glen "Hop" Barnett, the three civil rights workers were arrested by Deputy Sheriff Cecil Price while driving back to Meridian, ostensibly for speeding. Price jailed them and then released them once darkness fell. Only they weren't free. The young men's appearance with Price on the courthouse lawn signaled to the other conspirators that Chaney, Schwerner, and Goodman would soon be back on the road to Meridian in their station wagon, easy prey in the pitch-black night.

A convoy of stalkers, with Price back in the picture and in the lead, pulled the young men over and pushed them into another car. At this point, Price headed back toward the city limits, while the remaining conspirators drove their captives to a desolate road and shot them one by one. Their bodies were stuffed into their own station wagon, and they were brought to a nearby farm—with Schwerner still breathing—and buried in an earthen dam.

Acting on tips, the Federal Bureau of Investigation (FBI) coordinated the search for the civil rights workers, drawing in sailors from the Meridian Naval Air Station, while Department of Justice officials on direct orders from President Lyndon B. Johnson pressed agents to solve the case. Finally—after six weeks of silence, speculation, and international media coverage—the young men's bodies were pulled from their damp grave on August 4, 1964. In trials that dragged on throughout the rest of the decade, nobody was convicted of murder. Deputy Cecil Price and six others were convicted only on charges of conspiracy.

WHILE FEDERAL AGENTS poured into Philadelphia to investigate the disappearance of Schwerner, Chaney, and Goodman, coinciding roughly with the debate and passage of the aforementioned Civil Rights Act (1964) and the Voting Rights Act (1965) aimed at states like Mississippi, another brand of federal influence appeared in eastern Kentucky, home to young Rickie Lee (Ricky) Skaggs.

In that consequential year of 1964, President Johnson introduced the Economic Opportunity Act, the first salvo in his War on Poverty and the impetus for programs such as the Job Corps, Head Start, and Volunteers in Service to America. The following year he signed the Appalachian Regional Development Act, sending millions of dollars to improve highways running among isolated communities in the region.

These initiatives targeted urban and rural areas that were bereft of opportunity, but no region of the country felt the expectant gaze of Johnson more than Appalachia, the heart of which lay in eastern Kentucky and Tennessee, western North Carolina, and the Virginias. His predecessor, President John F. Kennedy, shamed by the poverty he witnessed while campaigning in West Virginia in 1960, had convened the Appalachian Regional Commission in 1963 just as journalist Harry Caudill's best-seller *Night Comes to the Cumberlands* hit the bookstores of America, painting the stark environmental and economic degradation in parts of eastern Kentucky as a result of decades of coal mining. Caudill had encountered miners facing starvation while pecking at the edges of exhausted coal pits. He wrote, "With low wages, lack of union membership and protection, and in most instances without even Workmen's Compensation coverage, such a miner is fortunate to keep cornbread and beans on the dinner table in the poor shack he so often calls home."

Parts of Skaggs's home county, Lawrence, though situated north of the abundant coal veins of Harlan, Leslie, and Letcher Counties, nonetheless resembled scenes in Caudill's book. More than 20 percent of the adult population in the county was functionally illiterate, and mining deaths, particularly in out-of-the-way pits such as Caudill described, were frequently reported in the county. No amount of federal dollars would dissolve Appalachia's rust, but within months of the passage of Johnson's welfare initiatives, Lawrence County residents sixteen to twenty-one years of age could sign up for paid job training in the Job Corps, and hundreds of thousands of dollars were dispersed to improve education and housing. In the spirit of Chaney, Schwerner, and Goodman in Mississippi, young idealists from Appalachia itself and other parts of the nation taught children, repaired and modernized homes, and brought medical and counseling services into the tiniest hamlets and hollows. Some were veterans of the Freedom Summer.

Headlines in Lawrence County's weekly newspaper hailed the American taxpayers' contribution to local development, but paradoxically warned of charity's corrosive effect on individual initiative, sentiments echoed even today by Ricky Skaggs:

> We never really saw at the time that it was bad. We saw the government wanting to help the poor, and maybe Bobby Kennedy in his heart wanted to help the poor people because he was from such a rich family, and that's very noble for someone like he and his brother to have compassion for the poor. But in many ways some became worse off than they were even before they came in. If people would let people work, they'd rather work than to have a [welfare] check. . . . I started seeing that after I moved away and people were getting worse off. It takes faith away from you, and it just erases our dependence on God.

Naturally, the influx of national media coverage, money, and volunteers sparked controversy in the 1960s, as many people of the mountain regions found newcomers patronizing or an affront to their religious and political convictions. Many suspected local officials and contractors of pocketing some of that abundant federal money. In some cases, the backlash reached Mississippi-like terror, especially when outside volunteers were thought to be communists. "A lot of them would be caught out driving and they would be run off the road into ditches," said a Kentucky musician who lived through those times. "The reason they did that was because they had these kids here starting to think. Starting to read material other than what we had been handed out in the classroom."

THE SKAGGS FAMILY prospered indirectly from the federal government's focus on eastern Kentucky inasmuch as schools and roads were improved, but Skaggs's people—with 150-year-old roots in the region—eschewed government assistance, relying on their small farms and temporary work in industrial Ohio and other states. Though a few of Skaggs's cousins and friends got caught up in the boom-and-bust cycle of coal mining, his father, Hobert, avoided that kind of work. "He just didn't like being back where there was no sunshine or where it was just so dark you had to take a carbide lamp," explains Skaggs. "So he just said to himself, as he's growing up, he never wanted to be a miner."

Hobert and Dorothy Skaggs, with their four children, Linda, Garold, Ricky, and Gary, lived on fifty acres, much of it on a hillside next to Hobert's parents, in a community known as Brushy Creek, or just "Brushy" to the locals. Their tract emerged near the bottom of a long hollow that awoke in a sweet glow just before the late-afternoon sun disappeared over the ridge. They raised milk cows and tended a considerable vegetable patch that yielded tomatoes, corn, watermelons, cantaloupes, and cucumbers. "I'd go behind Dad and put seeds in the ground," says Skaggs, "and drive stakes in the ground—about four feet high—for beans to climb on. They were a lot easier to pick when they're hanging up in the air."

There was more fun when the boy with the thick auburn hair ambled next door to see his grandfather.

> If he was going to go fishing, I would watch him put new line on his reels and get the hooks ready or I'd watch him milk in the mornings. He'd put his bucket around his arm, put him

in a fresh plug of tobacco, and walk down toward the barn to milk.

There was this big old cat that kind of hung around the barn and caught mice all the time, and that cat sat there every morning, which I could never figure out because my granddad would walk up kind of close and get his chewing tobacco real good and wet and he would spit and hit that cat right in the eye and it would take off at ninety miles an hour. But he had an old hubcap down there in the barn, and he would turn it over and he'd pour that cat some fresh milk.

After sunset on Saturdays, Skaggs called on his grandfather one last time for the day, jumping up into the old pickup truck parked by the barn where they listened to crisp transmissions of the *Grand Ole Opry* broadcast on WSM from Nashville. In the dark, while Bill Monroe galloped through "Molly and Tenbrooks," a classic based on an old folk song, the dim dashboard light revealed Skaggs's fingers in the air trying to keep up with him.

THE YOUNG BILL Monroe fan had known music from an early age. Dorothy—a devout Christian—loved to sing old hymns, and Hobert, who had picked guitar with his mandolin-playing brother Okel before Okel was killed in the Second World War, idolized Monroe and other musicians who played bluegrass music, although, as many experts have pointed out, Monroe's music had yet to be decisively labeled "bluegrass" when Ricky was born on July 18, 1954. Ralph Stanley in southwestern Virginia called his art "mountain music," distinguishing it from Monroe's style, though both lived under the bluegrass tent. Some ballad collectors and urban fans in the 1950s and 1960s simply labeled the bluegrass sound as "folk," while Skaggs himself preferred "mountainish country."

Almost everybody up and down the hollow and throughout the county knew Hobert's love of music, trading stories about the many trashed guitars he salvaged and his friendship with fiddler Paul Johnson when the two men lived in Columbus, Ohio, for a spell in the 1940s. Banned from picking in the tight quarters of their rooming house, Hobert and Paul jumped on a city bus with their instruments and tramped toward the back. "They'd buy transfers," says Larry Cordle, a neighbor of the Skaggs family, "and ride until way up in the night, sometimes until two or three in the morning. I said, 'Did you have people who were listening?' And he said, 'Yeah . . . sometimes people would get transfers and ride around with us so they could hear us play.'" Later, Hobert introduced Paul to Ricky, who would count the older man among his primary influences on the fiddle.

Like the Stuarts, the Skaggs family played at home and in their church, the Low Gap Free Will Baptist Church. But his parents also hosted serious jam sessions known to stretch deep into the night, fueled by Dorothy's cooking and bottles of moonshine tucked under the seats of visitors' cars to be sipped from on breaks because any form of booze was forbidden in the house. Cordle—who played guitar with Hobert's encouragement—mostly remembers the aroma of brewing coffee and the chatter of women playing Rook in a back room.

"People would start gathering in just about dark, and there'd be visiting on the front end of it," he recalls. "But Ricky's dad just couldn't hardly wait until the jam session got started. There'd be a houseful." Young Cordle—who would grow up to be an award-winning songwriter and performer—choked on the thickening cigarette smoke as he waited for the musicians to, as he says, "get the music out," as if the songs themselves had been carried in boxes like precious gifts. "Sometimes them things would go from early evening to the wee hours, until there wouldn't be but two or three of us around, you know. Hobert nearly had to fall over to call it off."

And in the center of the clutch of pickers was the half-pint Ricky, whose instrumental proficiency was discussed in the same breath as Hobert's attentiveness to music. The assumption was strong in observers' minds that father was grooming son for a life in music, perhaps even living vicariously through him—for the lad could sing harmony parts and his hands moved with exceptional dexterity on the fretboard of the mandolin, and he took surprising control of the fiddle and guitar. "People would come to the house and listen to little Ricky," laments Skaggs. "It was like, 'What's the big deal?' I'd have cousins or friends come by, and all the boys and girls my age would get out and run around outside and just have a great time and I'd be sitting in there entertaining grown-ups."

Together, mom, dad, and son played churches and community picnics and climbed onstage with national country stars passing through the region, including at least three times with the Stanley Brothers—in Prestonsburg, Paintsville, and Olive Hill. The family, with cousin Paul "Euless" Wright on fiddle, also trooped to radio station WCTR in nearby Ashland as the "Skaggs Family" for a weekly broadcast, where they performed an array of songs, including two George Jones originals: "Window Up Above" and "Cup of Loneliness."

"Euless could have been a really, really great fiddler if he'd been able to stay off the bottle," says Skaggs.

> I remember Bill Monroe came to Ashland, Kentucky, and bailed him out of jail to go play with him. I don't know how many nights he played with Monroe, but it wasn't long until Bill had to let him go. Euless would come down to [Brushy Creek] sober as a judge, and Mom would tell him, "Now, Euless, I love you, but you can't bring your whiskey in my house." So Euless would get up every so often and take a swig and come back and fiddle a while. . . . When I started playing fiddle at thirteen or fourteen we would go over to his house, and sometimes we would get to the door and he and his mom both would be sauced, and sometimes we would go over there and they would be sober as could be and it was a wonderful experience. So I learned a lot listening to him

play. He loved jazz and swing and Stéphane Grappelli and Joe Venuti and Stuff Smith.

The family, sometimes with Wright, also performed on WGOH, located in Grayson, Kentucky, pretaping their show at home. A regional band named the Bluegrass Playboys joined them to record while Hobert set up the microphones and plugged in his Wollensak reel-to-reel tape machine. Neighbor Cordle—who made guest appearances on the show—recalls Hobert as engineer, player, and producer.

> They'd get in the living room, and once they turned this thing on, the show from start to finish was taped without turning the tape recorder off. I've heard [Hobert] holler back through the house, "Dorothy, you all be quiet back there because we're fixing to tape"—because Ricky's mom might be back there fixing something for people to eat. He turned the tape on and Walter Adams [of the Bluegrass Playboys] emceed the show, and he would make it sound like they were in the studio at Grayson, and they had three or four sponsors. . . . It was seamless. When it was over, they turned the machine off.

Around this time, the six-year-old Skaggs had his storybook first meeting with Bill Monroe in Martha, Kentucky. Cordle, who had witnessed one or two of his friend's cameo appearances with the Stanley Brothers, was on hand to bear witness.

> I remember Mr. Monroe coming there with some kind of big car, like a Buick or a Pontiac. And it had that bass fiddle on top. Bessie Mauldin played bass. They came [into the school], and we people were packed in there like sardines. I think it was fifty cents to get in, and he sings three or four songs— and I knew Ricky and Hobert were there—and Monroe said,

"All right, this young man wants to get up here and sing a song with us. His name is Ricky Skaggs." A huge cheer went up because everybody in the area knew him, a lot of people were related to him. He gets onstage and plays "Ruby." We thought, "Can you imagine, our neighbor playing with Bill Monroe?" The next year he got on the TV show with Lester and Earl.

LIKE ELSEWHERE IN rural America, many eastern Kentuckians had fled to urban life when the industrial machine of the Midwest and Northeast cranked up earlier in the century, thanks to world wars and, later, skyrocketing global demand for American consumer goods. The heaving engine demanded workers into the early 1970s, emptying pockets of the South, including parts of Appalachia. In faraway cities to the north such as Baltimore, Chicago, and Dayton, migrants turned neighborhoods into unique enclaves awash in homegrown music and regional accents. The smells of home cooking fanned by white banners of drying laundry over the neighborhood streets attested to the tricky magic of jamming the spirit of rural freedom into a two-bedroom flat. But as volumes of oral histories and country songs make clear, the northward trekkers missed their old homes. It could be heard in the lonesome timbre of the Stanley Brothers' "I Long to See the Old Folks" and was visible in the snarled traffic on weekend highways pointing to southwestern Virginia or eastern Tennessee. In the summer, families sent children back to grandparents or aunts and uncles who had stayed, hoping to preserve inside them something deep and ancient that could not be articulated and, without nourishment, might wither and die.

The Skaggs family played it both ways. A welder by trade, Hobert disappeared with his tools into the urban jungles of Ohio, Pennsylvania, and New York, leaving his family behind in Kentucky sometimes for weeks before returning home. He briefly moved the family to Bay City, Michigan, where he worked on a Dow Chemical plant, but he could not tame the call of Brushy Creek.

Moving permanently to Ohio would have seemed like the natural next step for the family. There were always plenty of jobs for Hobert in the state's industrial cities, and Dorothy's folks lived in the Columbus area, where her father worked on a stud farm. But while his neighbors and countless other Kentuckians moved north, Hobert in 1962 chose Nashville, Tennessee, so his son might reach a major country music audience. In no way an industrial center like Dayton or Columbus, it was fast becoming a music business capital, thanks to national recording companies and music publishing concerns that had set up shop in town beginning in the late 1940s. Radio station WSM reigned over all, blanketing much of the nation with country music in the evenings on a clear channel and dealing in ancillary activities such as concert promotion and artist management. However, among loyal audiences, WSM meant the *Grand Ole Opry*, the country music jamboree staged in the Ryman Auditorium that rode the station's nighttime clear-channel frequency. It was the very destination Hobert envisioned for his son.

Renting initially in the city, the family bought a house in the suburban town of Goodlettsville, home to stars such as Bill Monroe and Patsy Cline. Hobert struggled to find regular work locally and had to work far afield at the Tennessee Valley Authority (TVA) plant in Paradise, Kentucky. On weekends, father and son campaigned for attention behind the high curtains of the *Opry*. The backstage was part bus station, part family reunion, with artists on the show hustling to and fro, listening for their cues, while strangers—admitted by a sympathetic guard—wandered about. Like many youngsters before him and after him—Carl Jackson, for example—Ricky sat down like a sidewalk busker and picked his mandolin until somebody influential noticed. Finally, Hobert won an invitation for his son to perform on Lester Flatt and Earl Scruggs's show on WSM-TV. Sponsored by Martha White Flour, it was a morning staple in Nashville. But although Ricky confidently chimed in on the legendary duo's "Foggy Mountain Special" and belted out his old standby "Ruby," father and son could not capitalize on the exposure. They resorted to playing in churches as the "Skaggs Family," like back home, and made a few master recordings should they ever decide to press albums to sell on their own.

Ricky just shrugged, the goal of making it big more his father's than his own. "I wanted to be in [show business] in one way," he told a writer in 1974, "but in another way it was boring to me because my dad wouldn't let me go out and play football and baseball. He knew what it might do to my hands and my fingers. I guess if it hadn't been for him, though, I probably would have laid out a long time ago." When his father severely injured his back on the TVA job in Kentucky, the family moved back to Brushy Creek on Dorothy's condition that Hobert install indoor plumbing.

But there would be more departures and arrivals at Brushy Creek in store for the family as Hobert's work and love for the hollow tore him in two. "Sometimes we would only stay away maybe for four months, like we'd just rent an apartment," says Skaggs.

But we were always going back to Kentucky, and then having to go back into that school system again, and things I'd learned in Tennessee may not have been something they were teaching in Kentucky, mathwise and that kind of stuff.

But to be with Mom and Dad together every night, no matter where we were, was worthwhile, 'cause he and Mom together was the family. At night we could play music together. Mom would sing and Dad would sing and I'd sing with them, even though he had to get up at four in the morning, to be at work. He just loved music and he loved his family and he just never liked being away, didn't matter how much money he was making per hour.

2

Old Southern Leanings

IN BETWEEN EPISODES of the Porter Wagoner television shows, so attractive to Marty Stuart and his sister, the national news bore down on Philadelphia's repugnant story line, including the conspiratorial reluctance of white jurors to convict white men in the murders of Chaney, Schwerner, and Goodman. The Stuart children picked up snippets of the story from news anchors and whispered conversations among parents and friends, but few discussed it in the open air. Says Stuart:

> I remember waking up in the morning and going, "Something's wrong and I can't do anything about it. It's not the same as it was when we were all happy." It was like this thing that hung over that part of the world. It wouldn't go away. I'd wake up as a kid and I'd walk outside the door and the sky was still blue, but the cloud was still there. The heaviness wouldn't go away. We couldn't do things the way we used to. We couldn't talk to people the way we used to. People couldn't come to my house that used to. I couldn't go to the Busy Bee Cafe and hang out and dance on the sidewalk like I used to.

Two years after the murders, as Stuart approached his eighth birthday, Martin Luther King Jr. and about twenty followers arrived in town to honor the victims' legacy and to shame Neshoba County residents who remained silent as federal authorities groped still for cooperative witnesses. But even King must have realized no white man in the state of Mississippi would be convicted for killing Chaney, a Black man, or Chaney's white civil rights friends from New York.

King appeared like a prophet to more than 150 local residents who joined his two-mile march from a Black neighborhood called Independence Quarters to the courthouse downtown where Deputy Cecil Price had held the victims before sending them to their deaths. One woman told local writer Florence Mars that if King could risk his life by coming to Philadelphia, she could, too.

But whites scowled and shouted brutal epithets along the march route, hurling bottles and firecrackers. A few drivers steered into the procession and veered away at the last second, although one car hit a boy in his side. As King prepared to speak, whites and Blacks traded insults while Deputy Sheriff Price glowered behind him. Expressing publicly his belief that the civil rights movement would triumph over murder in Neshoba County, King may not have been too sure. "This is a terrible town, the worst I've seen," he was overheard to say later in the day. "There is a complete reign of terror here."

On the edge of the downtown crowd, John Stuart parked his pickup truck and boosted Marty and Jennifer onto the hood so they could see the unusual commotion. "I remember Daddy saying, 'There he is,'" says Marty. "There were so many Black people there marching, I didn't know which one he was talking about, but I knew I had laid eyes on Martin Luther King at that time."

Nobody knows John's thoughts as he stood near the courthouse square, one foot propped up on the bumper of his truck, but the moment must have stirred serious reflection and carried him back to the fateful years after the birth of his children when he served shoulder to shoulder with Lawrence Rainey, Hop Barnett, and Cecil Price in the Neshoba County Sheriff's Department.

INVITED TO JOIN the force by Barnett, his friend and a member of the KKK who had also recruited Cecil Price into both the Klan and the Sheriff's Department, John Stuart served from 1960 to 1963. If Barnett also tried to bring John into the Klan, both Marty and his mother, Hilda, say he failed. "I think Daddy had old southern leanings inside of him that were instilled," says his only son. "But I believe joining the Klan would have crossed a moral line inside of him that he didn't quite have in him to cross. There's no doubt in my mind he would have been hit upon to be a member of the Klan. But that never, ever surfaced. First of all, I don't think he would have been able to keep Hilda if he joined the Klan because she wouldn't have put up with that for a second."

Though John's immediate family says he never spoke of witnessing racial violence inflicted by fellow deputy sheriffs, interpreted to mean he wasn't around it, he was at least on the payroll of the Neshoba County Sheriff's Department staff on Halloween night of 1962 when a Black man named Ernest Kirkland—a local activist—and four other Black men were absurdly arrested for stealing a white man's cow. In their definitive book, *We Are Not Afraid: The Story of Goodman, Schwerner, and Chaney and the Civil Rights Campaign for Mississippi*, Seth Cagin and Philip Dray claimed it was one of the department's "most notorious abuses of power."

Although Kirkland and his friends professed their innocence, Rainey and Barnett, along with two city police officers, attempted to beat "confessions" out of the four in the Neshoba County jail. Kirkland was spared physical abuse but overheard the torture of his friends. He heard one shout, "Go ahead, white folks, kill me! I haven't stolen no cow!" The men were stripped and held to the floor, their bare buttocks whipped with the heavy leather belt from a cotton gin, while county attorney Rayford Jones sat at a desk in the next room typing "statements" for the victims to sign when they were led out of "interrogation."

The anti-Black mood permeated every socioeconomic tier of white Philadelphia, traveling on many of the Stuarts' friends, family, and neighbors like lint on a sweater. But after 1964, says Hilda Stuart, the family backed away from the racists they knew, at least the hard-core haters. "Some of the people—without our knowing—had become members of the Klan, and we didn't participate in that. We just kindly stayed away, and after that you didn't want to follow along with them; they weren't too friendly to you anymore."

But the Stuarts remained friendly with Cecil Price's family when Price himself was sent to federal prison in Sandstone, Minnesota, in 1970 for conspiracy to commit murder. "Cecil's wife, Connor, and my dad had worked together at Hamill's Drug Store, so they were like family," explains Stuart. "I think it was absolutely heartbreaking to everybody involved that somehow Cecil wound up in the middle of all that. . . . My mother never quit loving Connor. And Cecil has a son named little Cecil, and my sister, Jennifer, just kind of had a heart for him because he didn't have a dad around during those times. They were just family friends."

Reflective, perhaps, at having worked amid the inhumanity of the Sheriff's Department, John appeared solemn in many of Hilda's pictures from that point forward in contrast to lighthearted scenes in pictures with family and friends in the 1950s. Nursing ulcers and fatigue from late-night shifts at US Motors where he worked after 1963, he focused on his son's music and recounted stories about busting moonshine stills rather than reflections on the department's interactions with people of color. "It was not going to get any easier [in the Sheriff's Department after 1963]," says Stuart. "I would think you have to be one of the gang to stick around, and I think his vote was that he did not stick around, and I'm glad he didn't because we might be having a different conversation had he stuck around."

Young Stuart continued to discern the cloud over his hometown.

I would get up every day hoping it was over and gone, but it just would not go away for a long time, and I just remember it confused me, and I just knew there was a lot of anger and a lot of hate and a lot of violence that seemed to surround the town and everybody was so uptight. But it was those Saturday-afternoon country music TV shows, especially *The Porter Wagoner Show*. When it came on, the world was all better for thirty minutes. Those rhinestones and those story songs and those characters on our TV made life better, and when they would go off the air the tangible heaviness seemed like it would come back to me.

BY THE TIME the federal prosecution of the mob who participated in the abduction and murder of Chaney, Schwerner, and Goodman neared a conclusion in 1970, Stuart had become a serious local performer and an ardent fan of bluegrass music, finally meeting the father of bluegrass himself when he wheeled down to Jackson, Alabama, to see Bill Monroe at the National Guard Armory with his father and a bluegrass player in the area named John Wesley Cook. Although, unlike Ricky Skaggs, he wasn't invited onstage to play, the sight of Monroe only clarified his vision of the country music family he yearned to join, and he walked away with an autographed album and a mandolin pick.

Similar to Skaggs and his father who sought out well-known performers as they traveled through Lawrence County, Stuart, his father at his side, presented himself to like minstrels, hoping to pick up a few tips and leave an impression that might seed a job offer. Country and bluegrass acts began to talk about the kid in Neshoba County who looked like Eddie from *The Munsters* television situation comedy; one of them was Little Roy Lewis of the Lewis Family whose voice invited comparisons to another children's television character, Foghorn Leghorn from the *Looney Tunes* cartoon shorts.

Lewis recalled Stuart approaching when his band pulled into Philadelphia in 1968 for a show in the county courthouse. He'd been waiting since morning, the same way Lewis used to linger as a child when his idols Flatt and Scruggs came to his hometown in Georgia. His sisters Polly and Janis admired the cute boy, but Stuart charted a direct course to Little Roy. "I got out of the bus, and he wanted to take my banjo and guitar in for us," says Lewis. "And then all the while I'm walking with him, this little fella is saying, 'What kind of strings do you use?' So I told him about the strings, and he messed around with us, sitting on the front row while we set up. That's the first time I ever laid eyes on him. We'd sing everywhere [in Mississippi]. We sang in Bruce, Philadelphia, and Vicksburg and all those places, and his parents would bring Marty to see us."

Music inundated Stuart even when he hadn't courted it. On the first day of the sixth grade, as Neshoba County experimented with racial integration in the schools for the first time, he eased into his chair knowing he'd have a Black teacher, his first ever. Unexpectedly, it was a man named Virgil Griffin, who fronted a band called the Rhythm Kings. Sure enough, you could find Griffin's singles on the jukebox in the Busy Bee Cafe, on a green label, the emblem of Reginald Records located up in the Mississippi Delta country. "The first day of school," says Stuart, "there's Mr. Virgil Griffin, my teacher, and I thought, 'I've got it made here. This guy's so cool.' Again, it was the power of music."

In the summer, he made his way to a pine-barrens pleasure park outside town replete with catfish ponds, picnic tables, a music hall, and an amphibious car that park owner Grover Willis drove across the ponds to the unending delight of visitors. But Stuart was magnetized by the array of gospel groups on the summertime program: the Downings, Dixie Echoes, the Lewis Family, and an act from nearby Kosciusko, Mississippi, called Coleman Akins and the Attala Four. "If I knew a gospel group was going to come to Grover's place, I'd sit up by my driveway, hoping to see somebody's bus pass. I remember the Hemphill Gospel Singers came by, and I couldn't believe it."

Stuart formed a small band with John Wesley Cook's son and a few other boys and continued to step up to tiny local stages with his Fender electric guitar and his sister, who sang lead vocals. He played electric bass for a group in neighboring Choctaw County known as the Prewitt Family, who sang gospel music and featured on guitar young Carl Jackson, the prodigy who proved to be a valuable influence on Stuart.

In addition to the guitar, Jackson played a hot banjo, and he often traveled with his father, Lethal, down to Neshoba County to play with the Page Family, the gospel group in Philadelphia who kept Flatt and Scruggs's old bus in their yard. Still in his midteens, Jackson's big score in music thus far was playing in Jim and Jesse's Virginia Boys, who starred in their own syndicated country music show.

When Stuart learned Carl and Lethal Jackson were rehearsing a new Page Family album in Philadelphia, he asked to observe and immediately connected with Lethal. "I guess from raising Carl," says Stuart, "he had a gift of taking kids under his wing and spending time with them, and he had a lot of patience, showing chords and harmony parts, and he had a great record collection which went back a long way."

Lethal played the guitar, but he also owned mandolins and sold one to Stuart. "My dad spent countless hours with Marty helping him on the mandolin and getting him started," explains Jackson. "Of course, Marty took it and ran with it. You could tell Marty was going to be a great, great musician. He lived and breathed it. He was just like me. He would spend hours and hours playing in front of a record player, slowing records down and learning."

By 1972 Stuart well understood the power of asking. It had gotten him audiences with towering bluegrass figures and access to stages around Neshoba County. So when Carl told him he'd be going on the road with an Alabama-based bluegrass gospel group known as the Sullivan Family Gospel Singers during the summer, the thirteen-year-old inquired if they might need a mandolin player. And then he asked his mother.

The Sullivan Family needed no introduction to those fans of bluegrass who attended Pentecostal churches in the South. The band started on the radio in Picayune, Mississippi, in the late 1940s, featuring the patriarch Rev. Arthur Sullivan, his brother Aubrey, and his sons Enoch and Emmett and Enoch's wife, Margie, whose fulgent vocals were almost always out front. Working an impressive network of churches, radio stations, and festivals, their sincere performances of "Walking My Lord Up Calvary's Hill" and "Working on a Building" were known throughout the South and up into the Midwest. In the 1960s, they struck a deal with Bill Monroe to perform bluegrass gospel shows together, a relationship that provided entrée to major-league festivals across the eastern half of the nation, including Monroe's Bean Blossom. But the whitewashed churches from Louisiana to Georgia remained their staple circuit into the early 1970s, with the core of the group composed of Enoch on fiddle, Margie on guitar, and Emmet on banjo. A skinny young bass player from Pine Bluff, Arkansas, with dark skin named Ronnie Dickerson joined in, too.

"The Sullivans had a good name," says Hilda Stuart, "and I thought Marty could do that on weekends maybe. But I quit thinking about what he might do because I almost knew what he was going to do. But you don't know how it's going to turn out. There's no way you can know. I couldn't say, 'You got to stay here and play with the Sullivans on the weekend.' That never would have worked. And he loved the Sullivans. That's where he learned the rest of the bluegrass . . . with them."

Slated to play almost exclusively on weekends in the summer of 1972, and mostly in Mississippi, Alabama, and Louisiana, Carl would pick up Marty in his yellow Gran Torino on the way to rendezvous with the Sullivans in their base of St. Stephens, Alabama. They chatted about music, girls, and sports, and Marty felt like he'd found a big brother. "It still stands out as some of the most fun I've ever had in my life," he says.

Uniforms and instruments stuffed into Enoch Sullivan's Town and Country station wagon, they actually sang or worked out instrumental arrangements on their drives to Hattiesburg or

Gadsden as if in a scene from a B-grade film musical.* Carl offered
Marty pointers on the mandolin, while Emmett cracked practical
jokes that usually involved removing his false teeth or joking on
Stuart's youth—gags that migrated to the stage. When the fuel
needle listed toward empty, Enoch would pull into Dixie Gas stations with bathrooms and a snack stand. "In most of those old
backwoods service stations," observes Stuart, "there was an eight-
by-ten or a poster of George Wallace, and sometimes you'd see
Kennedy, but always George Wallace."

Emmett and Enoch sported impressive white pompadours
that never seemed to deflate, even when the station wagon arrived
late, igniting a feverish scramble to set up the modest sound system and unload the clothes and instruments. "They were beautiful Civil War–looking characters, exotic-looking backwoods
guys," says Stuart, "and Margie Sullivan was just a state-of-the-art,
Pentecostal-looking lady. But, man, they would roll out of there
in those black suits, important-looking suits, and the dust boiling
from the station wagon finally stopping, and it was an impressive
sight. They were somebodies."

Their rousing arrangements of "Light in the Sky," "The Stone
Was Rolled Away," and "I'm Using My Bible for a Road Map"
reminded Stuart of the Singing Rambos, whose scintillating performance at a Pentecostal church in Philadelphia had so disman-
tled Jennifer emotionally that Hilda had to take her and Marty
home. If the spirit took hold at the revivals the Sullivans played,
the congregation might commence the mysterious practice of
speaking in tongues and shouting hallelujahs audible in the next
town. And then the performance ended and a love offering was
collected, freeing Marty and Carl to get to know the young people
in the teenager-to-teenager way. "I can remember we'd sometimes

---

*In middle age, Stuart learned from Mavis Staples a new term for rehearsing
in the car: "chin singing." It's when you're in the backseat working out vocal
parts while propping your chin on the back rest of the front seat.

stay in the parsonage," says Jackson. "People were accommodating. They'd feed us, take care of us. We'd come in and do a show for them and we'd get paid, not any kind of big money. But it was a wonderful, wonderful life and musical time. I know we laughed, and we had a great time. I don't want to say we didn't completely realize what a great time we were having because we did to a certain extent. But looking back on it, it's even bigger."

On the road, Stuart did more than just note the Wallace posters on gas-station walls; he and the Sullivans played rallies for the nation's archsegregationist, who was mounting his run for the presidency in 1972. He can't remember if Wallace actually appeared or if they performed only for local supporters, but there's a lot he does recall, like watching Enoch explain to a skeptical preacher that Ronnie Dickerson only *looked* like he was African American and realizing the difference between reasoned political oratory and demagoguery by comparing his interactions with the august US senator John Stennis of Mississippi and the race-baiting former governor Ross Barnett.

"Enoch Sullivan was one of the smoothest emcees of all time," says Stuart. "And a lot of times at those churches he would open with, 'The Sullivan Family Gospel Singers are proud to be here, and let's get things straight right off the bat. We love our Lord Jesus Christ, and we believe in states' rights and we're so happy to be here with our friend Ross Barnett and we love our friend George Wallace.' There was a razor-thin line between how religion and politics were presented to the audience."

Stuart joined a long list of country music show people dating back to the 1930s who had stumped for politicians. Country comedienne Minnie Pearl and "Candy Kisses" hit maker George Morgan took the stage for Tennessee senator Estes Kefauver in his 1956 run for the US presidency, and, later, Hank Williams Jr. hired on with Alabama politicians Carl Elliott and Winton "Red" Blount, while O. B. McClinton warmed up audiences for presidential candidate Edmund Muskie in 1972.

As Stuart soon learned, nobody mined the country world like George Wallace, who carried his own house band on the road and rarely met an audience without Nashville celebrities in tow. As his exhortations of "segregation today, segregation tomorrow, segregation forever" reverberated in auditoriums and town squares, Webb Pierce, Grandpa Jones, Billy Walker, the Wilburn Brothers, Hank Thompson, Marty Robbins, Hank Locklin, Ferlin Husky, Hank Snow, or Minnie Pearl—a big fan—might be there to sing the chorus. But nobody was more strident for Wallace than country music royals George Jones and Tammy Wynette, who for a period of time virtually gave over their careers to the segregationist's cause.

"I was really more interested in learning the Sullivan Family songs and me and Carl looking at girls and having fun than I was in listening to what a politician had to say that summer," says Stuart.

> But I knew that in the minds of a lot of people George Wallace seemingly mattered. I really didn't listen to his [rhetoric], but I knew that he could draw a crowd and we're there on his behalf. I got my old mandolin down the other day that I played with the Sullivans in the original case, and I flipped it open and I found two things that got me: one was the George Wallace bumper sticker that I just stuck in the bottom of the case from that summer, and then there was a little set list that Marzell Page used to have on the side of the mandolin when I bought it from Lethal Jackson. I think I saved everything.

UP IN APPALACHIA, the US government's War on Poverty attracted national journalists, policy experts, and health-care providers, many of whom unwittingly encouraged stereotypes in their scrutiny of characteristics and conditions tied to mountain people. Such attention was mostly unwelcome. "They'd find the worst-looking place they could find, and that's what they put on

TV," complains Larry Cordle. "We knew poor people—we were all poor—but everybody had this pride about their places and how things looked. Even people who didn't have money knew how to clean things up."

As Cordle's complaint suggests, more outsiders might have taken a page from sensitive folklorists who studied Appalachian music and other indigenous art forms, or looked to the ethics of psychiatrist and documentarian Robert Coles, who held up mountain ways as a model for all. He referred to Appalachia as "a culture strong on family life, on community affiliation; a culture tied to a *place*; a culture with a sense of *time* that transcends the immediate moment, the latest fad, cliché or hustle."

One persistent characteristic of rural Appalachian life, particularly in Kentucky, was constant relocation, the sojourns to the North for jobs with the dream of home always alive, a theme the Skaggs family embodied. It was present in their moves to Michigan and then to Nashville that were followed by anxious retreats to Brushy where the old house remained in the family's name, never put up for sale. In 1967 they were on the move again, heading inevitably to Columbus where Dorothy's father was ill and in need of care.

Sitting on a jagged line tracing Appalachian settlement in industrial Ohio, Columbus is between Cincinnati to the southwest and Cleveland to the northeast, its countless factories having employed thousands of migrants, many of whom came from Lawrence County. "If you were from eastern Kentucky or West Virginia," says Larry Cordle, whose father worked for General Motors in Columbus, "and you went to one of those places in Ohio, they knew your work ethic. You could have a job anywhere you wanted."

Naturally, Appalachian migrants in Columbus brought their musical tastes with them, so they flocked to the area's festivals and clubs that had sprung up to serve them. A few of these venues also drew college students from Ohio State University and other young people who discovered bluegrass music in the 1960s at the crossroads of country music and the folk revival.

Still, the music clubs featuring the rural rhythms were mostly visited by transplanted Appalachians in search of escape after a long day at the factory. They were no-nonsense joints, largely about getting a buzz on, as author and scholar Robert Cantwell discovered in the 1970s when he visited the Country Palace in Columbus to interview Ralph Stanley. "I went ahead into what turned out to be a vast, low, and largely empty room, faintly reminiscent of a parking garage, shrunken by shadows and set about with flimsy card tables that seemed ready to buckle under the weight of the checkered tablecloths that had been thrown over them," he wrote. "On the wall adjacent to the door was the bar itself, with its electric beer-clocks and advertising gadgets throwing off sinuous points of light into a panel of vertical mirrors in which the solitary drinker might regard himself, and in which the four or five men who were sitting at the bar were imperfectly reflected."

Former Bill Monroe banjoist and onetime boxer Eddie Adcock, another frequent visitor to Midwest bluegrass bars, knew to watch out when the imperfect reflections of Cantwell's experience came to life in joints such as the Golden Eagle in Moline, Illinois, where he encountered a tough guy showing his muscles and talking trash. "He had everybody buffaloed," says Adcock,

But he made one mistake: he threw a sugar bowl up at me and hit my mic stand and got up and walked out the door. I lay my banjo down, and he was getting ready to get in the car, and I caught up with him and I had another sugar bowl— this was raw sugar in a bowl with a spoon—and I said, "Hey, sweets, you forgot something." And I poured it on top of his head. And he said, "Well, you just had to come out here, didn't you?" I said, "I usually follow people who almost knock my teeth out with a sugar bowl and knock the mic into my mouth. I usually come behind them to whip their ass." By that time, I had grabbed him by the head and was holding him with my left arm and was beating him in the face with my right fist. I waited until he fell limp before I let him go because the way I look at it is if you're as bad as you bragged about all night, I'm not one to let you off easy because I want to know that you're not going to be back up and whip my butt. He talked his own self into what he got, and I never, ever in my life, started a fight with anyone.

During the Skaggs family's residency in Columbus, Hobert led his son into a spot not unlike the Golden Eagle or the Country Palace. The Astro Inn served up the usual list of factory beers amid dime-store decor, but the musical experiences—suggestive of the bar's name—could be extraterrestrial. The fourteen-year-old Ricky, too young for beer and barely out of Ovaltine, absorbed the scintillating mandolin performances of Earl Taylor, who was a regular and a veteran of the beer joints going back to his days in Baltimore in the early 1960s. It was Skaggs's first glimpse into the dark corners of tavern culture where so much bluegrass thrived because aching men who showed up after work to drink—sometimes with their wives and girlfriends in tow—craved the familiar tones of home and frank moral themes of the lyrics. Ricky claimed to have spent the whole summer of 1967 with his dad at the Astro Inn.

Word of Hobert and son's availability to play for any audience soon got around Columbus, so young Skaggs's weekend afternoons were often spent on tiny stages for folks either from down home or descended from down home. When young teens with whom he attended school cheered his performances, his musical confidence only grew. But not surprisingly, plenty of boys made fun of the newcomer, the kind of experience that has long occupied psychologists interested in the anxiety associated with Appalachian migration in and out of urban areas, a condition informally known as "nerves."

"I had a very strong hillbilly kid accent, and you can hear it on the Flatt and Scruggs show," explains Skaggs. "It sounded normal to me, but when I moved to Ohio I had some guys that would call me 'hillbilly.' That was my nickname, 'hillbilly,' and I took it as a badge of honor. I didn't get mad about it because I was proud of where I was from. But when they heard me play music, man, they became my guards. I mean these guys were big and they played football and they would bust somebody's head if they got in 'hillbilly's' grill, and so I was pretty happy about that. My music got me through."

In 1969 the Skaggs family moved back to Brushy Creek after Dorothy's father died and Hobert decided he could no longer bear Columbus with the hollow heavy on his mind. Within months of returning home, the prodigy finally met a peer with a big appetite for honky-tonk country but who also loved the Stanley Brothers as much as he did. His name was Keith Whitley, and he lived about twenty-five miles away from Skaggs in Sandy Hook and played with his brother Dwight in a band known as the East Kentucky Mountain Boys. A pair of black-rimmed glasses balanced on his nose, Whitley had grown up on his mother's George Jones records and, similar to Skaggs, had appeared on country music television and radio programs, while still in Toughskin jeans.

They bonded like carefree children, Whitley playing guitar and mimicking Carter Stanley's lead vocals, while Skaggs, gravitating back to the mandolin from the fiddle, emulated Ralph's high tenor. Pinging between each other's homes, they sang "We'll Be Sweethearts in Heaven" and other Stanley favorites, pulled from the duo's recordings on Rich-R-Tone, Columbia, and Mercury, which featured mandolinist Pee Wee Lambert whom Skaggs claimed as an influence. Their living-room sessions transitioned to live performances around their hometowns and then to the Skaggs Family's old radio haunt on WGOH, where they took care of business as the Lonesome Mountain Boys.

"We would tape a show on either Wednesday or Thursday night over at Keith's house," says Skaggs. "His dad had a garage and we'd close the door so it wasn't noisy and make a Saturday show and a Sunday show. My dad would play rhythm guitar and maybe sing a little bass in a quartet, but it was mostly me and Keith. Then it was me and Keith and Dwight, Keith's brother, that played banjo, and he'd sing harmony with us."

Spending the night in Brushy Creek or Sandy Hook, they promised to form a band together when they reached adulthood, falling asleep trading mountain songs, each one anticipating the other's choice within the first half breath. Family members and broadcast audiences marveled over how two youngsters could sound so much like the Stanley icons who had enchanted Appalachia, Carter's dulcet vocals in harmony with Ralph's, channeling the timeless mood of the hills and rivers. Carter had died in 1966, leaving Ralph to carry on in his own band with lead vocalist Larry Sparks filling the space if not the spirit Carter had left behind. But many in eastern Kentucky were certain that the true essence of the Stanley Brothers had come to rest in Ricky and Keith. "It put chills on your arms if you had respect and love for the tradition of the music of the Stanley Brothers," says bluegrass star Doyle Lawson.

Lawson first spied Keith and Ricky at Carter Caves State Park in Olive Hill, Kentucky, when he was with banjoist J. D. Crowe's band. "I was amazed at their ability as young as they were because I remember at fifteen I had quite a ways to go as far as some of that stuff, but I was impressed. Keith's another story, but you could tell right off that Ricky had the music fever, so to speak. He was pretty much consumed by it, and, even as a kid, he left no doubt he was going to be a force to be reckoned with."

Ralph Stanley lived in southwestern Virginia and frequently traveled with his band into eastern Kentucky, so it wasn't long— Skaggs estimates just months after he and Keith met—before the two boys got the chance to approach Stanley and check out Roy Lee Centers, the new lead vocalist and guitarist in Stanley's Clinch Mountain Boys, who had replaced Larry Sparks. They set out with Hobert on a spring evening to a bar in Fort Gay, West Virginia, on the other side of the Big Sandy River from the stubbornly dry Lawrence County.

For a while the youngsters fretted because Ralph and the band had broken down on the way to the tavern, but when the proprietor urged Keith and Ricky to fill the time (with Hobert on guitar), Hobert—always prepared for such moments—unloaded instruments from the back of his car. Ralph picked up the story in an interview with scholar John Wright: "We got there and they was onstage, filling in for us. And they sounded identical, I thought, to the way Carter and me sounded when we first started. They had it down better than anyone I've ever heard. And they knew more of our old songs than I did! They wanted to get started in music, so I took them on the road with me."

But not immediately. The boys returned to Fort Gay a month later to open for Stanley, and then they traveled with their parents to meet Stanley and his mother in Virginia, where they undoubtedly demonstrated how much they sounded like the old woman's sons. Stanley, encouraged in his musical pursuits by his own father decades earlier, was anxious to bring the boys on the road, where their reincarnation of the Brothers act was sure to please, and Skaggs's expertise on the fiddle, paired with veteran fiddler Curly Ray Cline, reintroduced twin-fiddle songs from the Stanley catalog, such as "Cry from the Cross" and new things like "Brand New Tennessee Waltz." (His mandolin mostly remained in the case until Clinch Mountain Boy Ron Thomason left the band.) "Ricky sounded good with Ralph," praises Terry Baucom, a teen banjoist in journeyman Charlie Moore's band at the time. "He was a good fiddle player, and he was a good mandolin player. And his singing . . . He always has been a songbird. Anything he wanted to do with his voice he could make it do. Him and Keith was there with Ralph, and he would just turn it over to them and let them do two or three songs in a row, and I remember sitting there with Charlie listening to him. 'Man, that singing is great,' I said. "And he said, 'It is.'"

The families agreed to let their boys appear with Stanley from time to time during the summer of 1970, anxious to start their children in the music business with one of the kings of traditional country music. Skaggs recalls playing two or three dates with Stanley in West Virginia and capping the summer at the Camp Springs Bluegrass Festival in Reidsville, North Carolina, where promoter Carlton Haney planned to honor the Stanley Brothers with one of his story tributes. "Ralph really wanted [us involved] to show that his music was touching a new generation, the young generation," says Skaggs, "and that we were still carrying on something that he and Carter had started in the mid-'40s. So that was important to Ralph to get us down there to Reidsville, and we didn't know how important it was until we got there and saw the response of the audience when we sung with Ralph."

Earlier in the summer the boys and their families, still phasing into the professional world, had made a surprise visit to Stanley at Frontier Ranch near Columbus, Ohio, a moment, in Skaggs's eyes, that finally drew a line between the teenage musician's aspirations and those of Hobert. "We just kind of showed up," says Skaggs.

> And Ralph told us to go get our instruments, and so I had to round up Dad because he was out listening to somebody else onstage. I said, "Dad, Ralph wants us to play with him on the show this afternoon, and I need to go to the car and get [the instruments] out of the trunk." And when I got to the car, I reach in for my mandolin case, and Keith gets his guitar case and starts walking towards the stage, and Dad reaches for his guitar case and I said, "Dad, Ralph wants me and Keith to get up with him on this one." So he said, "All right then." And I could tell . . . I felt in my heart, in my spirit, that that was like cutting off something. It wasn't cutting off a friendship or love for my dad or respect for my dad, but it was severing maybe a dream that Dad had.

Despite Hobert's bruised ego, he and the other parents remained invested in the boys' association with the country music legend, knowing its implications for their future in music. There was plenty of biscuits and gravy when the star's Aerocoach bus traveled through eastern Kentucky to pick up Skaggs and Whitley, and the fathers offered to help Stanley roll out the Carter Stanley Memorial Festival at the Stanleys' mountain home place in May 1971, Hobert hammering together the rough-hewn planks for the stage and Keith's dad, Elmer, who had lost part of a hand in the Second World War, laying electrical wire. The parents also pooled their money to fund sessions with the Clinch Mountain Boys that produced the 1971 Whitley-Skaggs albums *Tribute to the Stanley Brothers* and *2nd Generation Bluegrass*.

"After that," says Skaggs, "we would just try to do as many shows with Ralph as we could because we were still in school. We had to be careful about how much we tried to go out, and Ralph wanted us to finish high school. As soon as school was out, we had a job. So in '71 we kind of joined on full-time and played every show."

3

Down the Road

NEWS OF THE young Stanley acolytes sped down the bluegrass wire to Bill Monroe, who might have been sizing up Skaggs for a job when he encountered the teenager at Frontier Ranch in Ohio. He asked if Skaggs played guitar, but the excited teenager was more anxious to remind him of their first meeting in Martha all those years before. Monroe gazed blankly while Skaggs explained. "You let me play your mandolin," he said, losing confidence that the elder had retained any memory of it.

"Well," the old gentleman replied, "I don't remember letting a six-year-old play *my* mandolin. I believe you were thirteen or fourteen, wasn't you?" Skaggs, who wasn't much older than that right then, attempted to stir the old man's memory. "There was a lady in the band," he offered. "I think her name might have been Texas Ruby." Monroe froze, embarrassed by the boy's mistaken reference to his former road wife and bassist, Bessie Lee Mauldin. "Oh, no, no, no," he pleaded, "I never played with Texas Ruby." And the conversation ended, Monroe's interest in the boy sitting on empty. "That was almost like strike three before you even get up to bat," chuckles Skaggs.

In the late summer of 1971, many of Skaggs's peers in Lawrence County bounded up the high school steps for senior year, but the young student of acoustic stringed instruments would not

41

be with them very long. He stuck around long enough to have his senior portrait taken and then, like Ishmael on the *Pequod* who "plunged like fate into the lone Atlantic," he boarded Stanley's bus as an official member of the Clinch Mountain Boys. Skaggs's teachers objected, and Whitley promised to complete correspondence courses, but vows faded in the sunshine of the southeastern bluegrass-festival circuit.

"The only thing I really failed in was English," confessed Skaggs in a 1982 interview. "I had an English teacher who wouldn't let me make up none of my tests when I'd be out on the road. She wouldn't try to help me. She'd just tell me, 'Boy, you ain't gonna amount to nothin' unless you get you a diploma, get you a good education.' I said, 'Well, I [sure] ain't gonna come back to school a whole year for one credit. You can forget about that. I've got a job waiting for me as soon as I walk out this door.' My principal felt the same way the teacher did. He said, 'Boy, you'll not amount to nothin'.'"

If tone-deaf in the classroom, Skaggs and Whitley adjusted the grammar of their new boss's performances, reprising Stanley Brothers songs such as "The Angels Are Singing (in Heaven Tonight)" and "The White Dove" that had all but disappeared from Ralph's set list. Whitley's guitar leads conjured up the old sounds he learned from listening to vintage recordings, while Skaggs's surprising jazz flourishes on mandolin spiced the Clinch Mountain mixture.

Caught on film at Carlton Haney's 1971 Labor Day weekend festival in Reidsville by director Albert Ihde, who was shooting his documentary *Bluegrass Country Soul,* the band performed "Man of Constant Sorrow," long a staple of Appalachian songsters that had become a Stanley Brothers favorite. After only a few consecutive months with the band, Skaggs—clad in a crimson shirt and black cowboy hat while he picked the mandolin—blended with Ralph's and Roy Lee's compelling vocals, shuffling to the rhythm while scanning the audience and sharing an inside joke with bassist Jack Cooke as if he'd always been there.

"On some songs we all pitched in," wrote Stanley in his autobiography. "Keith would sing lead on one verse and Roy Lee would sing lead on the second. Then I'd sing tenor on the chorus and Ricky would sing tenor on the second verse. We all knew where the other men were; we got to trust each other, and the way we could harmonize really got to the crowd. They hung with us all the way, and it meant the world to me that they believed in what we were doing."

Ihde's focus on new bands, most prominently the Bluegrass Alliance with long hair and mod shirts next to the staunch Jimmy Martin, Earl Scruggs, and Stanley, highlighted the generational transition so much on the minds of the American citizenry in the early 1970s. Even Skaggs, though less an affront to the traditional look and sounds, embodied the future, squirming inside the taut bars of "Man of Constant Sorrow" while surrounded by men onstage as old as his grandfather.

The film cuts to an aged woman sitting in the crowd next to a young couple, presumably her son and daughter-in-law, worrying her fingers over a ticket stub or stray piece of a leaf she had picked up from the ground. Mother—a metaphor for Stanley and the other bluegrass veterans—will soon dissolve in this family portrait Ihde has provided, leaving the children to explore the world unencumbered.

Transitioning away from the generational tension, the director turns his eye to the star of the film: promoter Carlton Haney. One of the poet-philosophers of southern music, in a class of purveyors of hill-'n-delta hokum with Sam Phillips of Memphis and even Skip James of Yazoo County, Mississippi, Haney strolls through the festival grounds framing his Labor Day concerts as the distillation of humankind's spirit. "The bluegrass festival is where you can hear the soul of a man," he tells the camera.

Says Doyle Lawson, who appears with the Washington, DC–based Country Gentlemen in *Bluegrass Country Soul*, "I got to where I enjoyed talking to Carlton. I'd listen to what he had to say. So we were talking one day, and it was the time when kids started growing their hair longer and had a more progressive approach to bluegrass. But it didn't bother him. He said, 'Look, Doyle, if all the bunches sounded alike'—he didn't call them 'bands'—'I wouldn't need to hire but one.' So I thought, 'Well, that's pretty impressive, Carlton.'"

In the early going with Stanley, young Skaggs learned a lot about Carlton Haney. A force in country music, he had organized and promoted the first multiday bluegrass festival in Fincastle, Virginia, in 1965 and went on to produce a warm-weather circuit of festivals, which represented the heart of many a bluegrass artist's touring business. A native of Reidsville, North Carolina, Haney also promoted shows for Bill Monroe in the 1950s, which led to organizing country music package shows featuring greats such as Loretta Lynn and Conway Twitty. The corpulent promoter then used the capital from his country music activity to promote his bluegrass festivals. And himself.

"When I put on a show I give each one a soul of its own," he told *Hustler* magazine in 1977. "Each one will have one or two moments that will never happen again. I talk to the entertainers before the show and get their minds workin'. Then when they get on stage they hear things they wouldn't ordinarily hear and this causes them to create."

Haney's bluegrass festivals often climaxed with his trademark "stories," which recognized a bluegrass legend's status by assembling his past and present band members to play while Haney narrated the honoree's history in music. The first, titled "The Story of Blue Grass," was staged in 1965 to recognize Bill Monroe, the rustic spectacle proving to be one factor in helping Monroe—and his fans—understand his status not only in country music but on the spectrum of American music.

In an earlier stint with banjoist J. D. Crowe, Lawson had been ordered to approach Haney about playing one of his festivals.

"So he said, 'What would you need?'" recalls Lawson. "I had never booked a show, but I was caught in the middle because I'd worked my way in to talk to him. So I threw out a number. And he said, 'No, I don't work anybody that cheap.' So he bumped it up $100 a day."

Most artists active at the time acknowledge the saving power of Haney's festival movement in the face of rock and roll and pop-styled country music that flourished in the late 1950s and 1960s. Bands got regular work—and rest if they were booked to play a festival for the entire weekend—that minimized their reliance on the dreaded taverns. "I had no idea it would turn out that way, but Carlton talked to us all and had said the festivals are going to be the biggest thing for all of us," explains Bill Emerson, cofounder of the Country Gentlemen. "It turned out to be a real boon for all of us because at that time we were just playing anyplace we could find to draw a crowd or for somebody who would pay us a percentage of the gate or whatever. That's how all the bluegrass bands were operating at that time, and Carlton brought bluegrass up by its bootstraps, so to speak, when he came up with this idea for festivals."

Haney's work in festivals was inspired by a visit in 1964 to the Newport Folk Festival, produced by George Wein, who also handled the famous jazz festival in the same city. A guest of Ralph Rinzler, who worked for Wein and had earlier managed Bill Monroe, Haney, first of all, observed the crowds flocking to hear acoustic music, much of it based in his own southern backyard, but he was curious, too, about the multiple stages, which allowed the music to play on without pause.

Though the crowds at Haney's inaugural Roanoke Bluegrass Festival in Fincastle, Virginia, couldn't match Newport for size, the continuous performances on various stages that he observed in 1964 were replicated in Virginia and remained the template for his subsequent festivals and the competing festivals he inspired. "When you sit down at a table, how many different things do you eat," he asked bluegrass scholar and former aide Fred Bartenstein in an interview. "That's how I put on a show. Every 20 or 30 minutes you were eating something different with your ears."

Festivals in the South thrived in part on the era's manufacturing and research boom, as many northern-based enterprises chose the management-friendly region to locate their businesses and, as a result, funneled more disposable income into fans' pockets. Important, also, was the expanding interstate highway system, which sadly hollowed out neighborhoods in major cities but nonetheless eased the festivalgoer's long-distance journey across Tennessee or North Carolina, for example, to see favorite stars.

"Summertime stuff is the bluegrass festival," proclaimed Skaggs in the 1970s, "and they'll consist of 2,500 up to sometimes thirty-thousand people, depending on where they're at. But 90% of that thirty thousand are the type of people that come out to camp for three or four days and sit and stay high and boogie and dance and get up and have a good time. . . . The festivals are definitely the thing that kept bluegrass from being an extinct music, because it just about went out. If bluegrass festivals hadn't brought it back, it would be dead now."

The festivals also facilitated something of a cattle market. Bandleaders scouted pickers in competing groups whom they believed might be available, while record men and women from companies such as Rounder, Rebel, and Flying Fish pitched contracts to unsigned artists. Meanwhile, fiddlers hawked their private-label albums, drug users scored pills and pot in younger tour buses, and prowling pickers in wash-and-wear suits exchanged addresses with love-struck girls and women.

Dobro master Jerry Douglas describes feeling like a side of beef or, more charitably, a minor league baseball prospect when he looked out from a festival stage in Ohio to see members of the Country Gentlemen sizing him up. "I mean I could see Bill Emerson straight ahead of me in the back of the crowd, and I looked to the left and there's Doyle Lawson. And they're staring at me like they're going to sign me. It was a very strange day."

SOMETIMES, HANEY AND other promoters shorted the bands, even Stanley's, as Skaggs recalls. "But Ralph never took them to task over it. He'd get what he could from them, what they had. We always got paid whether Ralph got paid or not. That was the kind of man Ralph was." Even so, wages for Whitley and Skaggs were pitiable—due to the boss counting the exposure he provided as compensation—while the cramped bus traveling hundreds of miles in the space of a weekend would leave a teenager longing for home. And no matter how many festivals Stanley played, he still clocked time in the skull orchards of urban Ohio while many bands in bluegrass—like the Country Gentlemen and the Seldom Scene—were swearing them off.

Says mandolinist Thomason, "I knew after a while I wasn't cut out for what Ralph was doing, which was just beatin' around on the road all the time. One time we were out for twenty-nine days. And it was really tough because Ralph and I were the only ones who could drive the bus at the time."

Only the wide, growing community around bluegrass kept Thomason in the game. Festivals popped up across the American West, nurturing dynamic bands from the region and the blending of musical styles, while the US government sponsored decent-paying folk festivals gigs and international goodwill tours. New magazines documented the art form—notably *Bluegrass Unlimited,* published by player and enthusiast Pete Kuykendall in the Washington, DC, area—and provided a forum for fans and scholars alike. Ihde's *Bluegrass Country Soul* documentary film memorialized the phenomenon, and, later, Barbara Kopple's Academy Award–winning *Harlan County U.S.A.* (1976) employed the mountain-oriented style to accentuate the coal miner's deadly battle for rights in Kentucky, in contrast to the ironic use of bluegrass in *The Beverly Hillbillies* and *Bonnie and Clyde* of the 1960s. "I loved being where I was, and I loved being in that band," says Thomason. "I thought it was the greatest music. I loved driving down the road in the middle of the night and you're getting sleepy and Ralph Stanley comes up and stands in the well of the bus and sings songs to keep you awake. There's nothing like that."

Thomason, who later formed the beloved Dry Branch Fire Squad, handed over mandolin chores exclusively to Skaggs, who stumbled himself running at the marathon pace. But over the course of Skaggs's roughly two years with Stanley, his name and Whitley's came up in virtually every conversation about the new-generation performers, verifying Hobert and Dorothy's faith in the power of Stanley to lift their son. "The overall effect is a near perfect recreation of the Stanley sound from the late 1940's and early 1950's," raved *Bluegrass Unlimited.* "There's little doubt that we will be hearing more from this talented duo in the future."

The fanfare multiplied when they showed up on one of Stanley and the Clinch Mountain Boys' most beloved albums, which remains in print as of this writing: *Cry from the Cross,* recorded in February 1971 in a basement studio belonging to Roy Homer in Clinton, Maryland, when the boys presumably were supposed to be in school. Annotator Gary Reid traced the performances, "Sinner Man" and "Two Coats" chief among them, straight to the band members' evangelical roots. "It makes for some of the most haunting, earthy and chilling work of Stanley's career," he wrote.

Reid suggests Skaggs's love of sacred music inspired him to lobby Stanley to make *Cry from the Cross*—though the young player's ongoing role in reviving the Stanley Brothers' sound, including their gospel selections, may have been at work, too. Whatever the case, the album released on Rebel Records proved to be one of Skaggs's favorites for the mere fact that Stanley rehearsed the selections before the session in Maryland. The boss tended to look at live performance as practice enough for recording sessions, while Skaggs practiced for perfection—as he and Whitley had done after they first met. "We all knew a lot of these songs," said Skaggs in reference to *Cry from the Cross.* "Going down the road at three in the morning, driving the car and singing—to try to stay awake—we'd start singing Baptist hymns. We came up with twelve or fifteen songs that we knew right out of our heads and that Ralph knew. Like 'That Old Village Church.' Ralph and Carter recorded it earlier, but they did it with music. We did it a cappella."

AT THE SPRING Bean Blossom weekend in 1971 where Marty Stuart met Skaggs, he also sought an audience with Lester Flatt, the legend whose gently creased face was so familiar from the loop of Flatt and Scruggs's television programs he had watched in the 1960s. He hustled over to Flatt's bus to say "hello," and then he followed his entourage to the stage. Later, he'd write, "He walked very slowly through the dust and the sea of campers. People sort of changed as he passed, like the effect of a preacher walking through a poker game. Musicians, hippies, old folks, and kids all wanted to just touch him."

Although Flatt's former partner Scruggs now reached much larger audiences picking pop-rock music with his sons in the Earl Scruggs Revue, the man known as the "Baron of Bluegrass" held on to a major recording contract (RCA), hosted his widely heard Martha White Flour show on radio station WSM, and ranked among the bankable acts on the increasingly lucrative bluegrass festival circuit. He seemed as distant from Stuart's reality as Elvis Presley, but at Bean Blossom, the young admirer closed the gap by getting to know Roland White, the mandolin player in Flatt's Nashville Grass.

A native of Maine where he picked up traditional fiddle sounds from across the border in Canada, White and his brothers Clarence and Eric grew up in California, where they formed a childhood band known as the Country Boys that was central to the nascent bluegrass scene in Los Angeles. The band, which would evolve into the Kentucky Colonels, appeared twice on *The Andy Griffith Show* situation comedy and provided a showcase for

Clarence's innovative lead guitar that transcended the uniform rhythm playing of most bluegrass pickers. When Clarence rode his star into the Byrds, the nation's premier folk-rock band, the Kentucky Colonels broke up, and Roland briefly signed on with Bill Monroe and, then, Lester Flatt.

Sympathetic to child musicians and possessing an understated worldliness, White listened in Bean Blossom as Stuart explained his brief history with the mandolin and the bands he organized in Mississippi. "He was just really kind to me," recalls Stuart, "and he gave me picks and his phone number and one of his ties. And he showed me some stuff on the mandolin." The older player, as true and gentle a mentor as Carl and Lethal Jackson, promised to stay in touch.

STUART PHONED ROLAND White from time to time after Bean Blossom and, in July 1972, met him again at the Georgia State Bluegrass Festival in Lavonia, where both Flatt and the Sullivan Family showed up on the bill. Weeks later, Flatt and his troupe pulled into Neshoba County for the Choctaw Indian Fair, and Stuart invited Roland and Dobro player Jack Martin to Kosciusko Road for supper. Sister Jennifer fluttered when her father approached the house with the men, thinking they might be two of the Osmond brothers come to visit. But it was all part of brother Marty's scheme. "He's thinking ahead all this time," explains mother Hilda.

When Roland followed up a few weeks later, inviting Stuart to ride with the band to the Labor Day bluegrass festival in Glasgow, Delaware, Hilda and John recalled their congenial supper guest and—perhaps softened by Marty's Sullivan Family excursion— reluctantly put their son on a bus to Nashville. He arrived in the middle of the night and buckled in for the long drive to Delaware with the Nashville Grass.

Recalling the romance of Flatt and Scruggs's old bus in the Page Family's front yard, he imagined the interior of Flatt's two-level Scenicruiser would be like the bridge of the Starship

Enterprise. "But the first time I stepped up on it, there were bus seats and, two steps up, a string with a curtain on it and army cots. And I said, 'You got to be kidding me.'" He watched aghast as Flatt snuffed out his cigarette on the bus floor and tossed the water from his paper cup against the windshield, suggesting somebody should get busy cleaning the glass.

On the way north, Stuart and White plunked their stringed instruments in cautious duet, perhaps the old Flatt and Scruggs number "Down the Road" recorded in 1949. They almost definitely tried out "Love Come Home," luring Flatt from behind his tall seat back on the bus. He suggested the band perform it in Delaware with Stuart sitting in on guitar.

"We were in that park in Glasgow, Delaware, for two days and four shows, and at the end of the four shows, Lester offered me a job," says Stuart. "I was supposed to be back home in school about two days later, and so I started calling my parents and I said, 'You'll never guess what happened? Lester Flatt offered me a job.' They said, 'Well, that's nice, but you have to come home.' I begged and pleaded, and Lester said, 'If you stay on this week you can play the *Grand Ole Opry* with us and play on our Martha White radio show.' So that was begging rights to get me to stay one extra week."

Stuart quivered when he bunked down at White's house in Nashville and sifted through Flatt's stock of Nashville Grass costumes for one that would have to be altered for the *Opry* appearance. But at home in Philadelphia, Hilda's and John's stomachs churned. No doubt, John might have predicted the day and hour of his son's departure, having accompanied him to so many musical shows and helping him acquire relatively inexpensive instruments, and Hilda had patiently listened to his dreams and schemes, thinking, perhaps, he would grow out of his obsession. "We didn't push him in any way," says Hilda. "When he wanted to have friends over and play [music], it was his own idea. We just supported whatever he wanted to do. But I didn't know that I was supporting Nashville at the time. I thought we were doing local stuff."

They could feel young Stuart's place in the family fold slipping through their hands while Flatt transmitted his pitch over the telephone. No doubt there was some urgency in Flatt's invitation: Stuart's youth was a novelty to be exploited in stage banter and dealings with promoters, and Roland would soon be re-forming the Kentucky Colonels with his brother Clarence, leaving the mandolin chair open in the band. Besides, word about Stuart was traveling through the bluegrass world. Who knew when somebody else might grab him?

All parties agreed to meet in the town of Chatom, Alabama, where Flatt was slated at Bill Monroe's Dixie Bluegrass Festival, exactly one week after Marty's first appearance in Delaware. Marty's summer sponsors, the Sullivan Family, familiar faces by now to the Stuarts, helped organize the festival.

Recalls Hilda, "The day we went over there, I thought, 'We'll go get Marty, and he can go home and then go back to Nashville. We'll talk about it and see what we need to do and go to Nashville later.' But I think Lester thought if he ever went home, we wouldn't let him go with the band." Although nobody in the family admits to it today, the meeting must have been tense, Stuart's determination to join Flatt so strong in contrast to the family's desire to take it slow.

"After the first show that day," relates Stuart,

We all gathered in the front of that bus and that's when we had our talk, and I just remember sitting there and Mama looking at me and saying, "Is this what you want to do?" And I said, "Yes, ma'am." I did a lot of begging and a lot of pleading and a lot of pointing out the positives in the situation without considering any of the negatives because I didn't see any. There was a gap there of a couple or three weeks, and every day I was on the phone, saying, "Have you talked to Daddy yet? What are you guys thinking?" Just being a pesky kid, trying to get his way and selling something I was hoping for.

He remembers, "My parents had to get used to the fact that I'd be gone and out of their sight. Instead of playing with the Sullivan Family on a regional basis, I'd be running the roads of the nation with people they didn't know. There was the part about school and finances. It was just all unstructured, and it had to be discussed." In the end, everybody agreed Stuart would live with Flatt and his wife, Gladys—their marriage on the verge of separation—in the Nashville suburb of Hendersonville and take correspondence courses toward his high school diploma, while Hilda, John, and Jennifer would entertain moving to Nashville at some later point in time.

But that day in Chatom, Alabama, Hilda and John could have only felt stone shock when they left their thirteen-year-old behind with a bandleader known mostly to them as the guy who tipped his hat to "Granny" from *The Beverly Hillbillies* on network television. Meanwhile, Jennifer considered the empty seat next to her while the family's car departed the festival grounds. She climbed up to look through the back window at her brother waving from the door of the Scenicruiser, tears on both of their faces. "I felt like my right arm was taken off my body," says Jennifer. "But we knew we couldn't keep him home, not with that much talent."

Hilda assumed her son would go home with them to Philadelphia to collect his clothing and then rejoin the band back on the road. But in the spirit of Mark Twain as a new cub pilot on the Mississippi River, who was possessed by "an exultant sense of being bound for mysterious lands and distant climes," the teenager clambered up the steps of Flatt's bus for the long journey back to Nashville.

THROUGHOUT THE FALL, Lester Flatt and the Nashville Grass and their new teenage sensation (Stuart had turned fourteen on September 30) meandered through Lawtey (Florida), Myrtle Beach, Charlotte, and Atlanta, with the Stuart family following behind when schedules allowed. Despite Hilda's unnerving sense of loss, she documented with a steady hand her son's early days with Flatt. Portraits from Heber Springs, Arkansas, captured her son in his powder-blue stage shirt gazing worshipfully at Flatt and stretching toward the stage's corrugated ceiling while playing a mandolin duet with Bill Monroe. They drove up to Nashville for the *Grand Ole Opry* Birthday Celebration and DJ Convention in mid-October, where Hilda framed her son signing autographs as Jennifer looked on with sisterly concern, as if to telegraph, "Be as careful as you were when you signed them back home, Marty." Perhaps the family members discerned the sense of confidence their son exhibited in the pictures Hilda took, helping them come to terms with his new direction. Separations after brief reunions on the road grew less painful as their son's destiny solidified.

Hilda dreaded conversations with skeptical friends and family about her decision to let Marty travel. A fellow employee at the bank told her, "A boy that age don't know what he wants," and two aunts questioned her judgment, offering to pay for Marty's and Jennifer's college education. "And I thought," remembers Hilda, "'You all don't have a music school, so we'll pass.' I thanked them kindly. But they questioned me, and I could understand why. I didn't get upset with them. I knew if we were going to do that, and there was somebody like Lester that had an interest in him, then we better go through the door right then and give it a try."

LESTER FLATT'S COATTAILS pulled Stuart to the highest echelons of bluegrass music where the likes of Bill Monroe and Earl Scruggs dwelled. The bandleader had earned his status as a member of Monroe's Blue Grass Boys with Scruggs in the 1940s, where the core characteristics of bluegrass music first appeared together. The guitarist and lead vocalist in Monroe's band from 1944 to 1948, Flatt popularized the so-called G run, a flourish, like a punctuation mark, in a line or chorus that ends on a G string, and wrote some of the standards of early bluegrass, including "Little Cabin Home on the Hill" and "Will You Be Loving Another Man." But his lead vocals in the Monroe band, effortless and tempered like an October day, enchanted an audience, and when he left Monroe and formed Flatt and Scruggs and the Foggy Mountain Boys, he took all the lead vocals, his delivery the wry counterpart to Scruggs's brisk, syncopated banjo style.

Heroes in the country music world thanks to many classic sides on Mercury and Columbia, the men also rode the airwaves of the mighty WSM whose listeners relied on its invigorating morning broadcasts as much as their first cup of coffee. In the 1960s, their names were familiar in most pockets of American culture thanks to "The Ballad of Jed Clampett," the theme of CBS-TV's popular *The Beverly Hillbillies*, though Flatt's vocals were not featured on the theme song as it aired on the show. It nonetheless made Flatt and Scruggs household names and moved Columbia to sell their music across markets. One might find a Flatt and Scruggs LP such as *Town and Country* (1966) next to an office assistant's record player in Washington, DC, or a restless kid learning to play the guitar in Philadelphia, Mississippi. When the duo's trademark "Foggy Mountain Breakdown" accompanied the action in Hollywood's *Bonnie and Clyde* (1967), starring Faye Dunaway and Warren Beatty, they hit the pop charts and their following doubled again.

Although an exciting new discovery to mass audiences in the 1960s, in the insulated world of country music they had achieved divine status beginning in the late 1940s and early 1950s. Flatt's early work singing and playing mandolin for Bill Monroe's brother Charlie in the early 1940s was known and admired, while Scruggs excited legions of young banjo players with his fast three-finger picking style, its drive an essential ingredient in what we know today as bluegrass music. Though Scruggs didn't originate the three-finger approach, he moved it into the forefront of banjo picking, overshadowing the more elementary clawhammer style associated with *Grand Ole Opry* favorites Uncle Dave Macon and David "Stringbean" Akeman.

The power of Scruggs's picking as well as his godhead status among banjo players tended to overshadow his partner, but Flatt, too, claimed his followers, including a young fiddler named Terry Baucom who also played the banjo. "Earl was the best, but he had the best guitar player he could have found right next to him," says Baucom. "He knew Lester was going to be there and hit that G run. He knew it was going to be there and he was going to be right on it. Lester made Earl sound good, and he don't get enough credit for it. Listen to that guitar. Earl sounds like a machine gun going off. And so does Lester."

A hundred tales told across the South repeated the sheer thrill of Flatt and Scruggs and their Foggy Mountain Boys, stars of radio and records, visiting town as if they were Hank Williams or Jimmie Rodgers come to blow away the heavy humidity of a summer night.

In the mid-1950s, they traveled a weekly route through South Carolina, Georgia, West Virginia, and Tennessee, hosting their own television shows—sponsored by the trusty Martha White Flour company—in a different city each day. Little Roy Lewis, who let Stuart carry his banjo in Philadelphia, grew up in Lincolnton, Georgia, and rode his bike two miles with a packed lunch every week to watch his heroes' bus speed through an intersection on the way from Atlanta to Florence, South Carolina. "Every Wednesday morning that bus come down the road, and I'd sit out there for hours just to look at them. Earl later told me, 'If you'd'a knowed it, we didn't have no generator in the bus and we was sleeping under the tree up there in Washington, Georgia—thirteen miles away.' I said, 'Doggone if that ain't so. I could have come up there and be with you all.' But I followed them, and that's the greatest team that's ever been. Bluegrass wasn't bluegrass until Flatt and Scruggs went with Bill Monroe."

As young Skaggs and Stuart assimilated into the mainstream bluegrass world, they perked up at legends about Flatt and Scruggs, Bill Monroe, and Ralph Stanley that were shared in quiet reverence or hoots of disbelief. In a community where grudges sprouted like knotweed, the teenagers soon learned their respective bosses were entangled in a beef dating back to the 1940s.

"I don't think Earl ever had a harsh word with anybody," says Skaggs, "but Lester was a little more apt to confront and be ill-willed and be a smart aleck because he and Carter Stanley had words one day, Ralph told me, at WCYB in Bristol [Virginia] where Carter and Ralph were stars of the *Farm and Fun Time* show." Flatt and Scruggs had individually left Bill Monroe in 1948 and, searching for a radio home like Monroe's at WSM in Nashville, appeared on a series of radio stations, the latest WCYB, before the year was out. Radio spots ideally were an instant link to an audience who'd pay to attend local gigs the musicians advertised, and it could have been Ralph and Carter were loath to share their territory with yet another act. But, according to Skaggs, Lester—known on the air as "the man with the hat"—was ready with words about the brothers' irritating penchant for performing songs he had written for Bill Monroe:

> There was this confrontation in front of the hotel where WCYB studio was and Ralph said it came to fisticuffs and Carter just knocked the snot out of Lester. Lester confronted him and said, "You quit singing my songs." It got bad. Carter was a big old boy and wouldn't take it, and Ralph was like Earl. He was not a confronter, more soft and mild, but Ralph told me that story and he said, "That confrontation was the best thing that happened to the Stanley Brothers because Carter said out of his mouth, 'All right, I'll write my own blank-blank songs. And I won't need your songs.'" Or something like that.
>
> Carter commenced writing songs at that point, and he delivered even more songs to bluegrass than Monroe. Monroe wrote a lot of instrumentals, but he didn't pen that many lyric songs. Carter did. You go back and look at Carter's copyrights. It's amazing how many songs he wrote. Carter Stanley

is credited for writing "Who Will Sing for Me?" I learned that
song by listening to a Flatt and Scruggs record.* Is that ironic
or what? I bet that was sweet revenge when Carter saw a copyright check come in the mail as a result of a Flatt and Scruggs
recording.

On the other side of it were tales about the beautiful camaraderie among musicians who loved the country music they played
despite the low pay and long hours on the road. Skaggs's fellow
Clinch Mountain Boy Ron Thomason heard about those feuding
stars of WCYB competing in the darkness of a lonely hollow to see
who could sing the loudest and the highest. Along those lines,
Monroe's old sidemen told Skaggs of passing the Stanley Brothers' car on the road and, once the two bands recognized each
other, pulling over, unloading their instruments, and jamming
as one.

But internecine conflict finally ruptured Flatt and Scruggs in
the late 1960s, another zesty chapter in the long story of bluegrass
feuds. As Columbia Records tasted the sweet revenue of the duo's
crossover success, it sanded down their rustic edges and sidelined
the Foggy Mountain Boys, whose Paul Warren often came home
from the studio with his fiddle having never left the case. They
released well-worn standards of the folk music revival mixed with
covers of Chuck Berry's "Memphis, Tennessee," Johnny Cash's
"I Still Miss Someone," and Bob Dylan's "Like a Rolling Stone."
The title of a 1965 album, *The Versatile Flatt and Scruggs*, was reso-
nant of a Jerry Vale record.

Scruggs embraced the duo's new direction, inviting his rock-
oriented sons Randy and Gary to appear on recording sessions,
but Flatt's dissatisfaction over the songs—and problems with Earl's
wife, Louise Scruggs, their manager—had become so obvious by
1969 that the duo's financial adviser and super fan Lance LeRoy

---

*Skaggs took his turn recording "Who Will Sing for Me?" with Earl Scruggs
and Doc Watson for the live album *Three Pickers* (2003).

directed his son Lanny to start taping concerts for posterity on a Wollensak audio recorder. Indeed, young Lanny was behind the console on February 22, 1969, when between appearances on the *Grand Ole Opry* Flatt turned to Lance and said, "Let's go." Igniting the Godzilla of grudges in bluegrass that no festival reunion could heal, the pair never took the stage again.

Little Roy Lewis heard about the split back home in Georgia. "I never will forget, Flatt and Scruggs was part of my life so much. I was sitting on the bus cleaning it up, and my sister Polly came out and said, 'Paul Harvey said that Flatt and Scruggs split.' It got me so bad it took my breath. I was sad just like when Hank Williams died. I sat and cried all day." Although Flatt was out on the road with most of the Foggy Mountain Boys within weeks of the separation, it was some time before Lewis could listen to him without Earl Scruggs on the banjo. Nor could he enjoy Earl's playing once he and his sons formed the rock-oriented Earl Scruggs Revue. "I never did listen to what Earl did with the Revue because the banjo was getting drowned out by the drums."

OUT OF THE gate, Scruggs maintained the eclecticism that had begun on the Flatt and Scruggs recordings of the 1960s, his albums drawing from gospel and California-styled country-rock music first proffered by innovators such as Mike Nesmith and the Byrds. Albums *Nashville Rock* and *I Saw the Light with Some Help from My Friends*, the latter with Linda Ronstadt and Arlo Guthrie as guests, soured more than a few die-hard Flatt and Scruggs fans, but progressives embraced Scruggs's experimentation, part of a new mood in Nashville that was now open for business to the likes of Neil Young and George Harrison.

Lester exclusively worked the Flatt and Scruggs tradition, but Stuart cast hidden glances at the experiments happening all around him, particularly the Nitty Gritty Dirt Band's *Will the Circle Be Unbroken* album, released in 1972, within a few months of his joining Flatt. Driven by the band's love of traditional country, the three-record album assembled an all-star cast of pioneers, including Mother Maybelle Carter, Merle Travis, Roy Acuff, Doc Watson, and Scruggs, to reprise traditional favorites such as "Wreck on the Highway," "Wildwood Flower," and "Honky Tonk Blues." But when the sessions turned to "Nashville Blues," "Flint Hill Special," and "Earl's Breakdown," familiar numbers from the Flatt and Scruggs oeuvre, the father of the G-run was playing concerts with an unknown teenager.

4

The Soul of Bluegrass

AS *WILL THE Circle Be Unbroken* garnered rave write-ups in *Rolling Stone* and major daily newspapers across the nation, Robert Cantwell, writing in the *Atlantic Monthly* (March 1972), found Ralph Stanley at the pivotal Bean Blossom Festival of 1971 where Skaggs and Whitley's revival of the Stanley Brothers sound gripped the audience. Unlike the Nitty Gritty Dirt Band's epic album, whose collaborations between young and old created a template for future reunions, in effect moving country music forward in an attitude of tradition, the Skaggs-Whitley performance Cantwell witnessed was about "perfect imitation of the early Stanley Brothers," a vision from the past confined to that particular moment on the Bean Blossom stage.

Cantwell discerned the imminent spiritual death of the generation of rural people molded by the Great Depression and the Second World War, who may have remembered pushing an unwieldy hand plow but who now lived the Shake-'n-Bake mindset of 1970s America. It followed, he argued, that musicians like Stanley and his boys would merely memorialize hand-plow culture rather than narrate the contemporary story of a people in motion or transition. It was a role Stanley was most comfortable filling.

Bassist Johnny Castle, transplanted from a rock band in the Washington, DC, area, played progressive bluegrass in Eddie

Adcock's II Generation, and he concurred with Cantwell, though he gravitated to festival campfires after hours to play what he calls "the traditional stuff" and counted Ralph Stanley as his favorite banjoist. Nonetheless, he winced when Stanley referred to bands like the Seldom Scene as "hippies" and at the incessant requests from old-line fans—Cantwell's "bluegrass people"—to play standards "Foggy Mountain Breakdown" and "Rollin' in My Sweet Baby's Arms." "You'd get a request for them every night," he complains, "and I thought, 'Seriously?' It was like a rock band getting requests for 'Louie, Louie' every night. It's kind of an insult when you're up there trying to play your stuff and different stuff and people want to revert back to square one. Mountain music hadn't really progressed much even up into the '70s. It kind of stayed right where that sound was—a lot of Carter Family songs and things like that. That was what Ralph Stanley's role was, and Bill Monroe, too. They were place keepers, if you ask me."

Whether Skaggs had read Cantwell's critique of his role in Stanley's group or not, he nonetheless understood his future lay outside the Clinch Mountain Boys, though he couldn't have imagined at that moment his transformative roles in two pivotal bluegrass bands (the New South and Boone Creek) and, then, Emmylou Harris's lauded Hot Band, all before the decade was out. "I felt that there was more about me that I wanted to do," he says.

Recalling the spotlight he enjoyed in Lawrence County, Skaggs desired a more prominent stage, and he winced at the occasional indignities of riding as a Clinch Mountain Boy. On a New Year's Eve in Columbus, Stanley sort of loaned him out to fellow bluegrass star Jimmy Martin. Skaggs recalls:

> It was a big old beer-joint, dance-hall kind of place, and when we get there Jimmy and Ralph are standing there talking, and I just happened to walk up and Jimmy said, "You can sing tenor, can't you?" I said, "Well, yeah." And he said, "Would

you sing with me tonight because I ain't got a tenor singer, and I really need somebody to sing with me." And I looked at Ralph [as if to say] "Help me." I might have known one of his songs, but I really didn't know his songs. And Ralph said, "Well, it's up to Rick, whatever he wants to do." I'm like, "Ralph, that's not what I wanted you to say. I wanted you to come to my rescue." And so I was painted in a corner. I couldn't get out. I had to say yes. And so we got in a room somewhere and ran through six or eight songs, and I kind of learned the words to them on the chorus, which is all I had to sing. But, anyway, I played with Jimmy that night.

LARRY CORDLE, SKAGGS'S friend from Brushy Creek, enlisted in the US Navy in 1968 and only learned about his friend's ascendency to the Stanley band from letters he received from Skaggs's mother, who included clippings from bluegrass publications, which, by the early 1970s, regularly applauded Lawrence County's favorite son. Meeting Skaggs to fish while on leave, Cordle got the full, astonishing story. But shortly after his discharge, as he contemplated enrolling in college for an accounting degree, his friend baited a hook and revealed plans to marry Brenda Stanley, a cousin of Ralph's, and give up touring to settle into a day job.

He would hold on to his music, he explained to Cordle, but looked forward to leaving behind the arduous travel and the same old licks and harmony parts that went with them. "I was just fried," he later told prominent writer Alanna Nash. "I wasn't makin' very much money, and the accommodations were terrible—four or five in a motel room together. It was just very hard times financially."

Still keen to form a band with Keith Whitley, Skaggs nonetheless maintained his commitment to domesticity and moved to the Washington, DC, area, where Brenda found work with the Daughters of the American Revolution. Bluegrass music thrived in both the working-class enclaves and the white-collar communities of the region, but Skaggs says that was coincidental to their move: Brenda's job and the promise of work for him at a power plant in northern Virginia drew them.

But he knew too much about the bluegrass scene in the nation's capital to ignore it. With Stanley, he had recorded numerous sessions at Roy Homer's studio in suburban Maryland and played festivals, high schools, and clubs elsewhere in the vicinity, including the Shamrock Tavern in the Georgetown neighborhood of Washington, where the chatter of pro football players and politicians drinking beer often competed with the live music.

The Shamrock was also home to the Country Gentlemen. Founded in the 1950s by the sidemen of local star Buzz Busby, who found themselves at sea after Busby was seriously injured in a car accident, the group was one of the first to radically take bluegrass beyond the original sound of Monroe and company, employing a sprawling instrumental style and vocals that drew as much from the Weavers as the Blue Grass Boys. "They were a unique thing to the Washington, DC, area," says founding banjoist Bill Emerson. "The music they played wasn't a hard-grass. It was more of an exciting brand of folk music." Although Emerson soon left to work with other bluegrass bands and was replaced by Eddie Adcock, he was back by 1970, the band's bluegrass-folk orientation still intact at the Shamrock.

Already acquainted with the band from Stanley's circuit, it wasn't unusual for Skaggs to show up at the Shamrock to sit in before a late-night shift at the power plant. He'd play fiddle for thirty or forty minutes—Jimmy Gaudreau was on mandolin—before dashing to his job in Virginia. Skaggs also took in performances by the Seldom Scene, regulars at the Red Fox Inn, a wood-paneled listening room in suburban Bethesda, Maryland. The band, founded by Country Gentlemen alumnus John Duffey, also brought rock and folk licks into bluegrass music, innovations Bill Monroe or Ralph Stanley would have naturally found distasteful. (Although both veterans understood the innovations taking place in bluegrass and country music, they resisted: Stanley famously referred to progressive bluegrass as "shitgrass," and Monroe feigned confusion at the mention of the Nitty Gritty Dirt Band, linking the "nit" in "nitty" to larval matter.)

The impulse to create still alive in him, the new kid in town was particularly drawn to Seldom Scene guitarist John Starling, whose home in northern Virginia was a salon for musicians in town and those passing through. A surgeon, Starling invited Skaggs to jam whenever musicians gathered.

An unexpected turn of events at the power plant pushed him deeper into the Starling and Shamrock scenes. He arrived one night for work with his banjo and a smoking pipe—a gesture toward the settled life, perhaps—intending to practice in the clawhammer style modeled by Santford Kelly, a Kentucky musician he knew in his youth. But first he had to drain and clean a boiler and refill it with water. Then he planned to plunk on his banjo and smoke his pipe.

While the boiler filled with water, the job mostly completed, he retired to the break room. He recalls:

I'm sitting up there playing this banjo, and these machines are running and I'm playing some rhythm to these machines and I'm in my little world kind of wishing I was back playing music again, and all of a sudden I hear these really loud hazmat horns and sirens [for the boiler had overflowed]. So I threw my banjo in the case real quick so the evidence was gone, stuck it in the locker, ran downstairs, and I see my superior and he's standing in about knee-deep water with his clipboard out, and I'm just so ashamed of what I did. I said, "This is it. I'm cooked." And I saw these fifty-gallon drums and they were just floating on top of the water. So my supervisor said, "Mr. Skaggs, certain people are called for certain tasks, and I just don't believe the good Lord called you to be a high-pressure boiler operator." He had this great Virginia accent. And I said, "Cap, you are exactly right. This is it."

THE SIDE STREETS and storefronts up and down Wisconsin Avenue in northwest Washington and up into Bethesda, Maryland, were natively familiar to Bill Emerson of the Country Gentlemen. He grew up there listening to bluegrass and honky-tonk country and owned a copy of Bill Monroe's "Uncle Pen" record. As a teen, he also knew John Duffey who inspired him to buy a banjo and, later, showed him how to play it. "And that eventually led to John and Charlie Waller and I becoming the Country Gentlemen," says Emerson.

By the time Skaggs came to Washington, the Country Gentlemen also played regularly at the Red Fox Inn, which almost cost Emerson his life. The banjoist had witnessed fights throughout his career, in the parking lots of bluegrass festivals and, worse, in the Pine Tavern in Washington where he saw a patron stab another in the back in the 1950s. But hometown Bethesda was almost never like that. "Me and Doyle Lawson [a recent addition from J. D. Crowe's band] were going home," recounts Emerson, "and I was standing by the passenger door when somebody shot my banjo case out of my hand, hit me in the forearm above my wrist, and broke both bones. I dropped the banjo case, went back inside, and called the police, and an ambulance came and took me to the hospital and I got over it. Never found out who did it or why."

WHILE SKAGGS TURNED in his identification badge at work, the Country Gentlemen—Emerson's wrist back in working order—happened to be debating whether to hire a fiddler. Founding member Charlie Waller didn't want another mouth to feed. But Emerson hewed closer to traditional bluegrass than Waller and, practically speaking, believed a fiddle would lessen the burden on the rest of the musicians, who included Bill Yates on bass and Doyle Lawson on mandolin (who had replaced Jimmy Gaudreau). "You're up there playing a four-hour gig at the Shamrock," explains Emerson. "You're taking every other break. You're kicking off every other song and it's just a lot of work, and if you have a fiddle player, that takes part of that burden away from the instrumentalists and it rounds out the band and makes the band sound bigger and fuller and makes us more versatile. We can do other things that we wouldn't ordinarily do. Like some of the slower songs. The fiddle really helps out, and everybody else had a fiddle player, so why not us?"

Emerson and Waller were already at odds over Waller's lack of interest in rehearsing and introducing new material into the band, so one more conflict was one too many. Brokering a compromise of sorts, they invited Skaggs and his fiddle to get on their GMC tour bus—retired from Greyhound's fleet—to play a session in New York City for Vanguard. When Emerson broached it with Skaggs, the young man assumed Lawson must have left the band. "I thought they were going to want me to play mandolin and sing tenor," recalls Skaggs. "And Bill said, 'Doyle's in the band. We just want you to play some fiddle.' I said, 'Fiddle with the Country Gentlemen?' And he said, 'Yeah, we're going to do some different stuff. You got a clean slate. You don't have anybody to have to play like. Just be yourself. Just play your first read on our songs.' That was nice that I could just play. The fiddle I was playing was Stanley Brothers style, those mountain slides and that kind of stuff. I didn't know country fiddle, but what I got to play on I was happy with."

Always a draw in the Northeast, the Country Gentlemen's visits to New York magnetized the faithful. Their shows at the Washington Square Methodist Church (booked by local folk music promoter Izzy Young) and the YMCA on Twenty-Third Street reliably attracted college students and aging folkies alike, while engagements at the trendy Max's Kansas City club looped in broader audiences. "This quartet from Washington has a more varied and a more sophisticated concept of the potentials of the bluegrass idiom," wrote John S. Wilson of the *New York Times*, a consistent advocate. "It is completely at home in as contemporary a piece as 'Country Roads' (beautifully sung by Charlie Waller in a warm, full-bodied tenor), and treats 'Make Me a Pallet on the Floor' as a blues that swings with country touches. But the group also keeps one foot in familiar bluegrass territory, harmonizing on a spiritual, giving Bill Emerson a showcase for his banjo on 'Cowboys and Indians' and even playing the inevitable 'Orange Blossom Special.'"

The addition of Skaggs on a full-time basis was fortifying, the eighteen-year-old accomplishing the fuller bluegrass experience Emerson had foreseen. "He had been with Ralph, and so the Stanley Brothers were his thing and that's the way he thought bluegrass ought to be done," says Emerson. "Which suited the heck out of me because so did I. Charlie, on the other hand, thought a little differently. He wasn't as hard grass as Ricky and I, or even Doyle and I or Bill Yates and I. Charlie was more into people like Hank Snow and that sort of thing, but Ricky was hard grass at the time, so he fit as far as I'm concerned."

And when the band returned to New York in May 1973 to make its usual round of venues with their now full-time fiddler, critic Wilson was waiting to give "Rick Skaggs" the first in a long line of mentions in the *Times*.

IN AN INTERVIEW with an acoustic music magazine in the mid-1970s, Skaggs cited a Country Gentlemen show in February 1973 as his portal back into full-time music work despite whatever pledge he had made to himself and Brenda to avoid it. Playing New York University, he sensed a new momentum as the band sailed through its typical mix of bluegrass songs with overtones from pop, folk, blues, and gospel, a compelling mosaic that would also mark groundbreaking bands into which he would graduate over the next few years. "The show we did kind of changed my mind more than anything in the world because it was good. I'm not boasting on it, but I know what it sounded like. If the Gentlemen really wanted the sound, I knew I wanted to stay in there and pick with them."

Skaggs's tenor vocals—later said to be the "most expressive" since Ira Louvin—melded with the band's harmony, though he could sing other parts, and his fiddling was often praised by music critics. He wrote a reel titled "Irish Spring" for the band's second Vanguard album and diversified the concert set list with selections from his deep mountain repertoire. "He took us in a little bit of a different direction," says Emerson, "away from the folk music thing we had been doing—'It's All Over Now, Baby Blue' and 'Matterhorn' and all that sort of thing—and more into the bluegrass thing. He had some convictions about how the music should be, and I think that at some point there was a little friction between him and Charlie in that regard. Charlie would say things like, 'Well, we're not the Stanley Brothers. We play our own music.'"

Lawson, too, notes Skaggs's ambition in those days, but says the new player understood his place as the fiddler in a band that had not carried a fiddle in years. In any event, he adds, the young man's vocals were his real asset. "He brought the soul of bluegrass—the feel, the emotion in the singing. I mean he came from that part of Kentucky that, with east Tennessee, we consider the Bible Belt. His mom and daddy both sang, and you can hear what I call the church in their voices. He knew how to deliver a song, and, not only that, he understood harmony singing. He could do the baritone, lead, or tenor."

Suspicious of Waller over his unwillingness to innovate, the eighteen-year-old Skaggs also kept his distance from Bill Yates, the hot-tempered bass player in the band, but the arrival of Dobro player Jerry Douglas, an Ohio native, eased the Kentuckian's transition. The bandmates had spotted Douglas playing at an Ohio festival with the West Virginia Travelers, his father's band, and invited him to sit in on their set. "He was like sixteen or something like that," recalls Skaggs. "And I hadn't heard him that night. I'm standing onstage and I'm turning around toward Charlie and Bill Yates and Doyle, and I'm tuning my fiddle. And next thing I know here is a kid standing beside me with a Dobro wrapped around his neck. And I thought, 'Who are you?' We just kind of met onstage. But, man, when he started playing, it was like, 'Ooh, yeah. You got the gift there, son.' And he did and we became great friends, very close friends."

WHILE SKAGGS NEGOTIATED his way back into the workaday bluegrass world, Marty Stuart settled into the thick of it. Lance LeRoy, now Flatt's manager, secured the teen's membership in the Nashville chapter of the musicians' union and arranged for his salary to flow to Hilda with a portion held back for her son.

Roland White rehearsed Flatt's catalog with Stuart, the favorites such as "Foggy Mountain Breakdown" and "Flint Hill Special" and a few newly recorded songs, particularly "Backin' to Birmingham," recorded in 1970 before Stuart arrived. "He was really hot on that song," groans Stuart, "and I used to go, 'Oh, no. Here we go again.' It wasn't my favorite one to play, but he didn't do a lot of stuff from the RCA sessions. It was pretty much the same stuff he'd leaned on all those years."

Stuart's progression into Flatt's Nashville Grass band was enhanced by sessions at LeRoy's home in the Nashville suburbs. "Some of my favorite nights," says Stuart, "Roland and I would go out to Lance's and he would deejay. Lance introduced me to some phenomenal recordings. After shows, he would record Paul Warren in a hotel room—they would drink beer, and Paul would play these fiddle tunes. Lance LeRoy was a great archivist."

Like Warren, who joined the Foggy Mountain Boys in 1954, many of the Nashville Grass had a history at the forefront of bluegrass. Bassist English "Cousin Jake" Tullock and Burkett "Uncle Josh" Graves, idol of every young resonator guitar player in America, signed up with Flatt and Scruggs in 1955, and White had arrived in Flatt's company after serving with Bill Monroe.* The latest enlistee before Stuart was Haskel McCormick, who had grown up copying Earl Scruggs's banjo picking without realizing

---

* "Resonator guitar" (a.k.a. "resophonic guitar") is the generic term for the Dobro, which is a brand name.

Scruggs rolled with three fingers rather than two until he finally saw Scruggs live. In the 1950s, McCormick filled in with the Foggy Mountain Boys after Scruggs was injured in a car accident.

"They were monumental figures to me," says Stuart. "And I loved them, and I loved being on that bus. It was like being in the Navy, but it was an old fraternity. I felt diplomatic status around that bus that a lot of *Opry* acts did not enjoy. They were struggling to beat it out on that old country path. But we could play the *Grand Ole Opry* or we could play college shows or we could play with Patti Page or Steppenwolf or with a stripper or a country schoolhouse, and it all stayed the same inside that bus."

Stuart watched as the inevitable Flatt-versus-Scruggs debates raged in his community. Fans who lined up outside the bus to say hello praised the legend's choice to follow tradition, unlike Scruggs who, in their view, had joined a rock band. Flatt would tell reporters and fans that the split had not been acrimonious, but, in truth, he and Scruggs were in the early years of a decadelong silence, Flatt exacting his best revenge in his perpetual presentation of the Flatt and Scruggs favorites, one of the most admired catalogs in all of country music, feverishly anticipated among his radio and festival audiences alike.

Throughout Stuart's eight years with Flatt, not much else changed. Some band members came and went, but the boss seemed determined to maintain the old ways. He met his appearance obligations to the *Grand Ole Opry* and to his Martha White Flour–sponsored radio programs on WSM, which were like his natural habitat, and he kept up a relentless schedule of festivals, though he was cooling to them by the time Stuart joined.

Parked in his bus at festivals, waiting for his turn on the stage, Flatt objected to the long hair he saw on the campers and the interminable waits before showtime. "You generally have to stay at those festivals all day and half the night," Flatt commented in an interview. "It's kind of like the *Grand Ole Opry*. You do the eight o'clock show, and then you have to hang around till ten for the next show. . . . It gets to be a drag."

Flatt made it worse on himself and his players because he often pulled into a gig during the middle of the night before a show, refusing to get motel rooms. "I don't know where we took showers," says Stuart. "Gymnasiums, truck stops. I dreaded when we played a little town that had nothing going on because he'd pull the bus in there and set there. His general line was, 'Well, I guess we better go on over to the show. By the time we get our sound system set up, it'll be time to play.' It might have been ten in the morning when he said that, and we would just go and sit all day. That was hard on a teenager."

In the years after *The Beverly Hillbillies* and *Bonnie and Clyde*, the road should have been easier for Lester Flatt and the band, but the boss was still that hard traveler who had slept under the tree by the road with the Foggy Mountain Boys between television stations in Florida and Tennessee. Like their counterparts in the rhythm-and-blues world, the Nashville Grass had no choice but to ride on when a promoter couldn't pay up after a rainy festival weekend, and they just plain winced at Flatt's practice—dating back to the 1940s—of holding back five or ten bucks from their checks for a so-called Christmas fund that gained interest for Flatt during the year before finally appearing in their paychecks. "It was a salaried gig, but it was a little funny," says Stuart.

When they played the popular television show *Hee Haw* or accompanied Flatt on an RCA session—Stuart's first was October 18, 1972—compensation went directly to the Nashville Grass musicians, per union rules, and the same should have been true after appearances on the *Grand Ole Opry* and the Martha White show. But Flatt played by different rules. "There was a tiny radio scale that we were supposed to be getting, but it went to the office and it became part of our salary," explains Stuart. "And nobody questioned it. It was just the way business was done, left over from the Flatt and Scruggs years. Not many bands got away with it, but they did." The radio station money should have been above salary, but in funneling it through his organization and masking it as salary, Flatt could claim to be paying competitive wages.

"The other thing that needs to be said—and this goes back to Flatt and Scruggs as well—it was an absolute no-no to play on somebody else's recordings," says Stuart. "The way they put it was, 'We don't give our sound away.'" However, Uncle Josh Graves would sneak away with his Dobro to contribute to outside sessions, and Stuart followed him—at least once—to play "Lonesome Fiddle Blues" on the self-titled album by Vassar Clements, produced by John McEuen of the Nitty Gritty Dirt Band (Mercury, 1975).* But most of the band complied with Flatt's prohibition, including fiddler Paul Warren who watched at festivals while peers, like Kenny Baker and Curly Ray Cline, hawked their custom-made albums for extra cash.

"But Lester would not let Paul Warren make a fiddle album, and Paul wouldn't buck him on it," says Stuart. "And I remember going to Lester one night and saying, 'This is wrong.' And we had words over not being fair to Paul Warren. Basically, I was told to mind my own business, which I did after that. Sadly, those Lance LeRoy recordings of old fiddle tunes by Paul went away in a yard sale. That was something about Lester that I never understood and never agreed with."

The seedy condition of Flatt's bus also continued to annoy Stuart, who aspired to a sleeker form of travel on the highways of the southeastern circuit. "About once a year, we would back it up on a little bit of an incline and we would get all the Martha White songbooks out from under the bunks and all the junk and sprinkle Tide all up and down the aisles of the bus and get a water hose and the water would drain out the door, and [Flatt's wife] Gladys would come and take Lester's sheets and it looked like he had changed oil on them, that greasy hair. It was funky. It was chitlin' circuit."

---

* In the credits Marty's last name was misspelled as "Stewart." The album also featured Charlie Daniels and John Hartford.

THERE MAY NOT have been a tighter bluegrass ensemble in America than the Nashville Grass, but Flatt, like Monroe, was on an oldies tour. His sets and recordings relied heavily on the Flatt and Scruggs catalog, just as Ralph Stanley served the ghost of the Stanley Brothers with Skaggs and Whitley in his employ. New hires like Stuart preserved Flatt's sound, unlike Earl Scruggs's sons who pushed Flatt's former partner into new dimensions, or the Country Gentlemen who freshened up with Skaggs's fiddle and high tenor vocals. But Stuart's impact resonated beyond the borders of the band as young cats strategizing their own move into bluegrass, such as Jerry Douglas, stood up and paid attention. "I used to hear Marty on the radio with Lester in the mornings, and I knew Sam Bush said the same thing as me: 'If that guy can do it, I can do it.' Him and Ricky . . . those guys playing mandolins with Flatt and Stanley inspired us."

Flatt would remain atop the bluegrass world throughout his life because fans valued tradition and respected his life-giving contribution to the genre's birth and growth. But he was not interested in developing his musicians for life without him, not even Stuart, who would have to reinvent himself multiple times after he finally went out on his own.

Flatt never lacked for work and played stages in addition to festivals that most of his fellow travelers could only dream of. Thanks to pop culture status achieved with Scruggs, he skirted the murky "knife-and-gun clubs" that sustained Ralph Stanley, and he frequently appeared in civic centers, listening rooms, and concert halls.

Sweetening the ride with Flatt, a possible case of mistaken identity may have linked the band to profitable business on the university circuit. They had played a college-buyer showcase in February 1973 in Cincinnati with Chick Corea and Kool and the Gang at the very same time "Dueling Banjos" from the *Deliverance* movie soundtrack—copped from an old Arthur "Guitar Boogie" Smith hit—was scaling the pop charts as performed by session musicians

Eric Weissberg and Steve Mandell. It just so happened Flatt and company had been performing the hit as "Mocking Banjo" for years. "We played that song inside the set, and we encored it," continues Stuart. "It was one of nine encores in a forty-five-minute set." Within days, an agent booked Flatt on a reckless succession of college campuses and rock festivals, seventy-nine days in all. Starting in early April, the field-house favorites stormed through East Tennessee State University, the University of Southern Mississippi, Morehead State University in Kentucky, and others before winding up that leg of the tour on May 11 at Michigan State University on a bill with Emmylou Harris, Gram Parsons, and the Eagles. "This show changed my life," Stuart scrawled in his 1973 appointment book.

The money from the college venues welled up like oil from the ground, but Stuart understood Harris and the Eagles were moving into the future by finding rock and country's natural connections, while the Nashville Grass in their herringbone suits defined eclecticism as Flatt and Stuart clogging onstage like Jed and Granny in *The Beverly Hillbillies*. Flatt's understated vocal style, which many found so attractive in the 1950s and 1960s, seemed almost nondescript among the assertive styles of Loretta Lynn and Waylon Jennings, even the high-tenor proclamations of Bill Monroe. And Flatt's new recordings were often corny, influenced, frequently, by nativist tendencies that might have played well on the *Grand Ole Opry* but deterred programmers on progressive campus radio stations.

Echoing Guy Drake's reactionary "Welfare Cadilac [*sic*]," Merle Haggard's "Okie from Muskogee," and Ralph Stanley's "Are You Proud of America," Flatt proposed his own social commentary in the out-of-step novelty "I Can't Tell the Boys from the Girls," on the *Flatt on Victor* album of 1970. Programmed with the mildly patriotic "Let Our Love Shine Through" and "The Good Old Fashioned Way," it poked fun at the male tresses currently in vogue that offended old-time sensibilities at diners and bluegrass festivals. But it was no joke to some college students and denizens of the counterculture on the streets of Nashville where long hair drew elbow jabs and other hostile reprimands. Apparently, the sons of Earl Scruggs believed the "Can't Tell the Boys" took aim at them.

STUART HAD PICKED up the strong scent of old medicine-show sensibilities of southern-based performance when he went out with the Sullivan Family in the summer of 1972, where he saw blue-grass music framing slightly dubious religious dogma and fluid conversion stories proffered by itinerant preachers. It was the old mingling of country music and commerce that had helped put Jimmie "You Are My Sunshine" Davis in the Louisiana governor's office and Lyndon B. Johnson of Texas in the US Senate. Every indigenous southern style—blues and jazz as well—had taken root in the southern market by drawing crowds for hucksters peddling sex, cures for male impotence, groceries, cars, and the like. And if Stuart thought he'd left that behind by going to Nashville with Lester Flatt, he was pleasantly mistaken.

Within Stuart's first three months of employment, he was heading to Raleigh County, West Virginia, to campaign for Emerson Stover, the Republican candidate for sheriff who, according to Stuart, was known for "an incredible stuttering impairment." A local newspaper's account of the visit pointed out that Flatt was familiar with the campaign trail, having taken up banners for George Wallace and local politicians all across the South. In that, Flatt was hardly alone in the wider country music world, nor was he unique in swiping at Martin Luther King Jr., as he did while tape rolled at a 1966 Flatt and Scruggs show in Houston when, according to the band's comic routine, bassist Jake Tullock interrupted Flatt's greetings to the audience with a shrill cry. "Don't pay no attention to him," purred Flatt. "He's worse than Martin Luther King to wanna yak all the time." And the audience roared.

Candidate Stover of West Virginia revealed to the local newspaper that he had met Flatt through Everett Lilly, a veteran of the Foggy Mountain Boys who had played on iconic Flatt and Scruggs recordings such as "'Tis Sweet to Be Remembered" and "Somehow Tonight."

"Everybody liked Emerson because he helped the Nashville Grass boys back in the Foggy Mountain Boys days to get their used cars," says Stuart. "And he especially had an angle with old police cars. You could still see where the police decal was on the side when you'd buy the car. And Lester would buy one of those cars every now and then. He was always into buying and flipping cars."

On November 6, 1972, the band put its sound system on a flatbed trailer and pulled it to Guy's Furniture in Sophia, Shumate's Grocery in Coal City, Ray's Leisure Time Shop in Shady Spring, and, finally, the Beckley Plaza Mall. Local politicians also on parade awkwardly waited at each stop for Flatt and the boys to finish their brief set, so they could endorse Stover and trumpet their own accomplishments.

The next day Stover lost in Roanoke County to incumbent sheriff Okey Mills, a legendary coalfields baseball player. But Stuart found the hucksterism of his summer with the Sullivan Family still viable in West Virginia. "The medicine-show deal carried over into the very last day of Lester's existence," he promises.

5

Peace, Love, and Country

LITTLE MORE THAN six months after Stuart joined the Nashville Grass, his mentor and friend Roland White returned to California to re-form the Kentucky Colonels with his brothers Eric and Clarence. The recent breakup of the Byrds had stranded Clarence, a member since 1968 and guest contributor since 1966, but not before he had created vocabulary for the nascent country-rock sound with a mechanism on his electric guitar called the String-Bender (conceived by White and fellow West Coast musician Gene Parsons) that produced a pedal-steel sound. Even before the StringBender, his guitar parts on the Byrds' "Time Between" and "The Girl with No Name" from the *Younger Than Yesterday* album (1967) are considered primordial elements of country rock, and he bolstered recordings by other progenitors of the style, including bands led by Linda Ronstadt and former Byrds Gram Parsons and Gene Clark. "Just playing with Clarence for thirty seconds was enough to know this guy was from another galaxy," said John York, who played bass in the Byrds with White.

Says Stuart, "I tended to look toward people like Clarence White, who were absolutely grounded and based and established on traditional bluegrass. But he had taken that and gone beyond it. Instead of keeping it to himself, he carried it into the Byrds, in the recordings he was doing with progressive people in California.

That looked like the promised land to me. What was going on with former bluegrass musicians in Southern California might have made it the coolest place on the planet earth. And they had palm trees and it was warm and they had cool clothes and they had recording studios out there that were better."

Stuart might have left Flatt to go with Roland had he enjoyed that kind of mobility so early in life, but the alternative wasn't so bad. Flatt moved Stuart to the mandolin and revived the career of guitarist Curly Seckler, formerly of the Foggy Mountain Boys where he had sung lead and played the mandolin. He happened to be driving a truck and playing on weekends when his old boss called.

In the early summer of 1973, Roland contacted Stuart to say he and the Kentucky Colonels would be wrapping up a road trip with a show in Indian Springs, Maryland, right around the time Flatt was booked in nearby Pennsylvania, and he asked to catch a ride back to Tennessee while Clarence and Eric flew to California. "So we go to this truck stop [around midnight]," recalls Stuart, "and there's Clarence and there's Eric and there's Roland, and we had a late-night breakfast together and Clarence was kind of quiet, but he said, 'Is Curly Seckler still around?' I said, 'Come here, I'll show him to you.' I remember taking Clarence on the bus and opening the bunk curtain, and I said, 'There he is.' Clarence laughed. Lester was asleep, and they didn't think anything about it. I was the only one up, me and the driver. And that's the only time I ever shook hands with Clarence."

Six weeks later, Clarence White died when a drunk driver hit him as he loaded instruments into Roland's car after a gig outside Los Angeles. Shell-shocked by his loss, Roland eventually moved on to the admired Country Gazette bluegrass band, while Stuart observed for the first time the easy intrusion of death in the country music world. "I saw such pain in Roland and such loss that I would have given everything to fill those shoes for him. I knew I couldn't." But to help Roland with the pain, Stuart never stopped lifting up Clarence in public conversation and in the spirit of his

own music, joining an ardent corps of musicians and fans who
kept his memory alive in the many decades that followed.

TO FILL THE mentorship void left by Roland's 1973 departure
from the Nashville Grass, Stuart turned to Seckler, almost forty
years his senior. "Curly became 'the guy' as I was becoming more
aware of how the world worked and how show business worked.
Curly was the most solid and steady character that I had to lean on.
He didn't have one ounce of pop culture knowledge or rock-and-
roll knowledge or blues knowledge in him. He was a dyed-in-the-
wool, first-generation country music–bluegrass music musician.
And that's where he lived, and that's where he parked it. But Curly
was kind of my best friend in that band after Roland left."

How close could a teenage boy be to a fifty-five-year-old man
who, even Stuart points out, lived in a bluegrass bubble? The
answer was surely plain to Hilda Stuart's skeptical family and
friends back in Mississippi. But anybody paying attention, including Hilda, knew Stuart had long courted the attention of older
men and women—the country stars he targeted as they passed
through Philadelphia and mentors such as Enoch Sullivan, Lethal
Jackson, and Marzell Page. He knew how to engage them with
flattery and conversation about their craft. Indeed, like Skaggs
growing up in a community of older men and women who played
mountain music, young Stuart was an old soul.*

Still, there was nobody on the Scenicruiser invested in Stuart's
emotional security as deeply as Hilda and John Stuart were back
in Philadelphia. Banjoist Haskel McCormick—who energized
Flatt's shows performing "Mocking Banjo" with Stuart on mandolin—recalls censoring his adult banter around Stuart while he and

---

*To experience teenage Stuart's ease with veterans in music, one need only
consult the series of photos of the youngster buttonholing the much older
Sonny Osborne with a joke of some kind in Carl Fleischhauer and Neil V.
Rosenberg's *Bluegrass Odyssey: A Documentary in Pictures and Words, 1966–86*.
They guffaw like old men playing poker.

other bandmates indulged Marty's incessant after-hours picking on the bus, a no-no as far as Flatt was concerned. But generally the teenager was left alone to look after himself on the road.

The stern Bill Monroe, understanding perhaps of the boy's experience in light of his own, extended a fatherly hand when his bus and Flatt's rode in tandem on their way to shared gigs. "And I would ask Monroe if I could ride along and play mandolin because he just loved to play," relates Stuart. "So several nights, he'd sit on one side of the aisle and I'd sit on the other and we'd just play the mandolin in the dark, and he'd show me old tunes that he never got around to recording yet or old licks. He showed me how his Uncle Pen [Vandiver] would have played this or that on the fiddle. He showed me how other people played. It was an awesome classroom."

Back on Flatt's nighttime bus, where the red glow of cigarettes in the dark silence was often the only sign of life, he buckled the hasps on his mandolin case and let his mind wander to home. Was sister Jennifer sporting a new hairstyle? In his family's living room, who gathered to play guitars?

Stuart's young friend Carl Jackson, who had graduated from Jim and Jesse to megastar Glen Campbell's band, could relate. He says:

> If there was a downside to it, it was being away from my family, being away from my little sister. Marty would probably say the same thing about being away from Jennifer, being away from his mom and dad. We were both doing something that we loved so much, and we were having a good time. My first two-week trip with Jim and Jesse, I was alone. I was a homesick little boy. And I couldn't wait to get home and see my family. But I also wanted to go back to the road. I had two dreams: play center field for the New York Yankees or play music. And that music door opened wide for me, and it opened wide for Marty. And we walked through it.

I am so thankful—and I know Marty feels the same way—to have had parents that understood and saw. It was obvious to them early on that we had those abilities; we had that God-given talent inside that could take us places that maybe they had dreamed of. Nothing would have made my dad happier than to play music for a living, and I can't say that about John Stuart, but I know John loved music so much. I see kids have to spend some of the most wonderful years of their life in a classroom learning stuff that they will never use, kids who have special talents that are in some ways suppressed because the focus is on, "You got to do your homework to do well in chemistry." If you're going to be a doctor, then there's a lot of stuff you have to learn, and if your dream is to be a doctor, you need to learn it. But diagramming a sentence is not used very often in the music world.

Nor is long division. But growing up in close community with one's peers has merits, too, as does disciplining oneself to study tricky academic subjects. Such experiences passed over Stuart as the correspondence classes Lance LeRoy had arranged fell by the wayside. "I was supposed to have a relationship with my schoolbooks," says Stuart.

Part of the deal with me going to work with Lester was that education had to be addressed. Roland helped me, but Lester had a third grade education, and I don't know if Curly finished school. Paul Warren was an intelligent fellow. But I remember one day as I was trying to study English, I walked to the front of the bus while we were traveling and the guys were all playing poker, and I said, "Excuse me. Can somebody tell me what a pronoun is?" And Lester stopped and said, "Let's see. I believe that goes on a tractor, don't it? Give me three cards." I just threw my books in the air and said, "I give up." So I dropped out of school that minute.

Mandolinist Ronnie McCoury was just a boy along for the ride to his father Del's festival appearances, most within a half-day's drive of their Pennsylvania home, when he encountered young Stuart in Delaware among the many adults. They played catch together, such childhood games somewhere still in Stuart's heart. But when the older boy stepped on the stage, says McCoury, who hadn't yet begun to play an instrument, he was every inch the serious player, a scarf around his neck and a girl or two waiting for autographs when the set ended. "It kind of made me want to play, seeing someone young like Marty playing. I thought, 'Well, I can do that.' He was probably the first child prodigy in bluegrass. I can't think of anyone else that was in a band like Lester Flatt's or had the national attention in bluegrass."

Offstage, Stuart often wrote letters to Jennifer or waited for calls from Hilda and John. "We always, always remained in touch," says Jennifer. "I missed him and we'd cry a lot, but he was like a child in an adult world trying to make it on the road. That had to be weird for him."

By 1974 Hilda put in motion plans to move to Nashville, sensing the need to bring familial care to Marty. Accordingly, the parent company of John's employer transferred him to Nashville, and Lester helped Hilda find a job in a bank. Recalls Jennifer, who was fourteen when she moved, "My mom's father, my grandfather, he just said, 'You got to do what's right in y'all's heart. I'm gonna miss you guys, but you know where I am and I know where y'all will be.' And so that right there was like the crowning moment from my grandfather. That meant the world to us."

Not to say the four Stuarts coalesced into the unit they had once been. Stuart, though he moved home, had been essentially independent too long for that to happen, and Jennifer had grown into the unpredictable teenage years. "We had to get here and rearrange our lives and our thoughts and basically relearn each other," she says. "But it was all good. I'm glad that we had that time together because, after that, he was always gone."

In the context of postlynching Philadelphia, the Stuarts were pilgrims of a sort on a journey out of the Deep South, following their son's path away from the pall still over the city in the mid-1970s.

IN THE HEART of Skaggs's approximately two-year run with the Country Gentlemen, the band ran up and down the road like the Clinch Mountain Boys, even headlining its own festival in New England, where each member had to engage with fans and fellow pickers all weekend. So the band looked forward to a short skip down to Warrenton, Virginia, a community fast evolving into an outer suburb as the population of the Washington, DC, area boomed. The town had hosted country performances by local royalty such as Jimmy Dean and Roy Clark in the 1950s, before each had broken out nationally, and it staged bluegrass music when the festival movement of Carlton Haney's creation caught fire in the late 1960s.

The Eighth Annual Warrenton Bluegrass and Folk Festival in June 1973 in Lake Whippoorwill Park touted stalwarts from the circuit: Jimmy Martin, the Lilly Brothers and Don Stover, Red Allen, Del McCoury, and others. But the fliers hanging in drugstore windows and record shops throughout the area telegraphed something more than the Carlton Haney model: the Grateful Dead's Jerry Garcia would be with his Old & In the Way band, and pop balladeer Don McLean, still in the draft of his epic hit "American Pie," would be headlining, too.

This show was a Jim Clark production, a so-called multigenre festival, staged in cooperation with the local Jaycees, calculated to sell as many tickets as possible. Although promoter Clark traded on the "bluegrass" name, only a taste of the genre was on the plate. Still, bluegrass music's place on the fringes of popular music resonated with some in the underground audience and simply suggested to others the promise of good times to be had in the woods.

If Haney had been inspired by Newport, Clark—based in northern Virginia—embraced the Woodstock template.

Fred Bartenstein, who worked on a freelance basis for Clark while doing the same for Haney, embraced the fusion of styles he saw in the multigenre festivals while acknowledging the danger in tempting the imprudence of the rowdy generation. "There's going to be drugs," he says. "There's going to be rapes. There's going to be shootings and stabbings. There's not enough sanitation for these large crowds. It's going to be a problem." A drunk fan had drowned in a lake at Clark's Peace, Love, Blues, and Bluegrass Folk Festival in Stumptown, West Virginia, earlier in the season, a worrisome prelude to Warrenton.

Music critic Richard Harrington, who eventually joined the *Washington Post* in 1976, worked two festivals for Clark, liaising with artists and phoning parents whose kids had passed out in the grass. He can't specifically recall how he came to work for Clark but guesses he must have met him when the promoter, looking to buy advertising, visited the offices of an arts weekly he owned in Washington. "In his own way, he was a semivisionary," says Harrington.

> I think he just wanted to figure out a way to get more people to buy tickets, and so he realized the young audience he wanted to draw was not going to be interested in the Country Gentlemen or Jimmy Martin or anybody like that. But they'd come to see the Star-Spangled Washboard Band, John Hartford, or any of the other groups who fit into that particular category. What I remember of Clark is that he never struck me as being a rebel, like Bill Graham. He was not a provocateur. He was an opportunist, and he saw an opportunity to grow his audience and therefore grow his wallet.

ACCORDING TO BLUEGRASS historian Neil V. Rosenberg, Clark first channeled the youthful mood in 1971 with a concert in Alexandria, Virginia—a DC suburb—featuring hard-core bluegrass talent and nationally known experimentalists. It proved to be the blueprint for some of the more outrageous festivals Clark staged, including the welter at Warrenton.

With the gig so close to home, most of the Country Gentlemen arrived to the festival at Warrenton in their own cars, but Jerry Douglas, just out of school for the year and barely qualified to apply for a driver's license, arrived in the band's bus with bassist Bill Yates behind the wheel. The teenager who paid attention to everything marveled at the throng in tube tops and ill-fitting overalls drifting into the grounds. "The stage was at the edge of a pond," he explains, "and there was broken glass in the pond and people were wading into the pond and getting cut and doctors were fixing people up. And somebody threw a bottle at Eddie Adcock onstage, and it hit the mic stand and went into a million pieces. I remember Eddie onstage saying, 'If whoever threw that bottle comes down here, I'll kick your ass.'"

While traces of the Haney-type bluegrass festival were recognizable at Warrenton—jam sessions in between parked vehicles and workshops throughout each day—families and middle-age migrants from the South searched futilely for the "bluegrass" in "bluegrass festival." The Pagans motorcycle gang showed up to terrorize fans, Bill Yates socked a guy who offended his wife, and the Sunday-morning gospel sing was comically out of place amid the weekend bacchanalia.

"It was just wild, hippies-o-plenty," recalls Skaggs.

I think it was like people saw a candy store that had a lock on it and just decided to break in. I don't know how many thousands of people were at Whippoorwill Lake, but Jim didn't have money to pay the band. Or said he didn't. I remember seeing Rodney Dillard, because the Dillards were there, jerk a leaf off of a tree and say, "Here, Jim, write us a check on this." Just being very sarcastic with him. And Jim stuttered a lot, and it was really sad. I ended up feeling sorry for the guy, in a way. Here's all these thousands of people and no money.

What's up with that? You say, "Is he telling us the truth?" All of us went home and didn't get paid. There was a lot of people that didn't. And there was a lot of fights.

The Country Gentlemen scattered to their vehicles in the lingering vibrations of their final set, while Douglas piled back into the long bus with Yates for the short ride home. Fans young and in the way dotted the exit route, and Yates had just picked up speed when a man darted into the road. The bus swerved, throwing Douglas and the musical instruments into the aisle. Yates pulled open the door in a rage. "And I walked behind Yates to see what was going to happen," recounts the Dobroist. "I was sixteen, and I watched Yates hit this guy, and he landed on the yellow line and Yates picked him up and threw him in the ditch. And he was walking back to the bus, picking skin out of his ring. I'm watching that, and I say, 'This is going to be a hell of a summer.' Those words went through my mind."

When the last attendee had departed, the police counted thirty arrests on charges related to drug use, assault, and indecent exposure. A mountain of garbage had piled up, and Jim Clark never staged another show at Lake Whippoorwill Park.

"The *Bluegrass Unlimited* crowd really hated these festivals, saying they're going to destroy bluegrass," says Bartenstein. "'They're going to make it impossible for us to do our thing. No community is going to allow us to do a bluegrass festival because [Clark festivals] are giving us a bad name.' Finally, there's this festival called Stompin 76 which is held near Galax, Virginia, which is Jim Clark on steroids. And that one festival pulls down the whole multigenre phenomenon because bad shit happened at Stompin 76."

MARTY STUART RETAINS few memories of the much-discussed Stompin 76 festival in southwestern Virginia, promoted by Hal Davidson of Baltimore. Staged not far from the cradle of recorded country music in Bristol, where Jimmie Rodgers and the Carter

Family created seminal recordings for the Victor Talking Machine Company starting in 1927, the festival triggers images in Stuart's mind of Flatt's bus inching toward the festival in a crush of traffic and then flying by helicopter over the crowds to the stage. He met for the first time folk troubadour John Prine, who invited the seventeen-year-old to sit in with him, another inspiring connection that enlarged his world. "It was a gargantuan hippie event," says Stuart. "I felt like the Woodstock generation had run out of rock-and-roll shows to go to, so they adopted bluegrass."

The dangerous aura around Stompin 76 that Bartenstein describes intensified at the unwelcome appearance of the Pagans. The motorcycle gang swarmed the gate, separating fearful ticketholders from their six-packs, food, and even charcoal grills as they entered. Further, some fans recall, bikers roamed the grounds, pillaging campsites while occupants stripped to the waist, woozy after bouts with local moonshine and bad drugs, barely stirred. There were reports of rapes and vandalism. "They had piercings on their faces, and they were pushing people around and people were terrified of them," says an alumnus of the festival. "I think most people weren't familiar with that whole ugliness. They were doing what they wanted to do, and if you didn't agree with them . . . you just tried to stay away from them as best you could." Meanwhile, the Earl Scruggs Revue, Bonnie Raitt, Doc and Merle Watson, Lester Flatt, and others on the multigenre schedule performed their shows, the music merely incidental to the alarming dramas unfolding throughout the natural amphitheater and beyond.

But at least one ticketholder found beauty in the weekend. Linda McCawley Dillon, raised in a sharply class-conscious suburb of Washington, DC, spent her high school years paradoxically contemplating injured Vietnam War veterans trying to get their lives started again while her mother lectured on the necessity of proper dress and makeup for women looking to get married. By the time the first fliers advertising Stompin 76 showed up in the DC area, she was desperate. She was working as a hair stylist and coping with a recent divorce in which she'd lost custody of her three-year-old son to her ex-husband's family, who believed she was a woefully unfit parent. So when a friend with tickets and access to a pickup truck invited her along because she knew how to drive standard transmission, she climbed on board, trading her false eyelashes and carefully coiffed hairdo for a denim style of festival dress at which her mother would have gasped. "I came with the clothes I had on and a change of underwear. I had a pair of Frye boots—because Frye boots were very popular then—and I had on a jean jacket with no shirt, no bra, and a bandana."

As Dillon—a festival neophyte—piloted the truck south, her passengers under the camper top behind her sang bluegrass songs while she fretted over going without makeup and a hair dryer. And where would she bathe? The unsteady refrains of "Rocky Top" from the truck bed in her ear, she glanced down at the one-person tent rolled up in an orange bag she had purchased at K-Mart and the bag of peanut butter and jelly sandwiches resting on the floor.

DILLON'S GROUP SPLIT up once it reached the farmers' fields that were the festival grounds. With no specific plans to meet them at the end of three days, she passed through the Pagan line unmolested, thanks probably to her meager supplies—the sandwiches, a water canister, and a can of Tang drink mix—and crossed over a wooden bridge where "herds of people" strolled up and down the wide, rutted paths. A hay wagon carried her to a dell near a stream that was a focal point for her fellow campers. "And the people were naked," she says," and I remember sitting in the tent, going, 'Am I going to do that? Am I going to take off my clothes and bathe in the stream?'"

For what may have been the first time in her young life—she was twenty-four years old—the novice festivarian sat beneath blue skies and chanced to contemplate her life so far, to enjoy a moment free of judgment without the masks she wore in polite society. There was no place she was supposed to be, no child in need of dinner nor a husband waiting at home.

"He was very mean, my husband, and verbally abusive, and he always looked down his nose at me, and I just told my dad, 'I can't take it anymore.' And he goes, 'Why can't you have an affair like your mother does?' I'm like, 'Because I can't. My marriage is ending, Dad. I'm sorry.' I remember him crying. He goes, 'Well, what about the money?' And I'm like, 'Are you kidding me? You want me to stay because of the money?' And he goes, 'You're making a huge mistake.'"

She perched herself on the side of a hill facing the performance stage, tracking the helicopter bulleting to and fro with artists on board and the orderly procession of the hay wagons transporting campers between the grassy seating area and the various tent cities.

She absorbed the blues rock of Raitt and the rock country of the Nitty Gritty Dirt Band. But John Prine was her favorite, with Marty Stuart shuffling behind him. "It was right now, and it was live, you know, so it was cool," she explains. "It wasn't something like driving down the road and listening to the Nitty Gritty Dirt Band on the radio, you know what I mean? The fact that it was live made it even better."

When the festival ended, Dillon magically rediscovered her friends, took the wheel, and lurched away from the scene to begin the hours-long drive back to Maryland. Later, she quit her job in the hair salon and, through a friend from high school, hired on at a motorcycle shop.

"I was kind of trying to figure out where I was supposed to be. So that's why I was able to say, 'Sure, I'll go. I can drive.' I think Stompin 76 actually changed me in the way of, 'Wow, I don't have to wear makeup. I don't need a hair dryer. I can just be me.' I think it showed me that it's okay . . . to be imperfect."

6

New South

THE COUNTRY GENTLEMEN'S swift exit from the chaotic Warrenton Bluegrass Festival gave way to a slate of peaceable shows in
the summer of 1973. But the band was in flux. Bill Emerson had
recently resigned to join the US Navy's Country Current bluegrass
band, and Douglas was merely traveling with the band between his
junior and senior years of high school trying to decide if college
was a smarter route.

In Douglas, though, Skaggs had a willing partner in his explo-
rations of the DC music scene so rich in elements of folk music
and southern country, not unlike the West End of Nashville in
the early to mid-1970s, where a first-class songwriting community inhabited by Guy Clark, Rodney Crowell, Kris Kristofferson,
and others had coalesced. Although the federal city lacked the
major labels and publishing companies of Nashville that could
have nationally amplified the city's music making, clubs and studios abounded to help the considerable bluegrass community
fine-tune its picking and learn how to make a record. Skaggs, eyes
always on the horizon, meandered in and out of Track Recorders, just over the DC line in Silver Spring, Maryland, where he
contributed to the Seldom Scene's *Old Train* sessions and the fast-
rising Tony Rice's *California Autumn*. He traipsed the sidewalks
of the city's gentrifying Georgetown neighborhood where young

pioneers in country rock and folk of national caliber played at the Cellar Door. "You'd see Linda Ronstadt, Kris Kristofferson, Steve Goodman, and the list goes on come to the Cellar Door," says Doyle Lawson, "and, by and large, most of them would make their way down to the Shamrock. I remember going to see Kristofferson at the Cellar Door when he kept getting his chin whiskers caught up in the microphone."

But John Starling's invitations to his guitar pulls may have mattered most. Says Skaggs, "He'd call me and say, 'Hey man, we got a picking going on tonight. You ought to come.' I'd take the mandolin and fiddle and go, and that's how I met Emmy. I loved John, and, of course, I met so many people that was coming in and out of his house."

Emmy, of course, was Emmylou Harris, who had recently landed back in the Washington area, where she had grown up, after the death of former Byrd and country-rock pioneer Gram Parsons, who had hired her as a harmony vocalist and taken her on the road upon falling under the spell of her Faye Dunaway grace and shimmering vocals in a local coffeehouse.

Her career still taking form when Skaggs met her, she had paid her dues like the rest, chancing Greenwich Village in the late 1960s and waitressing and playing bars in Nashville, which had only pointed her back to Washington's kinder music halls. But her short-lived collaboration with the troubled Parsons, beginning in 1972 and ending with his fatal overdose in 1973, produced the landmark album *Grievous Angel*, which gained the attention of national record labels as well as the West Coast country-rock community—to the point where one of its bona fide stars, Linda Ronstadt, befriended her. As it happened, Ronstadt—gaining loft with early hits on Capitol Records—met Harris for the first time in Houston where Harris was performing with Parsons. "Clearly, something unusual was taking place up on that stage, and we in the audience were mesmerized," Ronstadt wrote in her 2013 autobiography. "Emmy has the ability to make each phrase of a song sound like a last desperate plea for her life, or at least her sanity. No melodrama; just the plain truth of raw emotion."

Ronstadt and Harris loved harmony singing, so central to bluegrass, with a particular passion for sibling duets by the Everly Brothers, whom Lennon and McCartney and everybody else adored, and the Girls of the Golden West of early country music, composed of the Goad sisters, Millie and Dollie. Whenever Ronstadt's tour landed in Washington, they stitched together girl-duo arrangements of old country songs popularized by the Stanley Brothers and the Louvin Brothers. Together, even if only in John Starling's living room, they created searing vocal performances akin to Dolly Parton's "Jolene," a current country music smash that conveyed human desperation worthy of the best murder ballads but in a modern musical context.

Mesmerized by Harris and her J-200 Gibson guitar when she appeared at Starling's house, Skaggs introduced both her and Ronstadt to the store of mountain songs in his brain and coached them in the intricacies of harmony singing, like how to jump among notes and parts. Plenty of Stanley Brothers favorites— "The Angels Are Singing (in Heaven Tonight)," "The Lonesome River," "The White Dove"—reached the ceiling in Starling's home, which he shared with his wife, Fayssoux, another sweet voice in the homespun performances.

Jerry Douglas, who by the spring of 1974 had refused a scholarship at the University of Maryland to join the Country Gentlemen full-time, first saw Harris at the Childe Harold, another DC club, and saw her again at Starling's house. "I'm sitting here on the floor with Linda Ronstadt thinking, 'What are people that I went to high school with going to think about this?' And I just didn't tell them because they wouldn't believe me anyway," says Douglas.

Douglas also saw Harris at the Red Fox Inn, where she supped on the bottomless pot of spaghetti and sauce on the kitchen stove while greeting the local bluegrass and folk cognoscenti. "But the difference between the Red Fox Inn in '71 and the same club in '74 was that more than just a few appreciative West Coast musicians were liable to show up in the crowd on any given night," wrote journalist Daniel Cooper in his definitive profile of Harris for the *Journal of Country Music*. "Emmylou was now a known talent, and she was being represented by Eddie Tickner, a left field industry mystic who had previously managed the Byrds and Parsons. He conducted business by speaking in parables."

Tickner had the story line of his next parable—something about the power of an artist's persistence—when he brokered a deal with Warner Bros. Records, whose A&R (artists and repertoire) woman Mary Martin endorsed Harris after catching two shows in the DC area. The label paired her with producer Brian Ahern, a Canadian with an unruly shock of curls, who had produced Anne Murray's big hits. Before even meeting his new charge, Ahern contacted songwriter Rodney Crowell—a Texas native and early denizen of Nashville's West End—who was gigging around in Toronto and living on draws from his publishing deal with Ahern.

The script forming in Ahern's mind had Crowell, the southern boy, suggesting country songs that might influence the rundown of the first album, *Pieces of the Sky*. "Emmy was playing at the Childe Harold, I think," says Crowell, "and I watched her show, and, of course, I was a fan of Gram's records and knew Emmylou's work there, so she wasn't somebody I didn't know, but we hit it off instantly and after the gig we just stayed up all night and sat on the floor and traded songs. We sang Louvin Brothers' songs back and forth to each other, and we became fast friends because Emmy was impressed by my wealth of knowledge about old country music that had been passed on to me by my father and that I was writing songs that she could record."

At the same time, however, Crowell's eyes were upon Texas, particularly Austin and its Cosmic Cowboy phenomenon, conjured up by Jerry Jeff Walker, Michael Martin Murphey, and, coming in on the last chorus, Willie Nelson. Curious, too, about the hippie chicks whom he perceived to be abundant in Austin, he had relocated there after meeting Harris and seemed bound to stay. But she and her band played Austin on their way out to record in Los Angeles, and in the time it took to consume a can of Lone Star, she persuaded him to come along.

Crowell animated Harris's country music sensibilities, moving her and Ahern—who would soon marry—to draw Crowell into their fold. He joined her band on guitar and vocals as she prepared for liftoff and contributed his "Bluebird Wine" to *Pieces of the Sky*, released in 1975.

Harris and Ahern also tapped Crowell's notebook for gems such as "I Ain't Living Long Like This" and "You're Supposed to Be Feeling Good," classics that first saw the light on her *Luxury Liner* album (1976). But the broader conversation about songs, believed Crowell, was his most valuable contribution to Harris's world. "I was always sort of self-congratulatory at having steered Emmylou toward Townes Van Zandt's 'Pancho and Lefty' [1976] and Johnny Mullins' 'Blue Kentucky Girl' [1979]," says Crowell. "I told Emmy, 'You can kill "Blue Kentucky Girl"'—I knew it from Loretta Lynn, and it was a really big hit for her. I was secretly proud of that."

Ahern's open door to strong and informed voices such as Crowell's was one of his signature traits as a producer. He seemed not to be threatened by the lanky Texan's influence on song selection, nor the band's role in shaping arrangements. "He certainly understood that creativity is a matter of cross-pollination now and again," says Crowell. "Brian was really good at creating an atmosphere where really talented musicians were given an opportunity to contribute to the arranging, rather than the old-school, more formal method of a producer and arranger that would direct the recording session and keep everybody in line. Brian himself was part of that arranging, but he also reached out to the really top-drawer musicians with years and years and years of experience who knew a lot about how to arrange music."

Although Nashville's studio system was breaking down in the 1970s, undercutting the dominance of staff producers and engineers, Ahern's choice to record in Los Angeles was more about acknowledging the West Coast influence on Harris than rejecting Music City USA. The musicians who populated her Hot Band, notably guitarist James Burton, drummer Ronnie Tutt, and pianist Glen D. Hardin, approached music in a universal frame of mind, having backed Gram Parsons and worked closely with the likes of Mike Nesmith and Elvis Presley, and helped free even the hardest country songs Emmylou recorded from a particular time, place, or tradition.

A sure sign of Ahern's involvement was his remote recording operation, the Enactron truck, parked in front of a rented mansion in the Coldwater Canyon section of Los Angeles, the production home of the entire run of Harris's classic albums of the 1970s and early 1980s. State-of-the-art recording equipment filled most of the truck, leaving some studio space for background vocals and instrumental fills, which Ahern dubbed "the comfort zone." Cables ran from the truck into the house, the primary performance space, though Crowell used the living-room floor as a bed during his first two weeks in California.

"If there wasn't a real session going on," says Crowell, "I had free studio time, and I could go into the truck and make demos and write songs, and Emmy would come in and Nicolette Larson and Mickey Raphael, and we would just sort of have a party. A lot of songs came from that, and Brian knew if he created a playground where that could happen, then he would benefit from it."

The set list for *Pieces of the Sky* would not have surprised anybody who had sat with Harris in John Starling's living room. She covered the Everly Brothers, the Louvin Brothers, the Beatles, and recordings from the country music mainstream by Dolly Parton and Merle Haggard. And lest anybody might be inclined to accuse Harris of selling out Washington, DC, Fayssoux Starling appeared on backing vocals. Record buyers from bluegrass could also hear the glistening fiddle of a young Kentuckian on her recording of Shel Silverstein's "Queen of the Silver Dollar." She had not forgotten Ricky Skaggs.

Within months, Skaggs forged his own path out of Washington searching for a stage of his own, but not before he recorded his first solo album—*That's It*—the result of a deal with Dick Freeland's Rebel Records, Ralph Stanley's home label. Friends such as Douglas and Tom Gray of the Seldom Scene appeared on his album, while father Hobert contributed several guitar performances and mother Dorothy took lead vocals on a gospel selection she wrote: "That Evergreen Shore." "That was the first time my dad had ever been on a plane. He was scared to death, and Mom, too."

An introduction to the recordings of gypsy jazz greats Stéphane Grappelli and Django Reinhardt had rekindled the hot jazz influences of Paul Johnson and Paul "Euless" Wright from childhood, and he showed it off in lucid arrangements of "Darktown Strutter's Ball" and "Sweet Georgia Brown," which competed on the album with a raft of fiddle reels. "Ricky is everywhere," noted *Bluegrass Unlimited* of the album, "moving with ease from old-time to swing fiddle, from straight bluegrass to jazzy mandolin; he plays a couple of beautiful lead guitar solos and some of the prettiest clawhammer banjo you could ask to hear."

The album fed Skaggs's desire to lead a band, impossible in the Country Gentlemen, which had begun to feel a lot like playing with Stanley. "The group was kind of at a standstill, as far as I was concerned," he said in an interview at the time. "For a lot of people it wasn't; we were playing some good music, but it was the same grind over and over. It wasn't developing like I thought it should." Skaggs had also lost patience with Charlie Waller's reluctance to rehearse, and he missed Bill Emerson, his entrée to the band. "There was personal stuff, too," says Douglas. "And he just wanted to take a step away."

EMMYLOU HARRIS, WITH the momentum of her new Warner Bros. album behind her, had offered Skaggs a place in her Hot Band. It was clear to him, however, that Rodney Crowell was her primary conspirator, filling the artistic void Parsons had left in her world. So he turned again to Keith Whitley, who he thought might lead him away from the status quo, despite Whitley's recent departure from Ralph Stanley to form the band Country Store with Jimmy Gaudreau and Jimmy Arnold. But a tragedy whose very mention still enforces reverent silence among bluegrass fans and players rudely shut down a Skaggs-Whitley reunion.

During his and Whitley's tenure with Stanley, the young men had admired and grown close to Roy Lee Centers, the lead vocalist who some thought had come closest of any of Stanley's lead vocalists to emulating Carter Stanley. A playful sort who had sung in rock-and-roll bands before joining Stanley, Centers's flashing grin and jet-black hair projected a sex appeal from the stage that was rare in mountain music. The truth be told, both Skaggs and Whitley had come looking to see Centers on that fateful night in Fort Gay, West Virginia, when they took the stage in Stanley's absence. But in May 1974, Centers was helpless in the face of an acquaintance named Bill Hurst, a deputy sheriff, who dragged the singer and his twelve-year-old son, Lennie, from a party in Breathitt County, Kentucky, after—some speculate—a disagreement over Hurst's wife. Shoving father and son into his pickup truck by gunpoint, Hurst drove in the middle of the night to a desolate stretch of road where local males were known to settle scores and pistol-whipped Centers and shot him three times—twice in the head—while Centers's son watched the whole scene from the tall weeds at the side of the road where he had sought refuge.

Scenes of murder and other pitiable deaths haunt most every corner of country music—the double murder of comedian and banjoist David "Stringbean" Akeman and his wife in 1973 and Hank Williams's slow-burning demise in the backseat of his chauffeured Cadillac in 1953 come to mind—but few are as contemptible as the death of Roy Lee Centers. "What happened there was just the most monstrous, brutal thing ever," says Skaggs, who not only lost a bluegrass hero but, collaterally, his dream of partnering with Whitley.

We went to the funeral, and I remember after at a restaurant up in Jackson, Kentucky, me and Keith were sitting in the booth together and Ralph was sitting across from us and said, "Keith, I'm sure going to need me a replacement for Roy Lee, and I'm going to need him pretty soon. Is there any way you could come back and work for me until I could find somebody—or you could work as long as you wanted to?" I remember Keith saying right on the spot, "I'll do that, Ralph. I can do that for you." So he did. He came back and worked with Ralph.

BRIEFLY STUNNED AT Whitley's pivot back to Stanley, Skaggs carried his tackle box to Grayson Lake with his old Brushy Creek friend Larry Cordle. Barely attentive to the fish, Skaggs bemoaned the loss of Whitley and added that a band in Lexington, Kentucky, wanted him, and it enjoyed a plum set-down gig at the Holiday Inn hotel, so the touring was minimal. The offer, he told Cordle, came from one of the towering figures in bluegrass music, J. D. Crowe, who had appeared with his banjo toward the end of the first wave of bluegrass music in the early 1950s. His many years in bluegrass king Jimmy Martin's band, starting in the mid-1950s, burnished his picking and the business sense he needed when he started his own band. "He had a real certainty about what he did," observes bassist Steve Bryant, who played with Crowe from the late 1970s through the early 1980s. "Crowe had that space between the notes. His timing was impeccable. He would take a break and back off the mic, and sometimes he would turn towards me, just looking at everybody, [and then resume] like a cannon going off. He had such power and precision."

But Martin's feverish touring in the 1950s unsettled Crowe, and when the time came to form his own band—the Kentucky Mountain Boys—he stuck as close to his mobile-home park as possible, working full-time outside music and taking gigs around Lexington, mostly "knife-and-gun clubs," which he detested. "It's hard to mix beer, whiskey, and women and men," he says. "You're going to have problems, and a lot of times there would be fights. Nobody ever got shot or nothing. But the fighters would upset the whole night. But, of course, the old adage is 'If a fight starts, don't stop playing.' Nobody ever got hurt, but mostly it was some feller's wife was dancing with some guy."

The better nights catered to University of Kentucky students in clubs where the faint smell of weed in the parking lot was easier to take than boozy brawls. Martin's Tavern in Lexington was his favorite. "You couldn't get in on Friday or Saturday night. It was totally packed," recalls Crowe. The patrons, of course, craved bluegrass music that seemed to them to be part of the folk music revival currently in vogue, but they also lived for Crowe's virtuosity on the banjo and his arrangements of rock-and-roll music and rhythm and blues. His eye always on Elvis Presley's latest hairstyles, Crowe with the Kentucky Mountain Boys devilishly tore into the king of rock and roll's catalog as well as the Beatles' and the Flying Burrito Brothers'. "We did some things that were a little off the wall for us, honestly," says Crowe.

> But we did them pretty good, good enough that people who was watching us there or listening to us liked them. I think that's why we held a crowd there as long as we did.
>
> One night we were playing there, and this group of people come in. I didn't recognize them because I hadn't seen them before, but in that group was the daughter of the guy who built Holiday Inns. They loved it, and she went back and told her dad that he needed to come down and hear us. He did come down, and I remember it was so crowded that he could hardly get in.

Roy Winegardner owned several Holiday Inn hotels in the Lexington area and would acquire even more as the Memphis-based chain spread across the nation to keep up with the American people's increasing penchant for driving vacations and business travel. Almost immediately after seeing Crowe's band at Martin's Tavern, he envisioned transferring Crowe's audience to the Red Slipper Lounge of his flagship Lexington hotel, and maybe filling a few more double beds at the same time. Crowe went along with it and agreed initially to play three nights a week starting in the summer of 1968. "They advertised in newspapers and even run television ads," says Crowe.

> They had on their tables in every room a big brochure of us that we were starting at the Holiday Inn. That's a lot of publicity back then. So the first night we were there, you could not get in. It was packed. The Thursday night, the Friday night, and the Saturday night, they could not get in because there were so many people coming in there. They had never seen anything like that. We did that two weeks, and the owner came back to me and said, "I would like to sign you up to a year's contract, five nights a week."

CROWE AND HIS guys, which in 1968 included Doyle Lawson on mandolin, agreed to play four sets a night for the rest of the year. In later years they asked for and received a proviso allowing them five months off for the lucrative festival season.

The long stretches in one location were often monotonous, but the deal kept Crowe close to home and allowed him to break in new players and work up new material out of the glare of a more critical audience. "People would have killed for a job like that," trumpets Crowe. When Lawson left Crowe to go with the Country Gentlemen, he was surprised his new employers—with their bigger national profile—made less per night than the Kentucky Mountain Boys.

With the dawn of the 1970s, Crowe, still the king of the Holiday Inn, watched his band approach the peak of its influence. At the time he featured the reliable bass player Bobby Slone, a Kentucky native who had played in California with the Golden State Boys and, later, the Kentucky Colonels at the invitation of Clarence White. And just to prove that bluegrass is nothing more than one hundred interlocking human beings, Crowe had replaced mandolinist Doyle Lawson with Larry Rice, brother of the burgeoning guitarist Tony Rice, when Lawson decamped to the Country Gentlemen. Tony was also in the bandleader's viewfinder, but he was planted for the moment in the progressive Bluegrass Alliance in Louisville, Kentucky.

Sporting contemporary fashions that departed from the matching outfits of many bluegrass bands, the Bluegrass Alliance boasted an ardent following in a Louisville community that revolved around Harry Bickel's Bluegrass Hotel, effectively a boarding-house for struggling musicians. Among traditionally minded bluegrass fans who saw them at festivals, they were something of an oddity, as they staked out lasting territory for rock, folk, and pop in bluegrass. (Fellow members Sam Bush, Courtney Johnson, Harry "Ebo Walker" Shelor, and Curtis Burch would go on to found the resilient New Grass Revival.) For the time being, Rice thrived in the Bluegrass Alliance, who welcomed his dying-ember vocals and soulful guitar playing.

But Tony kept up with Crowe's band, volunteering to stand in for Lawson who had returned and then left again to go with Jimmy Martin's band. Rice's transition to the Kentucky Mountain Boys occurred at Carlton Haney's Labor Day festival in Camp Springs, North Carolina. With cameras rolling for director Albert Ihde's *Bluegrass Country Soul*, the wiry lead singer and guitarist fulfilled his last day on the job for the Bluegrass Alliance in a paisley shirt, which he stripped off before joining Crowe in starched white.

In the early going, Crowe found Rice's guitar playing too ambitious, striving to include every embellishment rather than a sharper focus on the melody that Crowe preferred. He suggested the young man listen again to Lester Flatt's and Jimmy Martin's rhythm and Clarence White's melody. "Once he got into the groove and figured it out, it was so easy to play. He enjoyed it, I did, we all did. Tony was probably my favorite rhythm guitar player. As far as timing and singing and knowing where to put it, he was the man. When he learned it, he never forgot it."

Rice's pitch-perfect vocals rivaled Crowe's banjo picking for the audience's attention. At the same time, his love of Gordon Lightfoot, Steve Young, and other popular folk singers updated the group. Soon, the band added a drummer, assigned an electric bass to Slone, and installed pickups on acoustic instruments in place of the traditional reliance on freestanding microphones to amplify the sound onstage.

Crowe knew purists in the bluegrass audience would sneer, but he didn't care. "I called them 'grassholes.' You always have some flak if you're doing something different. There's always a few that want you to stay the same. They don't understand that if you stay the same, you stagnate, that if you're not out there trying to do something different, you're doing nothing. That's why I started doing different material, things that nobody did, bringing material from other genres of music into what we do."

Reflecting the new decade and the band's new thrust, Crowe proposed a new name soon after Tony Rice joined, in deference, actually, to Rice.

I did not want to have the "Mountain Boys" name attached to the band because then you're labeled. Three or four of my friends were sitting around talking about bands changing names, and I said, "I want to get out of the 'Mountain Boy' deal. Been in that long enough. I need to have something that pertains to the music but that can be any kind of music." It could be bluegrass, it could be country, it could be rock, it could be whatever. We brought up "New Country" and things like that, and this fella sitting there said, "New South," and it just hit me. I thought, "Man, that's it. That'll work." I don't even remember the guy's name, to be honest with you. I kept studying on it, and the more I thought about it, the better it sounded as a group name. We could be playing whatever type of music and the name would fit.

The New South presentation tickled the live audiences, but record buyers would have to wait. An album recorded for the country music label Starday in Nashville, which showed off the band's taste in country, folk, rock, and jazz, was put on ice by the company for financial reasons. As a result, the best example of the New South's excellence at the time was Tony Rice's first solo album, *Guitar*, released on the Red Clay label in Japan, featuring Crowe, Slone, and brother Larry behind him.* On the album, Crowe's eclectic players pulled material from western swing, folk, and bluegrass, including Bill Monroe's propulsive "Salt Creek" and Earl Scruggs's gritty "Lonesome Ruben," accented by Rice's impish riff on the Beatles' "Norwegian Wood." Larry Rice's mandolin undergirds Rice's cover of the anthemic "Freeborn Man," perhaps forecasting Larry's transition to southern rocker Dickey Betts's band in the late summer of 1974, which left Crowe in need of a new mandolin player.

RICE LOBBIED CROWE to choose Skaggs for the mandolin spot, the two having recently combined vocals on a loping cover of Cy Coben's "A Good Woman's Love," recorded by Bill Monroe in 1957, for Rice's *California Autumn* album. The guitarist added that the tradition-minded Skaggs would be an easier catch if the New South banished the drums and pickup amplification. Crowe consented, but Skaggs warned he could leave at any moment to start his own band. "Of course, Ricky knew us, and I knew Ricky," says Crowe. "I'd met him when him and Keith were playing with Ralph Stanley. I said, 'Come with us, and when you feel like you're getting ready to leave, just let us know.' He joined us late in '74, and he stayed until August of 1975."

Before teaming up with Crowe's New South, Skaggs matter-of-factly announced his departure from the Country Gentlemen,

---

* The album was later released on two American labels: King Bluegrass and Rebel Records.

and Waller and Lawson responded graciously. Lawson was particularly aware of Skaggs's powerful potential in their profession, but Yates, from his perch behind the wheel of the bus on a tour of Texas, lashed out in frustration. "Ricky was sitting up front," recalls Douglas, "and he had a fishing pole and he had a knife and he was cutting fishing line and putting hooks on the line. And he said something provocative, and Yates said something back. Then Yates slammed the brakes, and there's a big argument between Ricky and Bill. No punches were thrown. I thought they were going to, but it wouldn't have worked out for Ricky very well. It wasn't a pretty leaving sight."

Continuing the story today, Skaggs asks, "Who would ever come after Bill Yates with a Swiss Army knife? I said, 'I don't want there to be any hard feelings,' and he said, 'If you get up in my face, there will be hard feelings.' He had a lot on him, I know. He was driving the bus a lot to dates and tried to be awake to play in the daytime. It was hard. You wondered when people ever slept."

The Country Gentlemen had scooped up Skaggs from the power plant when the waters had risen to his neck and introduced him to progressivism never known in the Clinch Mountain Boys. But Crowe's band, with Tony Rice its beating heart, embodied youth and vibrancy, the future. "Every time that I made a move from one band to the next," says Skaggs, "it was like I saw myself climbing up the ladder, and it wasn't necessarily the ladder of success. But it was the ladder of knowledge and wisdom, and it was also the knowledge of music, different styles of music that I was getting into my head. And so I saw the New South as a stepping-stone to maybe having something someday for myself. It was something that could be really good for me because I would be singing a lot and playing mandolin, not fiddle."

Perceptive fans of Crowe immediately noted the richer harmony singing in the group, as well as Skaggs's energy on the mandolin, which he had rarely played publicly since the Ralph Stanley days. Crowe itched to bottle the new sound in the studio, and his manager, Hugh Sturgill, negotiated an album deal with the new Rounder Records label, home at that time to an eclectic list of artists who represented traditions from bluegrass to Cajun. Crowe believed competing labels who dealt in bluegrass tended to show a preference for Washington, DC–area bands, so Rounder—based in Somerville, Massachusetts—seemed ideal to him. But, funny enough, Crowe chose to record in DC, gathering at Track Recorders on the day after his Starday agreement expired—January 16, 1975.

IN AN ACT that demonstrated Skaggs's assertiveness in the New South band, as well as his devotion to Jerry Douglas and his talent, he recommended Crowe hire his Dobro friend for the session. "I had heard Jerry before," says Crowe, "and I knew he was a good Dobro player. At the time, I wasn't real hot on Dobro players because most of them I heard I didn't care for. The one I liked was Uncle Josh Graves for Flatt and Scruggs. Jerry loved Josh, and I think that's what got him into playing Dobro. Anyway, Ricky suggested using him on the session, and I thought he'd add something a little different on breaks and backup than what I'd been using."

Initially, Douglas was to play on one or two cuts and then return to the Country Gentlemen. "Jerry's very humble and everything," said Skaggs in an interview, "and starts playing and then he ends up playing on six or seven more songs, and he made a place for himself. His rhythm playing was so great. It was just the 'stank.'"

Among the youthful blossoming around Crowe, only he and Slone were old enough to apply for a credit card without a cosigner, but the leader welcomed youth's wellspring, flat out hiring Douglas. "I get down there with Crowe," says Douglas,

And we're like reinventing the wheel and especially with crazy guys like Tony and Ricky involved. That's where I learned that you turn over every stone when you're trying to work your way through a song, not just blow through it. These guys were digging into the details of it.

It just felt right, felt good, and it also allowed me to have the best guitar, the best of everything next to me. I mean, these guys were on the highest plateau. So I better step up, and so I did. I tried my best, and I learned so much from them about improvising. And I learned more about my instrument: where notes work, playing out the fingerboard, things like that, and, more importantly, just the sense of when not to play at all.

With the New South, Douglas observed communications among artists that he'd never known, including the distress signals from an individual member—Skaggs on mandolin, for example—who begins to express an idea musically but, in a sense, gets lost on the way. "You know, I might just play part of a phrase," explains Douglas, "and they'll go, 'Oh, yes!' It just unlocks that mental block or whatever it is. Tony was great at that, at leading you to a place you never thought you would ever go."

And if the balance of the band followed the leader's cue or redirect, it was liable to become a defining trait of the performance, just like a lyric, sort of fulfilling the unanticipated destiny of the song. "You don't talk about it," says Douglas. "It just happens onstage."

The signature songs that would appear on the New South's upcoming album—such as Ian Tyson's "Summer Wages" and Rodney Crowell's "Home Sweet Home Revisited"—were proposed by Rice. Douglas nominated "Rock Salt and Nails," written by Bruce Phillips, while Skaggs introduced the reel "Sally Goodin" and the traditional hymn "Cryin' Holy," whose harmonies, supercharged by Skaggs, rival Rice's lead vocals as the sterling performance on the album. Only Fats Domino's "I'm Walkin'" and three cuts directly from the Flatt and Scruggs oeuvre bear Crowe's stamp. "Everybody had ideas," says Crowe. "We'd discuss them and pitch them around. Whatever worked, that's what we did."

Skaggs proposed stacking multiple string tracks on "Summer Wages," walking up the street in Silver Spring to an instrument shop to rent a viola to add to the fiddle layers he envisioned, and he animated the various harmonies in the band. But it was Rice, observes Douglas, who stepped to the forefront of the sessions as the de facto producer.

> I saw Tony take more control over that situation, of being the director. And Ricky was still learning that but really, really fast, and he had opinions. . . . I know they were both competitive. Ricky more so, but I knew that side of him before going into that just by our discussions about being in the Country Gentlemen and how we wanted more, and they weren't moving fast enough for us. But I didn't feel that from Tony. Tony is much more quiet. He just was doing what he was doing, trying to figure it out, and he wasn't being competitive with Ricky or J. D. Maybe he was more cerebrally competitive with Crowe because Crowe's name was on the band, but Tony was the one changing everything. It was Tony's world when we got into the studio.

The self-titled album, affectionately known today by its catalog number, 0044, finally gave Crowe product to sell at festivals upon its release later in 1975, but, more important, it influenced perceptions of bluegrass among fans and musicians alike and deeply polished the reputations of youngsters Skaggs, Rice, and Douglas. Just like the progressive Bluegrass Alliance and New Grass Revival, it incorporated various innovations, testing the borders of bluegrass while still respecting them. All of a sudden, lead vocals on a bluegrass song were free to soar like a Graham Nash vocal recorded in California, and song selection could skip from modern Canadian folk to traditional Appalachian style in the same setting.

In a review of the album, *Bluegrass Unlimited* echoed the spirit of rock critic Jon Landau's "I have seen the future of rock and roll" pronouncement in reference to Bruce Springsteen, praising the "congregation of superb musicians gleaned from a number of pre-existing bands who offers us not only one of the better albums of the year but some revealing insights into the direction and growth of bluegrass." In a community known for angry adjudicators of what was and wasn't bluegrass, Jerry Douglas recalls little dissent in reaction to their genre-bending album.

> I think [listeners] were trying to figure it out. I think it was a surprise that we would just make that kind of record instead of just a hard-driving record all the way through, that we would have some balance, expressed in a more mainstream folk way and not just a pile-blasting, unrelenting kind of record. It was different in its subject matter for a bluegrass record. It was sort of a continuation in a way with the band that Ricky and I were both in with the Country Gentlemen because they were the first ones to take Bob Dylan songs and make them sound like they had written them.

Each element of the band's performance on the album found its own constituency. "The material, for one thing, was so great and the craftsmanship," says guitarist Wes Golding, who had hired Skaggs to play fiddle on a recording by his band Country Grass two years earlier. "It kind of blew me away and a lot of other musicians who were involved in bluegrass music at the time." Indeed, many aspiring musicians marked that album as their gateway to careers in bluegrass music.

Set free to play mandolin again under Crowe, Skaggs perhaps envisioned an album closer to his *That's It* solo album that liberally invoked tones of Brushy Creek. But he had encountered a roomful of stylists with their own aspirations and their own tastes molded by rock, rhythm, and folk, not to mention the bold experimentation of the Bluegrass Alliance. Friction among the leader, modernists, and traditionalists in the band may have generated the quiet spark of the album, rendering sounds both fresh and widely acceptable. It arguably remains the masterwork of each individual member of that edition of the New South.

But, like Emmylou and Gram's partnership, the New South of 0044 flickered and then vanished. By the album's release in the late summer of 1975, Rice was arranging his transition into David Grisman's experimental jazz band on the West Coast, essentially removing the keystone. Consequently, neither Skaggs nor Douglas desired to remain with Crowe.

"When Ricky joined, Tony had already been with me about four years almost, and I knew he was getting tired, I could tell it," recollects Crowe.

> And he had already told me about making a move, and I said, "I hate to lose you, but you got to do what you want to do."
>
> The last show we did was in Japan, 1975, and I tell you this, the last song we sung when we walked off the stage, Tony had tears in his eyes. He couldn't hardly talk to me. We were not only pickers together, we were friends. Losing him was like losing a brother, like family.
>
> But it's probably great that we broke up. Let's say we had stuck together another four or five years; it would have been just another bluegrass group. You get stale. It would have been a good group; I don't think anybody could have touched us. But it wouldn't have had the impact that 1974 and '75 did.

7

Close to the Fire

A BLAST OF frigid air tousled Skaggs's shaggy hair as he stepped out of the used Chevy conversion van he had purchased for his new band. Parked on the berm of I-81 north of Syracuse, New York, he shuffled around the vehicle, searching for the source of an ungodly screech that had interrupted his passengers' naps a few minutes earlier. But Skaggs knew less about engine repair than he knew about shearing sheep, so he hopped back in the van and resumed the journey to Canada. It was January 1976, and a run of dates awaited the boys at the Country Way Tavern in Ottawa.

Starved for space because nobody realized you could rent sound equipment in Ottawa instead of lugging it all of the way up there, the bluegrass players also coped with the broken heating system, which sent warm air to the left side of the dashboard exclusively, cooking whoever happened to be at the helm. But terse speculation about the van's troubles ceased when somebody spied a gas station with a glowing "mechanic on duty" sign.

Says Jerry Douglas, cofounder of the band:

We eased off the road and pulled right up in front of the glass door to the gas station, and Ricky went in and said, "You got a mechanic?" And he said, "We sure do." And we said, "We got this noise, and we got a long way to go and it sounds terrible,

113

sounds like the thing's about to blow up." And the guy said, "Well, bring it on in, and we'll put it up on the jack and have the mechanic take a look at it." They put it on the jack, and we all were standing around watching this thing go up in the air. But it only went up in the air about three feet, and we were thinking, "He'll crawl under there or something." But, no, out the back of the room walks a [little] mechanic in greasy, gray overalls, and he starts reaching up in there. He just started touching things and getting burned because it was so hot, and he finally just threw down the rag in disgust and walked away, and Ricky said, "Well, what did he find?" And the guy said, "He couldn't find anything wrong with it." And when we backed out of there, the van never made the sound again. It was just God going, "You got to see this." This was the kind of stuff that happened in Boone Creek.

IN THE AFTERMATH of Tony Rice's departure from the New South, Skaggs checked in again with Whitley about forming a band, but his friend balked, intent at this stage on finding a mainstream country path apart from bluegrass. It was the last time Skaggs attempted to partner with him. "My dad had said years before, 'Son, he don't want to be in a band with you. He wants a band of his own. He wants to be his own man.'"

But Skaggs had found a new musical collaborator in Douglas, and together they assembled Boone Creek, named for a stream near Lexington, with contacts made through their collected years in bluegrass, mostly Skaggs's. Terry Baucom, who had appeared on Skaggs's *That's It* album, came in to play fiddle but took on the banjo, too, when Marc Pruett, another *That's It* alumnus, demurred because he had just opened a music store in Knoxville. Guitarist and lead singer Wes Golding, who had been playing since high school, got the call from Skaggs while he was working in a hosiery mill in Mount Airy, North Carolina, and he promptly accepted. But Skaggs and Douglas's choice for bass, Lou Reid Pyrtle, was waiting for his family's tobacco crop in North Carolina to come in, leaving a question mark in the rhythm section for months to come.*

Skaggs's traditional orientation was clear to the other band members arriving in Lexington, but Boone Creek let in the same influences Crowe had permitted, mostly from rock and roll and mainstream country music. "I mean, we would go out and do 'Working on a Building' or 'Little Cabin Home on the Hill,' or we'd do 'Little Community Church' or 'Daniel Prayed' in a four-part harmony, just as Stanley-Monroe tradition as you could get," says Golding, "and then on the other hand we would come back and do something like 'One Way Track,' which threw it into another genre." Featuring a haunting Dobro solo by Douglas and shared lead vocals by Skaggs and Golding, "One Way Track" borrowed from southern rock and rhythm and blues and, as Golding suggests, represented Boone Creek's broad vision, tested nightly at the Sheraton Hotel in Lexington where they wrangled a long-term gig like Crowe's.

Golding says:

> I'd always heard about the New South playing the Holiday Inn in Lexington, and I couldn't imagine having a place like that to play every night of the week, so when I moved to Lexington we would continue to go out and see J. D. and some of the guys play there . . . and there was a lot of great music coming out of that area. We'd go out to a lot of different clubs and stuff, and Exile—the country-rock group—came out in that period of time, and I can remember Terry, Jerry, and some of the guys, we'd go out and watch them play and just run around with them during the week. It was just a special time for music.

---

* For a short spell, Vince Gill, a graduate of the Bluegrass Alliance on his way to mainstream country fame, played steel guitar and sang in Boone Creek.

Golding remembers the bandmates cramming into one of their hotel rooms in the Sheraton Lexington to watch NBC-TV's *Midnight Special* show on Friday nights, soaking up the rock, blues, and country-rock and whooping it up when Ricky and Jerry's friend Linda Ronstadt appeared. They learned songs by the Eagles and Marvin Gaye and processed them through the group's breezy, bluegrass style. "Ricky was bad to do that," recalls Golding. "He would sing a line or two [from a rock song] onstage between our songs and the crowd would just freak out, and all of a sudden everybody else would start playing in on it and before you knew it we were all playing some rock song or something that was popular at that time."

For the first time, Skaggs was the quarterback in the huddle, speaking his plays into the ears of his fellow musicians. The directions were relentless—arrangements of vocal parts, tempo, instrumental fills. Not to say the others were shy; they, too, spoke their minds. But nobody stored up more ideas nor were as quick to activate them as Skaggs. Like Brian Wilson of the Beach Boys, he knew in his head how a particular arrangement should sound and, deeper, the soul of each instrument, since he could play them all. Moreover, he had the wherewithal to communicate his vision. His was a rare, powerful mingling of skills.

"I've got a God-given talent," he said back in those days. "I was one of the chosen few that was gonna be a musician. I felt like that's gonna be my calling, that's what I was put here to do, was play music. What I do with it while I'm here is a pretty heavy burden . . . because you get to thinking it was given to you and it could be taken away as easily. That's why I want to try to keep my music pure and natural and country and not to make it anything it's not."

He remained wedded to the original mountain style, too deep and alive inside of him to be surrendered, but he experienced Boone Creek as a supply of new oxygen to bluegrass. The band flowed, sparking off nimble energy rather than plodding predictability and grafting new songs to the tradition if it made sense.

"I consider myself an old minded musical person," Skaggs told *Omaha Rainbow*, a music journal based in the United Kingdom, toward the end of Boone Creek's two-year life span.

> I know the technique, I know exactly the way bluegrass music should be played. I know what it takes to make five musicians click. I know what role each one has to play. So many young musicians think just as soon as you learn to go from one end to the other, then you've got it licked. That's bullshit, it ain't so. It's keeping from overplaying is where it's at. That applies to any kind of music. Save your hot licks for the time it's needed. It's a very interesting music and there are very few people that could sit down and rap with you about it. They don't appreciate the old Flatt and Scruggs or Bill Monroe stuff like I do. A lot of it had a lot of mistakes in it, but there is a feel there that you cannot get by. I'd rather have a good-feeling track with ten mistakes as to have no mistakes and a track that's real bland and straight forward and no movement going.

Though Boone Creek's artistic direction clarified in time, its early days as a going business concern waffled, sometimes comically so. They survived numerous car wrecks (the baptismal rite of struggling bands everywhere), and when the musicians showed up for their very first concert, a fair date in Harrodsburg, Kentucky, they had missed the gig by one day.

"Ricky always made me a little nervous driving," says Golding.

> I wasn't used to somebody driving aggressive. I called it "aggressive." It might not have been. But he was just gettin' it down the road, and I thought to myself, "I don't know about this." We were sitting in the seats eating, and he had to hit the brakes and the van runned off the road, went up the embankment, I think, and tore the van up. We had food all over us, instruments laying on top of us, and, luckily, nobody

got hurt. Shoot, Ricky, the businessman that he was, it wasn't two hours before we had another van and we were on the way.

Bassists continued to elude the band. Although the bass's propulsive rhythm would ultimately have everything to do with Boone Creek's sound, proving to be what Douglas calls an "informing instrument," the players they rehearsed tended to be rock-and-roll guys who mixed uneasily with bluegrass boys. One of the early candidates, with an impressive country-rock résumé, joined the gig at the Sheraton. Rues Douglas:

> But we had to fire him, because in the middle of a set one night while everybody went outside to smoke, he went around the tables drinking everybody's drink. We told him we can't take this anymore, and I remember standing onstage and we were playing our final song, "Foggy Mountain Breakdown," which goes from G to E minor, but the bass player, he was drunk enough and pissed off enough that he refused to go to E and went to B-flat. It was one of the craziest things I ever heard, but we all just went to B-flat, too, and that was his last gig. Then we got a guy named Steve Bryant right after that, and that was the total band.

Bryant, a native of southern Ohio schooled on Ralph Stanley in one ear and James Brown in the other, ignited Boone Creek's rhythm on electric bass. "We didn't realize how much difference there was going to be having an electric bass onstage with a guy playing it who had played in rock-and-roll bands," says Douglas. "And all these bassists had had to play disco at some point, so that entered the fray from time to time, just popping and all of the bass tricks, all the Jaco stuff started coming out, so to have this undercurrent with the band made us all play a little bit different.*

---

* Douglas is referring to the great electric bassist Jaco Pastorius, a member of Weather Report, known for his fulminant playing style.

It kind of slanted us all toward a more rock or a pop sound. But we're standing up there playing bluegrass."

"I don't remember us ever doing a poorly played show," says Bryant, who was a veteran of tours with Dobie Gray from rhythm and blues, Jerry Reed from country, and Buffy St. Marie from folk. "Some of those nights at the Birchmere [in Alexandria, Virginia] were really cool. I remember particularly a happening night that we did at the old Red Gate Festival in Knoxville, Tennessee, and we had a lot of fans in the crowd, and, man, we were hot that night. We were playing in front of several thousand people, and everybody got it. We were really hitting it. It felt like the bluegrass Weather Report."

Predictably, the old park benchers decried the high-energy young bloods and hoisted their "no electric instruments" signs at festivals, to which Bryant once responded by stripping off his shoes, socks, and shirt, leaving only his cutoff shorts when he hit the stage. "I remember doing a show, and I'd be the first one out there when we were changing out bands," says Bryant, "and I'd bring my small bass amp onstage and the sound guy was assisting me. And the guy who was emceeing the show said, 'We don't like electric bass here.' And the sound guy said, 'Did you hear that?' And I said, 'Yeah, to each his own.' That never did stop me. I'd get a little cheeky about it, but I wasn't offended."

The band's eponymous debut album on Rounder incorporated piano, synthesizer, horns, and background vocals with patently uneven results, but the use of the band as a laboratory to understand how much outside heat bluegrass could stand was not unappreciated. "It is all over the place with singing and instrumentation," commented *Bluegrass Unlimited,* "and these musicians are most successful with their most radical effort, 'Sugar Daddy.' It's essentially a Dixieland piece and reminds us as no other of the enormous similarities between that form and bluegrass."

Enthusiasm among young listeners picked up where 0044 left off, as they realized the New South lineage in Boone Creek. An awkward emcee onstage, Skaggs won the admiration of observers who pinpointed his central role in leading bluegrass out of the shadow of the fathers and into a new era, drawing young fans. Plainly, he was becoming as key a transitional figure in country music as Hank Williams, Patsy Cline, and Earl Scruggs, redirecting foundational elements of country music into the future-moving stream. "Ricky is one of these once-in-a-generation musicians," said Barry Poss, the founder of Sugar Hill Records. "That guy feels music down to his very soul, and he had the skill to take that soul and convey it to the rest of us with grace and power and real beauty. And that doesn't happen very often."

A YOUNG CANADIAN in Durham, North Carolina, Poss had crossed the border for graduate studies in sociology at Duke University but soon became enamored of the rich traditional music scene of the Southeast, picking the clawhammer banjo in a group called the Fuzzy Mountain String Band and collecting tunes from musicians who recorded in the 1920s and 1930s and who still lived in rural parts of the region. Younger artists caught his eye, too, particularly those who had grown up in the old-time traditions and were trying to marry them with new styles that had reached them through radio and records. It seemed to him an atomic collision, and he wanted to be intimately involved in whatever the fallout might be.

"I had some very sweet offers to teach at prominent schools, but the music was a real draw to me," says Poss. "So with just a little bit to go on my dissertation, I switched gears. I went to work for County Records, and that's where I got deeply involved in going to hear music and see music, in addition to what I was doing on my own."

The Research Triangle Park, in which Durham sat, connecting Duke, North Carolina State, and the University of North Carolina, was the economic marvel of the so-called New South, a term that had come into vogue about the same time J. D. Crowe had chosen the term for his new band. It was apropos, for as Crowe wished to be invigorated by outside influences, so did many in the South.

North Carolina's textile industry was fading, but by the 1970s the Triangle had attracted tenants such as IBM and Monsanto, as well as a host of federal government research facilities. "The park's success significantly altered the Raleigh-Durham-Chapel Hill area's demographic makeup by attracting highly educated, well-paid professionals," wrote scholar James C. Cobb in his *The Selling of the South.* "Many younger research personnel welcomed the opportunity to complete further graduate study at one of the three universities. . . . To complement the advantages offered by the park itself, promoters emphasized the area's social and cultural atmosphere and supported local efforts to strengthen the latter even further."

Not surprisingly, similar trends appeared in other parts of the South. The number of southern students pursuing college education had increased sevenfold since the Second World War, while the number of workers in manufacturing in the region had grown by more than 200 percent. Accordingly, many people with newly found jobs and more money to spend poured into bluegrass festivals that dotted the region. They also frequented a much-appreciated answer to the "knife-and-gun clubs": spruced-up listening rooms and college clubs such as the Pier in Raleigh and the Cat's Cradle in Chapel Hill, as well as the Down Home in Johnson City, Tennessee. Instrument stores and record shops prospered, too.

As dollars spent on music increased in the Southeast and in-migration and expanded education promoted eclecticism, Poss's employer, County Records, located in the small Appalachian town of Floyd, Virginia, stepped up to meet demand as did Charlottes-ville-based Rebel Records, home at one time or another to Ralph Stanley, II Generation, and many other talents. Together, the two companies represented a major percentage of record sales by bluegrass artists on the regular festival circuit.

In 1978, encouraged by the many roots-based styles thriving despite disco and the viability of bluegrass and folk labels outside North Carolina, Poss started Sugar Hill Records. "I made a statement, to stand for something, to have a bit of an identity," he says.

> And my model was Sun Records of the 1950s, where you might not know the artists but you trusted the label. So we recorded bluegrass, but we were not a bluegrass label. We recorded country, but we were not a country label. The same thing with singer-songwriters and folk and gospel. We were a mix of all these genres, stemming from my own interest in traditional music with roots. It's essentially what later became known as "Americana." The hidden sociologist in me liked the idea of cultural transmission—tradition and change—and Ricky was the living embodiment of it, along with Jerry. It was very interesting that the two artists who were defining the label all along were right there on the very first album.

Recorded in Lexington, *One Way Track* announced the fulfillment of both Poss's and Boone Creek's vision. Stripped of the first album's experimental adornments, its innovation lived in the creative use of the basic instruments, such as Douglas's Dobro, roaming freely, its player never more confident, and the mandolin handled now with the strut of a lead guitarist in rock and roll. The set list culled liberally from Monroe's and Flatt's standards and even further back in the old-time tradition, but the band rejected some of their peers' obsession with imitation, synching even the old songs with their own young heartbeats and those of their fans. "I don't know when I've heard a bunch of young men with this much soul," enthused a reviewer in *Bluegrass Unlimited*.

"We were writing a lot of our own material at the time," says Douglas, "so there was this freedom from what we've been doing for the last twenty years of our lives. Suddenly, we had the freedom to go ahead and express these ideas with each other. We were just in a band of like minds, and it jelled."

Widely hailed, the album's prized gift to fans may have been the spotlight on Skaggs. Many listeners heard for the first time his high tenor soaring above rather than merely blending in as it had on many previous recordings in his young career, and his lead vocals, newly prominent and a little gawky here and there, more than made up for any deficiencies with their alternating grit and boyish enthusiasm.

On the road to new gigs, Skaggs coached the band in harmony singing and phrasing as well as in the old Stanley Brothers river-gorge aesthetic. "It was that mountain sound that he got out of anything that he sang," says Golding. "He just had so much soul in it, and I tried to keep up with him and tried to learn from it."

Golding recalls the vocal performance on the album's title cut "One Way Track" coming to life when Skaggs got involved. The guitarist had brought the song into rehearsals, evidently intending it to be a shared vocal, but every time he sang a line, Skaggs repeated it with infinitely more verve, like an electric shock. "I thought it was a great song, still do, but it would have been a lot more plainer and in a different direction from the way he took it," says Golding. Consequently, the two shared a writing credit on the song.

Although Boone Creek recorded enough material for at least two additional albums, the road was the band's place of business. They filled their calendar with festival appearances and, as we've learned, disappeared into Canada in their Chevy van during the slack winter season. "One time we toured up there," says Bryant, "and we played some clubs, and Dobro players would drive three or four hundred miles to see Jerry. I think Jerry was nineteen or twenty, and even then he was incredible. You knew he was going to do some great things. He brought that instrument outside bluegrass."

They frequently wandered up the Eastern Seaboard and into New England, always stopping in Skaggs's and Douglas's former home in the Washington, DC, area, where they played the Charlie's West Side club in Annapolis, Maryland, and the Birchmere in Alexandria, which had become one of the nation's best-known listening rooms. During a Boone Creek set at Charlie's West Side, Skaggs learned Joe Venuti, the storied jazz fiddler of the 1920s, was playing that same night at the Show Boat Lounge in Silver Spring. "And I said, 'Oh my God, we got to go see him,'" recalls Skaggs. "It was late because we'd just finished our set. We just floor boarded over there, and I brought my fiddle inside. Was I that bold to think he'd want me to play fiddle with him? He was very nice to me and invited me up onstage to play 'Sweet Georgia Brown.'"

Linda Ronstadt caught the band after she performed a show in Lexington's Rupp Arena in late August 1977. "It was her and a couple of guys from the band Canned Heat, who she brought to our gig," says Douglas, "and they all got up onstage with us, and then we went back to Linda's hotel and hung out a long time that night."

Ronstadt wanted Skaggs and Tony Rice both to go on tour with her. "Tony was living in San Francisco," says Skaggs.

> She loved bluegrass and loved old-time country, and I think she just wanted us to go out and lend our knowledge of the music and everything. She wanted Tony to play a Telecaster, because it would be hard to get an acoustic guitar loud enough to play in her band. And she wanted me to play fiddle and mandolin and sing harmony with her. But we had a rehearsal, and though the singing was really good [it never went further]. I don't know why—she never really told me. The only thing she really told me was that the summer tour had been canceled, that she was not going to do it right then.

SKAGGS SAYS TODAY he would have joined the tour with Ronstadt but refused full-time membership in the band. Douglas figures the plans crumbled when Rice attached a capo to the electric guitar, signaling that he planned to play bluegrass licks on it.

Then Emmylou Harris beckoned a second time. She had featured Skaggs in guest roles on her albums *Luxury Liner* (1976) and *Quarter Moon in a Ten Cent Town* (1978), and invited Boone Creek to open for her and the Hot Band whenever she played Lexington. "We fronted for her three or four times," estimates Terry Baucom. "She'd always call Ricky up to the stage, and they would always sing a song and it would be killer. The more they sang, the better they were going to get because both of them can really hear the music. I knew that was going to be a win-win."

The prospect of Ricky going with Emmylou haunted the band like impending death: they foresaw his departure—the musical chemistry between the pair too obvious to ignore—and knew not the day. But in 1977, Rodney Crowell signed his own recording contract with Warner Bros. and tendered his resignation to Harris. Inevitably, the songbird turned to the man from Brushy Creek.

It was directly after Christmas of 1977—the eve of the release of *One Way Track*—and Douglas had spent a lot of money on presents, while Golding planned his wedding to a woman whom he'd met at Charlie's West Side. "It pissed me off, and it did everybody," recalls Douglas. "But I think I realized that if I didn't make my money there playing music, I would make it somewhere else playing music. I felt good about that. But I don't think everybody felt as fluid as that."

The last note of Boone Creek, recalls Douglas, sounded an indifferent tone.

> We had gone up and played the Sanders Theatre in Boston at Harvard and were on our way down to DC and the weather was so bad—and, again, it was wintertime and our van's fuel line kept freezing, and we'd have to pull over and it would thaw itself out, and we would go another five miles and we got to where we could see the whole front of our van was just totally frozen over, and we didn't have any more windshield wiper fluid or anything. We couldn't move, but we could look over, and we were right at the Newark airport, so we called Gary Oelze at the Birchmere and said, "We're not going to make it because our van is dead, but we can see the airport."

He said, "Get to the airport and fly down here. I'll pay the tickets, and I'll pay you for the night. Just get here and play your gig." So we had a guy with us that was sort of a sound-man who ran interference and other things for us, and we flew to DC, played the gig, and then he drove the van on down after it thawed out, and picked us up in DC. We went back to Lexington, and that was the end of it, the last one. It was sad, but by then Emmylou had hired Ricky.

SOMETIME IN THE months before Boone Creek dried up, the bandmates converged around a motel swimming pool in Florida, killing time in between their slated spots at a weekend festival, maybe in the town of Lawtey. Draped on the lounge chairs, the guys drowsily sat up when Marty Stuart, like a sprite, poked his head into their loose circle. Jerry Douglas says:

> We were a band of smokers and pot smokers, except Ricky, and I think Marty knew that, and he just needed to get away, be with somebody his own age. He hung out with us at this pool all day long, and we just smoked all day long, and we delivered him back to play his gig. That was one of the only times that we did that, but we saw he needed help, and we grabbed him and took him with us, and we were so pleasantly surprised to find out he was just like us. He could have been in our band.

Such stimulation outside the Flatt camp was Stuart's constant pursuit. Various bands on the circuit knew to expect his knock on the door of their campers and buses over festival weekends, seeking a spliff or merely conversation to pass the long hours until showtime. On the road, he encountered whiz kids such as Skaggs and Rice and, in their shadows, Vince Gill, Sam Bush, Stuart Duncan, Mark O'Connor, and Keith Whitley, who helped him advance his craft. He also found community in Nashville's West End, home to Vanderbilt University, singer-songwriter clubs, group houses bursting at the studs with starving musicians, and Centennial Park, where artists looking for an audience hung out on the grass.

Stuart ran across photographer Jim McGuire, documenting the front rows and back alleys of Nashville, and a young Black musician named Earl Peaks whose "wicked right hand" could pop the electric bass like he'd never seen. "It was kind of like Nashville's version of Paris in the twenties," explains Stuart, "because it was bohemian, it was adventurous, it was creative. Another way to look at it was there wasn't a lot of *Grand Ole Opry* [in the West End]. If there was, it was the pickers who smoked pot and took pills. It was hippies, and that was what I was bumping into on the road a lot with Lester, and I looked for a place to follow up on it when I got home."

So he ditched his Nashville Grass duds when Flatt's bus arrived back in town and, with young ones in the Nashville royal line such as Jody Maphis (son of recording stars Rose Lee and Joe) and Mark Jones (Grandpa Jones's kid), wheeled out onto the streets in his white-on-white 225 Buick Electra, sleek like a cabin cruiser, the counterpart to outlaw David Allan Coe's ghoulish black hearse creeping down the streets of the West End.

Creating relationships and experiences that helped build the foundations of his solo career that would begin in the 1980s, Stuart prowled the city's instrument shops, particularly luthier Randy Wood's Old Time Pickin' Parlor, and he popped up in music mills and private homes, belting out songs from blues, rock, and country for small audiences who never would have seen him perform otherwise. But, finally, Stuart seemed most at home among the *Grand Ole Opry* community where he was a familiar face, a vessel, actually, that many of the old-timers believed would carry their music and traditions long after they had strummed their last chord. He was always welcome in the veterans' dressing rooms, pig roasts, and square dances, says Stuart, especially if Grandpa Jones was hosting. "Grandpa was just blazing hot on *Hee Haw* at that time, and during taping season for *Hee Haw*, he and his wife,

Ramona, would host folks who came in from California to do their parts on the show—executives, stars, and songwriters. To me, it was the social event of the season. If you were in country music society, you wanted to be invited to Grandpa Jones's pickings and square dances." Mingling with Roy Acuff and Buck Owens while observing deal making among music and media executives under Grandpa's shade trees seemed in its own country way to be as cool as Elliston Place, and he could also pick up artistic lessons as useful to him as a folksinger's showcase in the West End.

> One of those nights out there was when I met Merle Travis, and that really was one of the things that unlocked a whole lot. I was trying to write songs a little bit, and I asked Merle if he would write out the words to "Dark as a Dungeon" for me, and he did and he signed it for me. I said, "I'm trying to write songs, but I only went to the ninth grade in school, and I don't have a broad vocabulary." He said, "Well, who are you writing songs for?" I said, "I reckon people we play music for, country folks." He said, "They don't have a great vocabulary either. Just speak the plain truth." He was probably the most profound figure that I ever encountered out there.

Flatt was not the songwriting tutor that Travis proved to be that evening, even though he ranked among the most prolific writers in country music history. To wit, he avoided music when he was off the road or away from the studio. He preferred to fish from his dock on Old Hickory Lake in the Nashville suburbs, and, in the end, Stuart got only one writing credit on a Lester Flatt album, for the instrumental "Bluegrass Shuffle," a studio creation with producer Arthur Smith from 1978's *Pickin' Time*.

Although partial to the age-old musical arrangements from the Flatt and Scruggs days, Flatt generally respected the unique personality each musician brought to bear on his instrument, and, accordingly, Stuart took as many liberties as possible on the mandolin. His older self now regrets it, believing he should have replicated as close as possible the original arrangements in the Flatt and Scruggs canon.

In the wake of Flatt's loss of his RCA contract in 1974, manager Lance LeRoy struck a single-album deal with Canaan Records, a gospel-oriented company out of Waco, Texas. The session, recorded at RCA-Nashville's Studio B, called for "Let the Church Roll On" and "God Loves His Children"—both part of the Flatt and Scruggs discography—to be performed with three-finger guitar picking, as if Scruggs were playing the instrument. Young Stuart thought he could handle it, and Flatt let him have a try. "I went back in my bedroom when I lived at his house and just really woodshedded on that style of guitar, and I'd walk in the living room with the guitar, and I'd say to him, 'If you don't mind, would you sing?'—which he hated doing at home. And I tried to play it. I'd say 'Thank you' and walk off. But I look at that as probably the purest and the closest to what those licks were originally supposed to be. So that little after-hours collaboration with Lester is sweet to me. I cherish it."

FOREVER AND ALWAYS the youngest member of Lester Flatt's band, Stuart had become one of the veterans by 1978. Uncle Josh Graves had jumped to the Earl Scruggs Revue within a year of Stuart's arrival, replaced by Jack Martin, raising eyebrows all over Nashville.* "I don't know if he quit or was sent home," says Stuart. "I don't remember any part of it. I just know he resurfaced with Scruggs wearing a concho belt and groovy clothes, and it pissed Lester off." Banjoist Haskel McCormick resigned, too, tired of driving the tour bus or just plain tired of the bus, still a musty vessel despite Flatt's purchase of a brand-new Silver Eagle bus after Graves was cut loose. Stuart says:

---

* Martin had also done a stint with Flatt in the early 1970s.

When Lester got that bus, me and [bassist] Jack Hicks flew to Jackson, Mississippi, and I had a cashier's check for $58,000 in my pocket to hand to the guy. It had been shipped over from Belgium, and we rode it back to Nashville. I had dreams of it being customized very, very nicely. But Lance LeRoy and everybody had plywood and shag carpet on the walls, and they bought some living room furniture from a store in Nashville. And I suggested putting a radio in it, and I thought I was going to get run out on the rails. That was not their thing.

Nonetheless, Flatt remained an enviable gig, his royalty still intact. But departures of sidemen and the loss of the RCA contract cracked the soundboard. Inevitable comparisons to Scruggs, who would hold on to his Columbia Records contract into the 1980s, found Flatt wanting, and fans, although still faithful to the stature of the originators, sought out younger voices like those in Boone Creek who carried the traditions. It was as if the momentum of the Foggy Mountain franchise was finally petering out in front of Flatt's eyes.

Fifty-nine years old when he recorded his final album for RCA—a treasured live performance at Vanderbilt University on March 18, 1974, featuring a rollicking guest appearance by Bill Monroe and his band—he had been struggling with heart ailments for almost a decade and had withstood gallbladder surgery as well. Little more than a year later, he entered the hospital for open-heart surgery, which cleared three obstructed arteries, followed by another hospitalization a few months later arising from severe cases of pneumonia and the flu.

IN THE MIDST of Flatt's slow demise, the downside of Stuart's early entrance into popular entertainment with a group of adult men, some of whom drank heavily and fed an unhealthy appetite for amphetamines, became apparent. The long tour of colleges and universities on the strength of "Dueling Banjos" in 1973 taxed his resilience. "I learned the effects of drugs and what it can do to your life," he told a reporter in 1978. "I got to where I couldn't look myself in the mirror. Whenever I was alone in a room, I [was] jittery and nervous. I had a bad grass habit, and I knew that the rate and speed I was living, I wouldn't last two years. After one [recording] session with a major rock group that was visiting Nashville, I wondered about where I was going."

He understood shortly after arriving in Nashville that pills were as staple as road maps and two cans of deodorant in the glove compartment. Converging on concert halls or festivals, musicians gathered to swap uppers and downers as if they were candy. "There were prescriptions on the bottle," recalls Stuart.

> They were legal, and nobody thought anything about it. And in those days, fairly enough, musicians were hired a lot of times not so much on their musical ability but on their driving ability. After a picker plays a show, who gets the first turn at the wheel? Well, what do you do? You pop a pill to stay awake. The next thing you know, it's a vicious cycle, and you're going home and there's a family and you're grinding to drive home, and you have to go to Junior's Little League game. It does not work out. It never works out. And it tears your health apart.
>
> When I got to the *Grand Ole Opry*, I noticed there were people that we all revere that, as soon as the lights faded, they had huge problems. Whether it was drinking too much or taking too many pills or running around on their wives. It was just always there, and it was like sticking your hand in the fireplace. At some point, I went, "That looks kind of entertaining to me. I think I'll do it, too." I knew better. I was taught better, but it doesn't matter what you teach a child. The child's going to figure it out for themselves, right?

In later years, Stuart passed a few nights in jail as a result of his drug and alcohol abuse, but in the early days of his experimentation he managed to sidestep the probing eye of Flatt, who often boasted of his show's family-friendliness. "I knew what the standards were," says Stuart. "I knew my ass would get sent home real fast if there was a problem. Lester never had to call me down. But I look back on a lot of photographs, more toward the tail end of that run now, and I see that I might have been standing too close to the fire."

8

Roses in the Snow

FLATT'S VOICE WEAKENING as the 1970s marched on, he often rested on a chair during shows, and some observed that he seemed to be more band member than leader. But he deflected questions about retirement, promising to return to the road after bouts of illness. His band, like troops waiting for instructions, always reassembled. But now even the faithful Stuart acknowledged the fat raindrops splotching the bus window, puzzling over each and every one of them.

"They'd been playing the same places forever," observes Jerry Douglas, "and they practically knew everybody in the audience. I'm sure Marty met a lot of nice old ladies that baked pies and dinners for him. They didn't look at you as a musician. You were more looked on like, 'Oh . . . you're with Lester, come on in. We'll bake you a pie or give you a jar of something out of our garden.' It was all very sweet stuff that wasn't Marty. He loved the music, and loved playing the music."

He might have flown ahead on the wings of superstar Glen Campbell, who played a concert in Nashville and invited Stuart and his Mississippi buddy Carl Jackson, now Campbell's banjoist, to his hotel room and offered him a job. Recounts Stuart:

And it was more money than I ever dreamed of making with Lester, and I could go to California and get into all that stuff. And it became this big, churning fire in my belly. It was an opportunity, and it was scary. But I also knew that I'd be betraying Lester at a time in his life that was probably not the best. In the hallway of our bus one day, I said, "Lester, I need to talk to you. Glen Campbell has offered me a job." I laid it out there, and he put his arm around me and said, "It sounds good, and I'd be the first one to say go do it, but you're not quite ready yet." And from this vantage point, looking back several years later, he was exactly right, as he always was. I think he knew that I was not quite mature enough to go jump into the middle of California on my own. I'd probably come home in a boxcar.

Mindful, perhaps, of the tempting opportunity Stuart was forgoing and his own failing health, Flatt did not protest when Stuart was asked to record outside the band. Slim Richey, a big lover of hot jazz recorded in the 1920s and 1930s, contacted Stuart about making an album for his Texas-based Ridge Runner label. Often dipping into the bluegrass world for talent, Richey had released an album by Roland White, *I Wasn't Born to Rock 'n Roll*, in 1976, and, in 1977, the ensemble recording *Jazz Grass*, featuring contributions by Ricky Skaggs. It was all the endorsement Stuart needed. He jumped at the chance to redeem his six-year investment in professional music, showing off his command of various instruments and his relationships with top-notch musicians.

But even with members of the Nashville Grass and Flatt himself joining the cast, as well as bluegrass star Jesse McReynolds and veteran session musicians, the album *Marty* (1978) disappointed Stuart's expectations, skittering among bluegrass, gospel, country, rock, and rhythm and blues. Strong on swagger, his lead vocals lacked seasoning, and the album's clashing styles defied easy digestion.

However, his risky choice to cover country music troubadour Johnny Bond's "Love Grown Cold" in an explosive funk arrangement bespoke his audacity, he who would daringly, playfully, launch into Bill Monroe's signature "Raw Hide" if the legend were within earshot. Driving the jubilant performance of "Love Grown Cold" was bassist Earl Peaks, an admired player on the gospel and R&B scenes in Nashville, whom Stuart had met on his Elliston Place rounds. "He was just one of those kids that was around for a moment," says Stuart. "He was brilliant and then he was gone."*

THE RCA RECORDING company's decision to drop Flatt and other bluegrass artists in the mid-1970s complicated the legend's professional life. Manager Lance LeRoy was left to scrape together one-off deals with the aforementioned Canaan, as well as Flying Fish out of Chicago, then a major player in folk and bluegrass music with roster artists such as New Grass Revival, Doc Watson, Vassar Clements, and John Hartford. When Flying Fish released its only album on the bluegrass star, titled *Lester Raymond Flatt*, in late 1975, fans may have noted Stuart's growing prominence on the guitar and Lance LeRoy's comprehensive liner notes in the gatefold, but at this level of record production there could be a price, like unimaginative cover art and the unfortunate misspelling of bassist Jack Hicks's name, which reduced him to "Jack Hick."

When a more reliable contract tendered by CMH Records arrived, Flatt had little choice but to sign. Based in Los Angeles where founder Christian Martin Haerle (CMH) had worked in major-label merchandising, the label scooped up Flatt and other homeless bluegrass artists such as Mac Wiseman and the Osborne Brothers. Those artists dealt with Haerle's southeastern representatives: engineer Jack Linneman in Nashville, formerly with Starday, and musician-producer Arthur "Guitar Boogie" Smith in Charlotte.

---

*Peaks died in Nashville in 2020.

A co-owner of CMH with Haerle, Smith had been a fixture in North Carolina since the 1940s, where he regularly appeared on Charlotte's fifty-thousand-watt radio station, WBT, and its sister television station. By the 1970s, he boasted investments in publishing and real estate and produced syndicated radio shows for personalities such as Johnny Cash. He hosted his own thirty-minute TV show announced by his composition "Guitar Boogie," which he recorded under his own name for MGM Records in 1948.

While presiding over his Tarheel State empire, which also included grocery stores and a fishing tournament, Smith attracted national attention when he sued Warner Bros. over its use of his song "Feudin' Banjos" in the popular film *Deliverance* (1972), which was about a group of urban men on a backwoods excursion who find themselves in the grip of menacing rural folk, an allegory apropos to the uneasiness in the South over northern investment and people streaming into the region during the 1970s. Smith took action when he learned about the appropriation—by the musical director of the film, banjo player Eric Weissberg—as it climbed the pop charts in 1973 in sync with the film's soaring box-office receipts.

Warner Bros. tried to wait out Smith and then offered to settle. But Smith's lawyers waved his 1955 copyright in the face of the federal judge while Weissberg admitted under oath the obvious similarity between his and Smith's recordings. "It was a long drawn out thing," said Smith after the judge ruled for him in 1975. "But right is right and wrong is wrong. I fought the case for two years—not for the money, but for the little guys that get ripped off by the biggies."

His studio open to local talent or big stars traveling through town anxious to commit a groove to tape before the muse disappeared, Smith recorded James Brown's "Papa's Got a Brand New Bag" in February 1965 and, later, an obscure artist's double-sided tribute to the slain Kennedy brothers on 45 rpm—RFK on the A side and JFK on the B. Fearless on the crest of a possible trend, the entrepreneur persuaded rhythm-and-blues journeyman Roy

Roberts to switch to country music. A native of Tennessee who backed soul sensation Eddie Floyd in the 1960s, Roberts himself figures his relationship with Smith revealed not only the wily producer's eye for the unexpected but how easily racism heeled to music on the southeastern circuit, if only in the fever of a live performance:

> He had a big recording studio down in Charlotte, North Carolina, Arthur Smith Studios. I would go down there in the early days and record myself or with somebody else. That's how I got to know him. Through the '70s when disco came in, I was playing nightclubs, and every one of those nightclubs within thirty days called and canceled all of my gigs because they were going to go disco. I didn't know what in the world to do, so I told Arthur about what was happening and Arthur chuckled, like always, and said, "You can come down here and play bluegrass music with me." And I said, "Arthur, there's no way I can come down and play bluegrass music. I can't do all that fast picking like that, an old blues guy trying to play bluegrass music like that." So he laughed again and said, "Roy, you ought to go into country music." I said, "There you go again. These white people aren't going to let me in their clubs with an all-Black band playing country music." He said, "Roy, you can get along with the devil. If you give it a shot, I think you could be successful with it."
>
> The doors started opening for me. It was the hottest thing I've ever done, country, in the whole sixty years I've been playing music. People were just rolling into the clubs to see this Black band playing country music. My first show would always be nothing but country. I'm doing George Jones, you name it. I was doing them all. And then we'd take a break, and then some folks would come up and say, "Do you think you could play 'Brick House' by the Commodores?" And I'd hesitate for a little minute and I'd say, "I don't know. We might be able to do something like that, play a little funk for

you." It was like throwing a rabbit in a briar patch. I'm home then. We'd play some funk and just tear the place up. They'd be dancing, going wild. I had them for the rest of the night. I could switch it up then, doing country and funk, ballads, all that stuff.

And I never had no problem at all, and we were playing clubs where the Klan was in there. [There was] one club in Lillington, North Carolina, and my band was so hot 'til I had tons of fans that would go there and tell him, "You need to book this Black band down here because this is the hottest band around playing country music." And they talked him into it, and, sure enough, the old guy called me and wanted to book me in the club. He was a member of the Klan and we went down there to set up, and I walked in and on the wall was these pictures of Klan guys out there burning crosses at their meetings. I said, "I must be crazy to be up in here." Shoot, I had one of the best times I ever had playing there. We turned that joint out. The owner loved my band, and he'd do anything for me.

As Roberts tested his new turf, Smith concentrated on his role in extending the recording careers of his bluegrass veterans, which at least in Flatt's case meant rerecording old classics and as many songs as possible controlled by the CMH's publishing arm. Stuart says:

One day I woke up in Charlotte in the parking lot of Arthur's studio, and when we left the studio that night we had recorded a double album, and it was one of those things that Arthur produced—and "produced" might be a stretch. We'd do old titles, and the publishing on these things were just a complete joke. . . . That's where it got really chitlin' circuit. They would record these titles just to start bagging up content. I remember a joke going around town was that they'd record a skid mark on the street outside the studio if they thought they could get the publishing on it. The thing I hated about it was it took all of that monumental work that Flatt did in his early career and just ground it down to dust, and there was not much of any kind of value to it. It was just the same old title one more time.

Flatt's intermittent touring felt the same: a hapless, hopeless grind. Traveling with his nurse on the bus, which was disorienting to the members of the all-male club, he made only a handful of dates during the 1978 festival season. But his spirit rallied when they followed the road into North Carolina, welcome territory since Flatt's days with Bill Monroe. Stuart recalls:

> We played some of those school auditoriums, and they raised the windows because there was no air conditioning and people would sit out there and fan themselves and listen. A lot of times the men wouldn't come in. They'd talk with their foot up on the bumper of their trucks, too cool to come in, and they could drink if they wanted. One night we were doing Lester's recitation of "Father's Table Grace," and I happened to look out the window and there was a bunch of pickup trucks and cars out front where these men were congregated, and when he was doing it he was feeble and it was twice as powerful. And I looked out there, and every one of those men had their hats off and standing statue still. That really touched me that they knew him as one of their own and they claimed him.

Although Flatt continued to avoid Earl Scruggs, despite handsome offers from promoters who imagined a reunion, it was also a season of reconciliation. "The Foggy Mountain Boys were such a unit," says Stuart.

> They invented bluegrass music to a certain extent. They invented themselves and each other. They worked so much

and spent so much time together that when you talked to one, you were talking to all of them in a lot of ways. After Josh left the Earl Scruggs Revue, we were playing a concert in Missoula, Montana, and I looked at the [marquee] and we were opening for Josh. And somehow Josh probably said something to the promoter because it got flipped around to the way it should have been. But I went to Josh, and I said, "Will you come over here and see the old man?" And Josh said, "I ain't got nothing against him." I said, "Bring your Dobro." So when we were warming up, I went and got Josh, and he come walking in playing and just walked right up to Lester and picked up where he left off, and there wasn't one word said other than smiles. Later, Lester invited him back up onstage with us, and at the end of the night I saw somebody hug somebody else's neck and everything was fine.

A brain hemorrhage sidelined Flatt in November 1978, and he did not appear in public again until a shaky *Grand Ole Opry* performance in March 1979. Flatt took to bed soon after. Whether he mulled over his defining relationship with Earl Scruggs while his oxygen machine hissed and trilled in his room is unknown, but the old partnership came to Stuart's mind when Bob Dylan— introduced to Stuart by the troubadour's guitarist Billy Cross— asked if the two old bluegrass cats were on speaking terms. Relates Stuart:

> I said, "Not really. Lester's always talking about it, but it never quite happens," and Bob said, "That's sad because the same kind of thing happened with Laurel and Hardy. The little guy was always going to talk to the fat guy and it never happened."
> And when he said that, I went, "Oh no." And I left Bob's concert and went to a pay phone and called Lance LeRoy and asked, "Will you get me a number on Earl Scruggs," which was heresy for anybody in Lester's camp to reach over those lines. So I called Earl, and Louise answered, and it

wasn't very warm. I asked Louise if I could talk to Earl. "What do you want?" "I just need to tell him something that's very important." There was silence, and then Earl came on the phone, and I said, "Earl, this is Marty Stuart." He said, "I know who you are. I like your playing." And I said, "Thank you, sir. I have something really important that I need to talk to you about. Can I come out and see you for a minute?" He said, "Yeah. C'mon, son." We were leaving that night to go on tour, so I left the concert and got in my car and drove to Madison to Earl's house and it was pleasant. And then it got really quiet like, "What did you come here for?" "Well, Lester's back in the hospital, and I believe with all my heart that he won't come home this time and I know from the bottom of my heart that he loves you. I think it would be a tragedy if he left the world and the two of you didn't get to say good-bye. I will do anything I can to help arrange this. If you need me to clear the halls of the hospital, find you a back elevator, whatever it takes. Would you please consider going to see Lester?" And Louise is sitting over there glaring, and she didn't say one word. And I wrote down the number of the hospital room and my number, and I said, "If I can help, please call me." He said, "I'll think about it." And I left it with him. So we got on the bus and we went and played two or three shows [as the Nashville Grass only], and when we got back to town, Lance LeRoy met the bus and Lance with tears in his eyes said, "I just want to tell you Earl went and saw Lester." And I just thought, "Okay."

His flinty profile already embossed on country music's expansive brass portrait, Flatt died on May 11, 1979.

ONLY ABOUT FIVE miles in the car from the storied Laurel Canyon of Joni Mitchell and Neil Young, Coldwater Canyon in Los Angeles nurtured a music community of its own, thanks mostly to Brian Ahern's truck parked in his and Emmylou Harris's driveway. Rodney Crowell recalls his excitement upon arriving for the first time to discover Bernie Leadon (cofounder of the Eagles) with girlfriend Patti Davis Reagan and John Hartford jamming and goofing off. Willie Nelson and Booker T. Jones came later to record the smash album *Stardust* (1978), followed by Rosanne Cash, Billy Joe Shaver, and Guy and Susanna Clark, chiming a Nashville West bell in the canyon. Now Skaggs, with a retinue of musical associates from his own career, mixed in more southern flavor.

Skaggs, after at least ten albums in mainstream bluegrass on which he had played various roles, had never worked with an auteur in the producer's chair. To even say he had worked with producers was something of a stretch, in that his early bands relied on recording engineers' ideas about sound, and, in matters of song selection, the tastes of senior members mostly prevailed. Even the New South and Boone Creek albums were strongly collaborative, though his assertiveness in Boone Creek was undeniable.

Rarely shy in his opinions about instrumentation and repertoire, he was also gifted with executive function, rounding up bookings, transportation, and personnel for Boone Creek and marshalling any vocal talent on hand for the sweet harmonies that stole live shows, jam sessions, or albums in which he partook. But in bluegrass music there was little need for a commanding producer. Most arrangements were worked out onstage or in the bus, and dismal recording budgets prevented the kind of marathon sessions legendary in rock and roll where songs could be built up and broken down and rebuilt. You generally showed up to play when the engineer hit the "record" button.

But not in Emmylou Harris's studio. Hers was a curated process overseen by Ahern, with ample time for inclusive discussions about songs and arrangements, fueled by major-label advances to pay for musicians. Just as Ahern had welcomed the strong creative input of Rodney Crowell, he embraced Skaggs's intimacy with the mountain canon and his ideas as to how to meld it with Emmylou's

Ricky Skaggs on stage with his parents, Dorothy and Hobert,
Blaine High School, Kentucky, 1960.

(Ricky Skaggs Collection)

Marty Stuart flanked by childhood friends,
Butch and Ricky Hodgins, Philadelphia, Mississippi, 1970.

(Marty Stuart Collection)

The Skaggs home
place in Brushy Creek,
Kentucky.

(Photo by Michael Streissguth)

Toddler Ricky steadied by his father outside Brushy Low Gap Free
Will Baptist Church. Brother Garold sits next to them.

(Ricky Skaggs Collection)

The Stuart home in Choctaw Gardens, Philadelphia, Mississippi.
(Photo by Michael Streissguth)

Marty's sister, Jennifer, picks Johnny Cash's *At Folsom Prison* album.
(Marty Stuart Collection)

John and Hilda Stuart.
(Marty Stuart Collection)

A volunteer with Students for Appalachia works with children in Berea, Kentucky.
(Berea College Special Collections and Archives)

Protest against strip mining in eastern Kentucky by the Appalachian Group to Save the Land and People.

(Photo by Phil Primack; Berea College Special Collections and Archives)

George Wallace, at podium, campaigns in Whitesburg, Kentucky, 1968.

(Photo by Mike Clark; Berea College Special Collections and Archives)

MISSING
CALL FBI

THE FBI IS SEEKING INFORMATION CONCERNING THE DISAPPEARANCE AT PHILADELPHIA, MISSISSIPPI, OF THESE THREE INDIVIDUALS ON JUNE 21, 1964. EXTENSIVE INVESTIGATION IS BEING CONDUCTED TO LOCATE GOODMAN, CHANEY, AND SCHWERNER, WHO ARE DESCRIBED AS FOLLOWS:

ANDREW GOODMAN   **JAMES EARL CHANEY**   **MICHAEL HENRY SCHWERNER**

RACE:	White	Negro	White
SEX:	Male	Male	Male
DOB:	November 23, 1943	May 30, 1943	November 6, 1939
POB:	New York City	Meridian, Mississippi	New York City
AGE:	20 years	21 years	24 years
HEIGHT:	5'10"	5'7"	5'9" to 5'10"
WEIGHT:	150 pounds	135 to 140 pounds	170 to 180 pounds
HAIR:	Dark brown; wavy	Black	Brown
EYES:	Brown	Brown	Light blue
TEETH:		Good: none missing	
SCARS AND MARKS:		1 inch cut scar 2 inches above left ear.	Pock mark center of forehead, slight scar on bridge of nose, appendectomy scar, broken leg scar.

SHOULD YOU HAVE OR IN THE FUTURE RECEIVE ANY INFORMATION CONCERNING THE WHEREABOUTS OF THESE INDIVIDUALS, YOU ARE REQUESTED TO NOTIFY ME OR THE NEAREST OFFICE OF THE FBI. TELEPHONE NUMBER IS LISTED BELOW.

DIRECTOR
FEDERAL BUREAU OF INVESTIGATION
UNITED STATES DEPARTMENT OF JUSTICE
WASHINGTON, D. C. 20535
TELEPHONE, NATIONAL 8-7117

June 29, 1964

FBI/DOJ

The FBI sought help in the 1964 search for
Andrew Goodman, James Chaney, and Mickey Schwerner.

(Archives and Records Services Division, Mississippi Department of Archives and History)

Cecil Price.
(Library of Congress)

Bill Monroe's Bean Blossom Festival, Indiana, 1968.
Butch Robins, a frequent banjoist in Monroe's Blue Grass Boys,
faces the camera, eyes cast down.

(Photo by Doc Hamilton)

Fiddler Curly Ray Cline on the outside as Ralph Stanley and the rest of the Clinch
Mountain Boys do their thing. Left to right: Stanley, Keith Whitley, Jack Cooke,
and Roy Lee Centers. Country Gentlemen Festival, Webster, Massachusetts, 1972.

(Photo by Fred Robbins)

Whitley in the middle. Left to right: Eddie Adcock (mostly obscured),
Courtney Johnson, Doyle Lawson, unidentified, Whitley,
Peter Rowan, unidentified, and Charlie Waller. Country
Gentlemen Festival, Webster, Massachusetts, 1972.

(Photo by Fred Robbins)

Skaggs and Whitley harmonize with Stanley. Ron Thomason is over
Skaggs's shoulder. Curly Ray Cline on fiddle and Ed Ferris on bass.

(Photo by Ron Petronko)

The Country Gentlemen. Doyle Lawson, Bill Emerson, Charlie Waller, standing left to right. Bill Yates is seated.

(Emerson Family Collection)

Skaggs with Bill Emerson, 1971, Port Huron, Michigan.
(Emerson Family Collection)

Carl Jackson, left, with Enoch and Margie Sullivan of the Sullivan Family
Gospel Singers playing a Wallace rally in Mississippi, 1972.
(Photo by Hilda Stuart; Marty Stuart Collection)

Enoch Sullivan with Stuart, 1972.

(Marty Stuart Collection)

Early Flatt and Scruggs.
(Archives of Appalachia, East Tennessee State University)

Impromptu festival picking with Bill Monroe and the Blue Grass Boys. Monroe is flanked by Kenny Baker (fiddle) and his son, James Monroe (guitar).
(Archives of Appalachia, East Tennessee State University)

Monroe and Flatt,
together again.
(Photo by Doc Hamilton)

Festivalgoers make their
own bluegrass music.
*(Archives of Appalachia, East
Tennessee State University)*

Stuart's new road family,
genuine commodores
of bluegrass, The
Nashville Grass. Left to
right: Roland White,
Burkett "Uncle Josh"
Graves, Paul Warren,
and Haskel McCormick.
(Photo by Doc Hamilton)

The new Nashville Grass player with veteran Roland White,
Arkansas Bluegrass Festival, Heber Springs, 1972.

(Photo by Hilda Stuart; Marty Stuart Collection)

Rodney Crowell.
(Author's Collection)

J. D. Crowe at a
Lexington, Kentucky–
area festival, longtime
bassist Bobby Slone
behind him.

(Photo by Doc Hamilton)

The New South lights up in Lexington, Kentucky. Left to right: Bobby Slone, J. D. Crowe, Jerry Douglas, Tony Rice, and Ricky Skaggs.

(Photo by Doc Hamilton)

Boone Creek's Terry Baucom, Skaggs, and Wes Golding, left to right, near Lexington, Kentucky, 1977.

(Photo by Doc Hamilton)

Jerry Douglas.
(Photo by Doc Hamilton)

Skaggs in the Boone Creek days, near Lexington, Kentucky, 1977.
(Photo by Doc Hamilton)

Stuart in the Nashville Grass, Dripping Springs, Texas.

(Photo by Doc Hamilton)

The Nashville Grass in the late 1970s.
Left to right: Kenny Ingram, Stuart, Curly Seckler, and Flatt.
(Marty Stuart Collection)

Flatt in the later days. Curly Seckler in the background.

(Photo by Doc Hamilton)

Skaggs drives it home in Emmylou Harris's Hot Band with Harris, center, and legendary guitarist Albert Lee.

(Courtesy of the Country Music Hall of Fame® and Museum)

Ricky Skaggs and Linda Ronstadt.

(Author's Collection)

Legendary producer and entrepreneur Arthur Smith, left, with audio engineer Hank Poole in Smith's Charlotte, North Carolina, studio, 1976.

(Author's Collection)

Back home in Lawrence County, Kentucky,
Skaggs is honored by the city of Louisa.

(Author's Collection)

A family affair. Skaggs and, left to right, father-in-law Buck White,
wife Sharon White, Rosie White (her back turned), Jerry Douglas
(partially obscured), and Cheryl White.

(Author's Collection)

Stuart with Johnny Cash.
(Marty Stuart Collection)

Compadres on the set of Cash's "The Baron" video, 1981.
(Marty Stuart Collection)

Skaggs presents a gold copy of his *Country Boy* record to his hero Monroe, who played on the album cut "Wheel Hoss," a Monroe composition, Nashville, 1984.
(Author's Collection)

Working on the George Jones duets album *The Bradley Barn Sessions*, produced by Brian Ahern, 1994. Stuart, Ahern, Alan Jackson, and Jones, left to right.
(Author's Collection)

Monroe toward the end, Bell Cove Club, Hendersonville, Tennessee, 1995.
(Photo by Michael Streissguth)

Skaggs with parents
Dorothy and Hobert.
(Ricky Skaggs Collection)

Stuart with Tony Brown on the right.
(Marty Stuart Collection)

Stuart with the Staple Singers, left to right, Yvonne, Mavis,
Roebuck "Pops," and Cleotha.

(Marty Stuart Collection)

Brian Setzer, Skaggs, and Stuart, left to right, burned down the house on an
episode of TNN's *Monday Night Concerts with Ricky Skaggs*, 1997.

(Author's Collection)

Way out West. Stuart with the Fabulous Superlatives, left to right,
Chris Scruggs, Kenny Vaughan, Stuart, and Harry Stinson.

(Marty Stuart Collection)

modernism. In turn, Skaggs's nascent ideas about production evolved in Ahern's company, a prelude to the sterling productions he helmed in the days of his solo fame in the 1980s and 1990s.

He watched and learned as Ahern mixed audio with the precision of an open-heart surgeon and warned the band away from playing in the range of Harris's vocal because the instrumentalist and the singer can easily cancel each other out. Skaggs drooled over the vintage microphones Ahern kept on hand, and when Skaggs brought in Jerry Douglas for recording sessions in 1979 the old buddies together acquired a brand-new vocabulary. "Brian just made things sound great and taught us all a lot about gear," says Douglas, "about different microphones and such and the chain that goes from the instrument to the tape and when to play and when not to play at all. Just the little things like that, that he wouldn't beat you up with. He would just say, 'Well, don't play anything right here,' and then you'd listen to it back and you'd go, 'That's symmetry. That's the way it should be.' He really shaped Ricky's ideas in the studio, and they were beautiful and they were good."

Skaggs learned how to create a big and ultimately commercial sound with Ahern, observes Barry Poss, who from his perch at Sugar Hill was keeping a close eye on him as the market buzzed about Boone Creek's *One Way Track*. Indeed, since Harris vied for FM pop and country airplay, Skaggs learned the necessity of emphasizing the beat, pushing vocals to the front, and modulating the sound of instruments to create more ear candy. "That's in the nature of the creative genius, people reflect on one another," says Poss. "The gumbo comes out depending on what was in the mix. I was thrilled with Ricky working with Emmylou."

This refined, highly planned, and assuredly unbluegrass style of recording took root as Skaggs passed more hours in the Enactron truck. "Ricky was a utility guy at first," says Douglas, "and I mean that's what they got first, and then he got into the studio and he started having ideas and they go, 'Oh shit, this guy's a producer.' . . . I mean, can you imagine *Blue Kentucky Girl* [Skaggs's first Harris album under Ahern] or one of those without Ricky? It's just his record, and he'd been around Brian enough to know when to say something. I mean, Ricky's not afraid to say anything. That's just not him."

NEWS OF SKAGGS'S initiation into Harris's Hot Band ignited speculation in the bluegrass community about his future, but in light of his very public maturation as an artist and regular appearances on earlier Harris albums, his arrival to a larger stage couldn't have been surprising. As one writer commented, "He had never once played in the minor leagues."

Playing guitar and fiddle to the right of Harris onstage and flavoring her recordings with pronounced bluegrass sounds, Skaggs achieved a robust platform for his oft-discussed desire to bring bluegrass to new places and promote his own career. "Emmylou saw the gold mine that Ricky could bring," says Jerry Douglas, who was one of a handful of Skaggs's friends who ended up on Harris's albums. "She was ready to do something more traditional, and Ricky was the piece of the puzzle she needed."

Along those lines, he introduced her to Cheryl and Sharon White, old friends of Skaggs from the festival trail who had performed with their father, Buck, as the Down Home Folks. They added prominent vocal support to three tracks on *Blue Kentucky Girl*, which was Skaggs's first album appearance with Harris post Boone Creek. During the Boone Creek days, Douglas watched his friend and Harris sing together on hotel-room floors and little clubs when they crossed paths on the road, amazed that some producer hadn't put them together. "It was magic," he says. "It was bound to happen, and when Rodney left, Ricky slid right in. He, in fact, gave her more: gave her a fiddle player, mandolin player, another guitar player—all kinds of things she didn't have before. And Brian Ahern saw it, too, and these records started coming out that were just unheard-of and started the traditional country movement."

Still smarting from Boone Creek's demanding tour schedule and the attendant breakdowns and snowstorms, Skaggs had looked forward to a less demanding travel schedule, which evidently had been promised by Harris. Instead, he was away from home and family in Lexington more than ever as each new Emmylou Harris release topped the last and big magazines such as *Rolling Stone* paid attention. But even when the show's engines cooled, he programmed his dial to work, pursuing additional recording projects and tours with the Whites, presaging his marriage to Sharon White in 1981 after Skaggs's union with Brenda faltered.*

"Getting the divorce seemed like I'd failed," he wrote in his 2013 autobiography. "I was raised to believe a marriage was supposed to last forever. Mom and Dad had been married for decades. . . . I felt like I had let them down. Not to mention the guilt I felt over what my divorce would do to my children."

DESPITE THE POP music culture's admiration of Harris, linked in part to her loyalty to roots music and the ongoing fascination over her former association with the charismatic Gram Parsons, she danced at the edges of commercial country music as it lived in Nashville, spurning Music City in favor of Los Angeles, as Johnny Cash had in the late 1950s, where at least in Coldwater Canyon eclecticism tended to overrule the soft-rock country music formula gaining traction on Music Row. Indeed, by the end of the 1970s, country music was beginning to transmit the ethos of a slick Bee Gees album jacket. Many producers had shorn familiar country embellishments from recordings by artists such as Kenny Rogers, Ronnie Milsap, and Crystal Gayle in order to reach the

---

* Sharon had been married to Jack Hicks, the bassist in Flatt's band.

profitable popular audience, as if the reverence for traditional sounds in the *Will the Circle Be Unbroken* album, recorded earlier in the decade, had never existed. Indeed, as far back as the boogie in Hank Williams's hot singles of the 1940s and 1950s, and Eddy Arnold's honey vocals of the same era, country music had always courted popular tastes in order to fill the cashbox. But many in establishment Nashville seemed intent on draining the very last drop of creek water from the sound—one reason bluegrass music of the southeastern circuit, though niche, remained powerfully niche, a refuge for fans who believed the city had gotten above its raising.

The *Urban Cowboy* film and soundtrack album of 1980 would prove to be the worst offender in the eyes of many traditionalists. Directed by James Bridges, the film's plot transplanted lead actor John Travolta from a discotheque in Brooklyn to a massive dance hall in Texas, creating a screen world where tight-fitting cowboy wear and mechanical bulls became the emblems of country music, at least as the mass media saw it. To make matters worse, Top 40 numbers by Anne Murray, Boz Scaggs, Kenny Rogers, and others appearing on the soundtrack album only accelerated the seepage of country glitz into Nashville recording studios. "We called it the *Urban Cowboy* scare . . . mechanical bulls and shit and people line dancing," says Douglas. "We hated all of that stuff, and it just wasn't country music. It was like disco country: T. G. Sheppard, Barbara Mandrell, and all that. Everybody hated playing that, and I actually played on a Barbara Mandrell record once, and I couldn't tell you what happened."

Harris reflected on her reaction to the influx of pop in an interview a decade later: "I thought, what is this stuff they're calling country music? Or music, period? It didn't move me on any level." Though gloss had shown up in Harris's work from time to time, on album covers and in the music, not necessarily to ill effect, Harris responded to disco-era trends with *Roses in the Snow*, a resounding declaration of bluegrass.

As she told Patrick Carr in the interview:

I'd been wanting to do a bluegrass album for a long time, and Ricky Skaggs was in the Hot Band at the time, so bluegrass is what we'd all play when we were just sitting around. Also, I thought the timing was right; around then, the late 70s, every musician I met was saying they wanted to do a bluegrass album. But the record company thought it would be a commercial disaster. My *Elite Hotel* album [1975] had been a very successful record, and they thought we should follow it with another album of very good basic Hot Band tracks we'd already accumulated. . . . But I really wanted the bluegrass album. I said that I was willing to bear the brunt of a commercial disaster in order to make an artistic statement, and I needed Warner Brothers to take that chance with me. And they did.

Since it was strictly an acoustic album, most of the Hot Band sat out the session, replaced by Douglas, who was now touring in the Whites, and Tony Rice, who was close by in California with David Grisman. Skaggs also recruited the White sisters to reprise their harmonies from *Blue Kentucky Girl*.

Whether it was discussed or not, Skaggs understood Ahern knew little about how bluegrass was played and recorded, so he emerged as something of a producer on *Roses in the Snow*. And, says Skaggs, Ahern later admitted to him he should have received actual producer's credit as well as a cut of the album's receipts. "Brian let me produce a lot of the overdubs with Tony and Jerry," says Skaggs. "Brian said, 'You know more about this music and these punch-ins and stuff than I do. So, you just kind of drive if you want to.' The way it was put together overdub-wise and instrumentation-wise . . . he didn't have the experiences working in that configuration . . . how to make a band sound out of an acoustic guitar, mandolin, clawhammer banjo, and Dobro. He allowed me to have input, and I was welcoming of it."

The album, released in 1980, followed the template of Harris's five previous albums by borrowing from the Louvin Brothers ("You're Learning"), sneaking in a cover of a monster pop hit

(Paul Simon's "The Boxer"), and nodding to mainstream country music (this time with guest appearances by Dolly Parton, Willie Nelson, and Johnny Cash). But the straight-ahead bluegrass arrangements and the bold decision to release the ultratraditional "Wayfaring Stranger" as a single set it apart. And for the first time, she had forgone a Gram Parsons's song and, then, as if to further acknowledge the passing of an old order, shared lead vocals with Skaggs on two transcendent performances, including another chestnut from the Carter Family catalog, "Gold Watch and Chain," which had conjured tearful memories of her grandparents when she first heard it.

The album shrugged off Music Row's doubts about bluegrass music's commercial appeal at the turn of the new decade as the single "Wayfaring Stranger," featuring Rice's lead guitar, reached the top ten and a space opened again in the market for the pure sounds that gave the genre its start. And although press reports and album reviews merely footnoted Skaggs's involvement, the message inside the music industry was clear: in helping usher traditional elements into a top-selling country music album, Skaggs sounded something like the future.

"That was as much Ricky's record as it was Emmy's," says Douglas.

> I mean, you hear his influence much more than hers on that record. All those string arrangements. Brian was the master engineer, master producer, and he would meld these things together and it would sound great . . . , but Ricky put a fiddle track down and then he would put a viola track down and then he would put another violin on top of that. They called it a fiddle sandwich, and it was a beautiful sound which took the place of a keyboard. But the big bed was coming from the harmonies; he was teaching Emmylou harmonies and songs. Brian's the brains, and not one of us will ever say different because he taught us a lot of stuff. But Ricky went to school right away.

WHILE IN HARRIS'S employ, Skaggs recorded an album's worth of traditional material—with artists who made guest appearances on Harris's recent albums and other friends such as Marc Pruett and Peter Rowan—and he showed up on Nashville sessions for Bobby Bare, Janie Fricke, and, prominently, Johnny Cash, who was recording his impressive *Silver* album (1979) with Brian Ahern producing. In addition, Skaggs traveled to Arch Street Studios in Berkeley, California, with Jerry Douglas to play on Tony Rice's *Manzanita* album (1978), a classic from Rice's West Coast period. Each pursuit only displayed Skaggs's genius anew.

Rodney Crowell brought in Skaggs on tenor vocals and fiddle for his recording of "California Earthquake," a saga song recorded in Coldwater Canyon that showed up on Crowell's first album. And though a dash of the Glaser Brothers might have better reinforced the song's theme, Crowell marveled at the Appalachian patina Skaggs provided. "My point being is that Ricky impressed me because he adapted his musical roots to work with a particular musical form that I was experimenting in. And it seems that when he took my place in the Hot Band, then Emmy started to draw from that and bring it into her own realm."

Little more than a year later, Crowell recruited him again, this time for Rosanne Cash's *Right or Wrong*, her first US album for Columbia.

And that's when Ricky blew me away because his musical creations were really, really creative. It wasn't so much from the bluegrass world that his creativity impressed me, though it was there. But Ricky just completely took control of ["Couldn't Do Nothing Right"], and he just blew it wide open with this kind of reggae acoustic-guitar part he came up with and this beautiful riff for twin fiddles, and I was thinking, "Oh man, you're so creative, so fresh." . . . It's not like I sent that to him in advance and he showed up in LA. It's like you get in the studio and say, "Well, we're going to do this." And you start playing and Rosanne's singing and Ricky picks up the guitar and starts his thing. Just instinctively in a matter of seconds, which triggers something else. And a feel starts to develop and then nuance starts to happen and arrangements start to take shape. It was a matter of taking those basic music instincts that he had and running it through the filter of the tone of the music we were creating.

Further, Crowell took notice of how Skaggs thrived creatively without drugs, which were abundant in their Coldwater Canyon world, though Skaggs did wrestle with alcohol during his time with Harris. "Piles of cocaine and a lot of marijuana didn't seem to faze Ricky that much," observes Crowell. "I'm sure he was looking at it, knowing Ricky, and saying, 'These people are going to hell.' But it didn't keep him from contributing. There were people in the scene for whom piles of cocaine was a part of the creativity . . . but after a while I was like, 'We don't need this stuff in the studio.' It took a while to learn that, and I imbibed plenty myself. My vision was impaired oftentimes when I was judging someone else's vision to be impaired."

Apparently, Skaggs was not going to give up the opportunity to be in the studio, part of the creative community, even if drugs offended his sensibilities, though any indignation rarely if ever showed. "I knew I didn't want to do drugs," explains Skaggs.

I would drink a beer every now and then or I'd have a glass of wine every now and then, but I never would cross the line into the drug scene. I loved my music too much to let it own me. I'd seen so many people be owned by what they ingested. I just couldn't do it. I wasn't walking with the Lord like I am now, but I had morals and a lot of prayers that my mom had prayed and I knew she was praying for me every day. At first, some of the Hot Band thought I was a goody two-shoes, but they accepted me, and I was okay with them doing whatever they wanted to do as long as it wasn't driving the bus.

TO NOBODY'S SURPRISE, Skaggs's major side project during the Harris years, pursued while she was on maternity leave, was his second solo album, *Sweet Temptation*, shepherded by Barry Poss, who had yearned to tap into Skaggs's experimentalism. Sugar Hill had followed *One Way Track* with releases by artists such as Doyle Lawson, Carl Jackson, John Starling, and New Grass Revival—familiar names on Skaggs's artistic trail—and polished up their mom-and-pop marketing practices.

Like the majors, the North Carolina–based label set up record-store appearances coinciding with artists' tour schedules and ran ads for retailers in local newspapers. But Sugar Hill lacked the resources of the big fellas who sprayed the market with product in hopes that one record might break through and sell a million. "We were much more of a catalog label," explains Poss. "The idea was we would sell a modest amount of records but over a much longer period of time. Like a Doc Watson record in its tenth year would sell almost as much as it did in its third year."

Sugar Hill excelled at niche marketing, finding the sweet spot among the masses by winning reviews in alternative weeklies and major dailies alike and by courting public radio whose broad array of programming in the pre–news/talk days might feature genres close to Sugar Hill's heart and catalog—blues, Cajun, folk, bluegrass, and old-time country—often programmed all in the same weekend. Poss and his staff also showed their wares at progressive bluegrass and folk festivals such as Winterhawk in New York, Telluride in Colorado, and the Strawberry Bluegrass Festival in California. "I remember the endless discussion in *Bluegrass Unlimited* about 'What is bluegrass?'" says Poss. "I found that boring. I was lucky because by the '80s, New Grass Revival had broken down a lot of the barriers for bluegrass. In my mind all these things were connected, but in the world out there they weren't so connected. I had all these bluegrass bands, but I also had singer-songwriters— Guy Clark and Townes Van Zandt—and acts that were in the middle. We licensed *Old and in the Way*, which opened up the world of Dead Heads to us."

On the cusp of Sugar Hill's eclectic surge, Skaggs hoped his *Sweet Temptation* on the label would open more ears to bluegrass music. "If I could sell 100,000 albums, oh man, I'd be flying sky high," he mused in an interview in 1979. "Hopefully I can really do something for bluegrass. That's . . . one of my main missions." Indeed, Skaggs's new album slotted orthodox bluegrass arrangements next to familiar country performances, kneading together both styles according to his own tastes and vision in a way that sounded completely natural. "If we had to do it over again," says Poss, "Ricky might want to mix it some more, but at the time it was pretty revolutionary. And you could see the transition right there on the vinyl. There was the best of both worlds presented right in front of me."

So Skaggs's choice of Lester Flatt's "I'll Stay Around"—announced on banjo by Marc Pruett—captured verbatim the spirit of a Bean Blossom festival, while Carter Stanley's "Could You Love Me One More Time" summoned a honky-tonk dance floor replete with steel guitar and Buck White's tasteful piano. But all of it soared on modern embellishments, such as the underwater electric guitar effect straight out of a Brian Ahern production.

Poss comments:

> We knew that was a special kind of record, blending bluegrass and country in this new way. So we decided to make a single. The idea of this little label making a single was kind of a joke. We didn't really know what we were doing. And we thought, "We'll send it to country stations." When the singles arrived, they came in an envelope with no logo, and I thought, "We're going to look like the nobodies that we really were," and I convinced our local print shop to open up at midnight to do a special press run to print our logo on the sleeves. You'd couldn't put the 45 through the printing presses so you first had to remove all the 45s and cut pieces of paper to fit inside the sleeves so they would run through the press, and then

remove the piece of paper and then insert the 45 and then send them out to the station.

IT WAS LIKE Lucy and Ethel packaging chocolates, remarks Poss, citing the classic episode of *I Love Lucy*.

Machines were packaging *Roses in the Snow* for release over at Warner Bros. when word came up from Houston that *Sweet Temptation*'s country attitude had not gone unnoticed. A record distributor there suggested if Sugar Hill made Carter Stanley's "I'll Take the Blame" the A side of Skaggs's single, he could get it played on radio station KIKK, the city's flagship country broadcaster. "I didn't want to do it," admits Poss, "but he was pretty certain we had the wrong side, so we made a special run and flipped the sides and, sure enough, it went to number one for four weeks on KIKK."

ON A PLANE bound for Nashville, while "I'll Take the Blame" appeared briefly on the national charts, Skaggs adjusted the volume on his Sony Walkman tape player, which singer-songwriter J. D. Souther had traded to him for a few tortoise-shell guitar picks. The flight attendant had just moved him from his cramped seat in the back to first class, when he began to review tracks for his follow-up to *Sweet Temptation*. At some point on the flight, a man seated next to him asked about the tape. Skaggs introduced himself as a member of Harris's band and handed the headphones over to his neighbor who was about to be among the first to hear his "Honey (Open That Door)," a strapping country song first recorded by Webb Pierce in the early 1960s. The fellow passenger was Jim Mazza, a Capitol/EMI executive who later signed David Bowie, and when the song ended he was like a changed man. "You could get a record deal with this," he confided. And then he invited Skaggs to stop by the Capitol offices on Nashville's Music Row in the morning.

"I get over there and all the Capitol people are waiting and Jim Mazza is waiting," Skaggs told interviewer Mitch Gallagher. "I play the tape and he's up rocking and dancing around. And there was another thing called 'I'm Head Over Heels in Love' [written by Lester Flatt] that I played a lot of guitar on. They love it, and they offer me a deal."

But it wasn't as simple as that. The executives in Los Angeles quashed the offer, leaving it to Lynn Shults, the head of the Nashville office, to preserve the flame. He called Rick Blackburn at CBS Records, the parent company of Columbia and Epic, on the twenty-six-year-old's behalf. "It's real stuff," Shults told Blackburn. "It's fresh. It's not *Urban Cowboy.*"

Possibly the most successful label executive in Nashville at the time, Blackburn had arrived in 1974 to keep an eye on his employer's half-interest in Fred Foster's Monument Records. In 1979 he rose to chief executive officer, overseeing the contracts of Willie Nelson (currently on top of the music industry), Merle Haggard (who had come from Capitol), and the emerging Rosanne Cash, along with a bench of solid hitters in between. In country music, said Blackburn, Willie Nelson's multimillion sales had turned the Nashville music industry from a sleepy town happy with fifty thousand in album sales to a goliath craving ten times that.

Consequently, Blackburn was always on the lookout for fresh voices to replace older artists who were cycling off the sales charts, and when market research revealed country fans might look past *Urban Cowboy* in search of basic stylings, he paid attention. "They wanted a traditional sound with energy . . . ," said Blackburn. "So we knew *specifically* what we were looking for with Skaggs. When he showed up with that sound—I can still remember the demo—I said, 'Yeah, okay, let's talk.' I think he was amazed because he was getting a lot of turndowns. That was in an era . . . when the contemporary side was really going crazy. So to do a traditional signing was really against the grain." Skaggs watched Blackburn sketch out a contract for him on the proverbial paper napkin over lunch. And then he turned to Barry Poss and the matter of the second album he owed Sugar Hill.

THE YOUNG KENTUCKIAN'S success with Barry Poss lifted Sugar Hill's name. Distributors across the country who had moved plenty of *Sweet Temptation* albums now were more likely to purchase from the label whether they knew the artists' names on the cover or not. "And certainly for recruiting new artists [*Sweet Temptation*] was important," says Poss. "Some of it was a little silly—people would send in a demo and say, 'We're the next Ricky Skaggs.' I'd say, 'I'm not looking for the next Ricky Skaggs. We had the original.'"

Poss suspected from the beginning Skaggs would slip through his hands, and rather than scuffle with a corporate giant or even Skaggs himself, he persuaded Blackburn to jointly release one of Skaggs's upcoming albums on Epic. "Ricky would get the major-label push that he wanted and deserved, and we would get the expanded notice that we wanted and deserved with a release with our name on the label," says Poss. Finally, the co-release proved to be Ricky's third with Epic: *Don't Cheat in Our Hometown* (1983).

Skaggs made one more exclusive recording for Sugar Hill before he completed his transition into the uncertain country music mainstream. Breaking away from some of his last sessions with Ahern in Coldwater Canyon, he headed back to Berkeley and Arch Studios to partner with his old friend Tony Rice, soon to be prominently dubbed "America's greatest unsung country musician," to record an album of straight-up bluegrass and old-time music, featuring interpretations of "Memories of Mother and Dad" and "Will the Roses Bloom," as if to settle a debt accruing since childhood.

It was strictly an acoustic performance, just the two of them: Skaggs on mandolin and Rice on guitar, both portrayed on the album cover in jodhpurs and Stetsons, recalling the spirit of the Blue Sky Boys, the Delmore Brothers, the Monroe Brothers, and Carter and Ralph Stanley, among other chieftains of rustic harmony. "At times it's hard to remember that this isn't a 1940s field recording made in the Virginia mountains," observed critic Rich

Kienzle. "Though both are known for their hot licks, there is nothing here but simple accompaniment, as it should be." Where the two young men with shared roots would go from there was the subject of a thousand conversations. But, in time, hard living on the West Coast and a broken romance dispatched Rice back to the southeastern circuit, where he formed the Tony Rice Unit and pursued many fruitful collaborations such as the Bluegrass Album Band, the Rice Brothers, and the Rice, Rice, Hillman, and Pedersen foursome. And Skaggs, with his own struggles still ahead, ushered in a new dream of country music that few had suspected was possible.

9

New Traditionalists

WHEN THE NESHOBA County Fair flung open its gates in 1980, Philadelphians awoke like Ole Miss football fans witnessing a fourth-quarter comeback. Craving the front-porch camaraderie of the fair's residential village, along with the music and horse racing, fairgoers this year also zeroed in on one special politician among the many who visited in their rumpled summer suits. He was Ronald Reagan, the affable star of television and movies past, who had just sewn up the Republican presidential nomination in Detroit and chosen Philadelphia, Mississippi, as his first campaign stop as the party's standard-bearer.

Convinced the White House was within his reach after two failed attempts—1968 and 1976—he emphasized not the skyrocketing interest rates and hostage crisis in Iran currently plaguing the nation but an age-old concern in white Mississippi: states' rights, the dog whistle of demagogic politicians who decried Washington's meddling in local affairs, including civil rights. "I believe in people doing as much as they can for themselves at the community level and at the private level," he pledged. "And I believe that we've distorted the balance of our government today by giving powers that were never intended in the constitution to that federal establishment. And if I do get the job I'm looking for, I'm going to devote myself to trying to reorder those priorities and to restore to the states and local communities those functions which properly belong there."

While the crowd hurrahed on that August 3, Reagan made no mention of the Freedom Summer victims for whom federal agents combed the thickets and swamps of Neshoba County only sixteen years earlier. The omission was at best insensitive or, at worst, conspiratorial. But in the eyes of many Philadelphians, somebody of national standing with a strong shot at the White House had finally visited to survey their needs and dispel the dark cloud. It must have felt good to absorb a new narrative, even if it might have been an old one in disguise.

The candidate's ascent coincided with growing social and political conservatism in the land. Disillusionment with Jimmy Carter's leadership had moved some voters to join the *Watergate does not bother me* chorus and reengage with the Republican Party, while hot-button issues such as women's rights and court-ordered school busing inspired many southerners and other longtime conservative Democrats to join the Republican Party, then in the early days of decoupling from the spirit of Lincoln.

Evangelical Christianity, always widespread and often aligned with a conservative political platform, also rose in America. It had moved into the spotlight largely on the coattails of ministers such as Oral Roberts and, particularly, Billy Graham, a native North Carolinian, whose active constituency included droves of young people, US presidents of both major political parties, and celebrities such as Johnny Cash and singer and antigay activist Anita Bryant.

If Graham's massive rallies in arenas across the country didn't adequately illustrate the nation's new revivalism, then Carter's election to the presidency in 1976 should have. A Sunday-school teacher in his Southern Baptist Church in Plains, Georgia, Carter freely discussed his faith and provided journalists and scholars a way into broader discussions about religion in American life during the 1970s. His new prominence also invited speculation about the interplay between religion and political power as commentators wondered how his faith might steer his leadership, not unlike the conversation around President John Kennedy's Catholicism in the previous decade.

Out on the front lines of evangelicalism, televangelists had moved into the living rooms of millions of Americans. Appearing in the mold of Graham, they did him one better by showing up on television on a daily or weekly basis. Preachers on local TV and nationally syndicated personalities such as Jimmy Swaggart, Pat Robertson, and Jim and Tammy Faye Bakker peddled their brand of Pentecostalism in exchange for millions in donations. Although many would be exposed as charlatans, the sentiments they encouraged probably found their way into the market research Rick Blackburn of CBS Records cited when he spoke about people yearning for a return to the fundamentals of country music.

But come 1980, evangelicals looking to attach to a political figure forsook the Southern Baptist Carter, turning to Reagan, who represented a strong masculine archetype and staunch anticommunism, though he rarely attended church. But over the decades he had determinedly built a political base resting on Technicolor dreams of America's past glory, as well as strict policy positions on criminal justice and taxes. In the 1980 campaign, Reagan hired the executive director of Jerry Falwell's Moral Majority to manage his relations with the Christian Right and, according to scholar Bruce Schulman, "was the only major presidential candidate to appear at the Religious Roundtable's National Affairs Briefing, a two-day 'revival meeting cum political rally' that attracted 15,000 evangelicals to Dallas." Accordingly, Reagan rejected abortion rights and the Equal Rights Amendment, which represented a reversal of the Republican Party's support for both.

Reagan's resounding victory over Carter in the November election highlighted the nation's resilient conservative streak and cemented the role of evangelical leaders in the political arena. The Christian Right's voice echoed throughout national politics for decades to come, while its perceived traditionalism, coupled with the former movie star's election, immediately impacted mass entertainment. Network television reintroduced the western genre and dusted off the careers of all-American actors such as James Garner and Andy Griffith, while the film industry made room for family-oriented titles and swashbuckling features harking back to Errol Flynn's heyday.

On Music Row in Nashville, it was much the same. With an ear to conservatism's refrain, executives turned down the volume on Waylon and Willie's outlaw movement as well as the Studio 54 vibrations in Tanya Tucker's act. The iconoclastic Rosanne Cash, newly signed by CBS, was told by marketing executives she should always appear predominantly chaste in promotional material but with traces of "fuckability," a typical American duality.

The industry demanded no such unholy mingling of saint and sinner in Ricky Skaggs. His corner-store countenance and well-known travels on the tradition-drenched southeastern circuit unequivocally made the point. He was Nashville's perfect answer to Reagan-era conservatism.

IN SKAGGS'S NEGOTIATIONS with Blackburn, guided by his manager, Chip Peay, he had received a rare concession: artistic control. Few artists in Nashville could claim it, and others just didn't care to have it. Most cooperated with producers who were either on staff at major labels or worked on a freelance basis—familiar names in Nashville such as Billy Sherrill, Bob Montgomery, Allen Reynolds, and Jack Clement. But Skaggs would not tolerate unfamiliar hands behind the glass meddling with his music. "The same ten or twelve guys were making all the records before Ricky came here," says old friend Larry Cordle, who had begun writing songs for Skaggs's sessions. "It's amazing to watch them work. But Ricky didn't want that. He wanted what he wanted, and Rick Blackburn let him have it."

That meant Skaggs chose the songs and selected his own session players. Picking up where he had left off at Sugar Hill, he supervised the mixes, arm-in-arm always with engineer Marshall

Morgan, and, as in Brian Ahern's studio, branded arrangements with his personal stamp. "He had come a long way from the kid who was working with Ralph Stanley," relates Cordle. "He knew a lot of stuff. By the time I was in the studio with him in 1980, I was amazed at what he knew about equipment and microphones and preamps. I could have cared less about any of that stuff, but the guy was up for it."

While insiders around town marveled at the newcomer's freedom, the public read about his credo, announced in every interview of consequence in his early days with Epic: to present traditional country music, including bluegrass, in a modern context, in effect reintroducing time-tested themes and songs to the masses. "I want to give these old songs new blood, new life," he said in a 1981 interview. "People just don't write that way anymore. As soon as I hear one I like, I start thinkin' about it and how I can change it to get my own interpretation. It's important to me to try to do it different from what anybody else has."

Who in country music expressed a mission like that—or any mission at all? Maybe Bill Monroe in speaking of the "ancient tones" he kept alive, or Johnny Cash's endorsement of folk music in the late 1950s. But most just strived for hits and good business on the road—a practical mission, no doubt, but one unmindful of a tradition. About a year into Skaggs's public life with Epic, the *Chicago Tribune*'s Jack Hurst, at the forefront of country music scribes in America, concluded the same: "One of Skaggs' most notable accomplishments is showing that some of country music's most potentially powerful strengths lie in its own heritage, in largely ignored Appalachian values that sustained people in hard times."

Skaggs, his public professions of religious faith increasing with his fame (he was baptized in 1980), spoke of his mission in biblical terms, lifting up overlooked songs, what the world considers weak, "in order to shame the powerful," paraphrasing from 1 Corinthians. Somehow, the contrast exposed the genius of the plainspoken songs that had fallen from the lips of Ralph Stanley and Bill Monroe.

"I was feeling that I was confirmed when I came to Nashville to get a record deal for the first time," he says.

I was playing some music from *Sweet Temptation* around to some people, and they were saying traditional country music doesn't sell and "What's this bluegrass music you're playing?" But I know that God uses the same things, insignificant things, to confound the wise. And that's what I felt about bluegrass in the years after I left Ralph, when I started to really see how the big world of country music felt about the little, insignificant, no-record-sales music—although this music was drawing thousands and thousands of people to bluegrass festivals that the country people were not. They were lucky to get a gig in a beer joint, or maybe four big-name country acts would get together and draw two thousand people when bluegrass was drawing twenty thousand people in some places. That was almost like a big "aha" to the country music industry.

Skaggs's first album on Epic, *Waitin' for the Sun to Shine*, established the template of every other album he released in the 1980s, his most successful decade on the country music charts. Echoing the mixture of country and bluegrass found in *Sweet Temptation* and Emmylou Harris's albums, he leaned heavily on the classic country of Roy Acuff, Jim Reeves, and Webb Pierce, but he also showed his bluegrass roots in covers of Flatt and Scruggs's "Don't Get Above Your Raising" and "Crying My Heart Out Over You." And, as if to signal his abiding loyalty to the man who first employed him, Ralph Stanley's "If That's the Way You Feel" was the first cut on the album.

Teammates from the 1970s joined in, too, and became teammates of the 1980s. Jerry Douglas on Dobro sparked up numerous performances, and the Whites played substantial roles, Buck behind the piano and Sharon and Cheryl with vocal support.

Production standards, always tasteful in recordings Skaggs had taken part in throughout the 1970s, were blemish-free on his new album and accomplished the radio-friendliness demanded by the major labels. "The quality of the instrumentation was top-notch," says Skaggs,

> And it wasn't like we were putting something up in the mix that barely made the grade. I think we didn't try to pull the electric guitar down or pull the steel down, but we pushed up the acoustic things. We had great microphones, great compression, good analog tape. It was something fresh and something very welcoming to listeners out there. And I think it was the same with the background singing. We put those harmony backgrounds up there where they really, really sounded like an instrumental almost. They blended so well with my vocal. I was hearing something fresh, and I was going after it.

Observing that modern country music muted the potential of the acoustic guitar, he tutored engineers in liberating the instrument, pushing up the low end and midrange of the instrument, when they'd been accustomed to strictly emphasizing the top end of the strings. "I'd say, 'This is what carries the rhythm in a bluegrass band. We don't have drums.' I felt like I had to keep educating every new engineer."

WITH VIRTUOSO BOBBY Hicks playing fiddle in his band, formerly a major role player in Bill Monroe's employ, Skaggs rumbled into the Cowboy Club in Memphis anxious to show off his new album, but his mood changed when he unfolded a note from a skeptic in the audience: "A lot of your bluegrass fans are here," it read. "Please don't disappoint us." That his first single on Epic was a Flatt and Scruggs standard cruising up the charts made no difference to some purists who grimaced at the prominent bass and electric guitar and were assuaged not one bit by the brief acoustic set in his shows. No doubt, Skaggs balled up the note and chucked it in the garbage bin. "A lot of bluegrass people ought to stop and think that what I'm doin' on my records and what I've done with Emmy . . . has done more for bluegrass than anybody has done in the past 10 or 15 years," he complained on the heels of the Memphis show. "They don't realize that I've got the ball right now, and I'm runnin' with it—and if they'll just leave me alone, I'm gonna make a touchdown for bluegrass."

The goal line still somewhere down the field, Skaggs's initial tour routing was manic—and barely remunerative as he fronted many of the expenses. He stopped at the Birchmere, Walt Disney World, and the Crystal Palace Saloon and Dance Hall in Paramus, New Jersey, before landing at Breeding's, a club in Lexington where he planned to meet Larry Cordle, who had ditched an accounting career to perform and write country songs, some of which he had pitched to Skaggs. Cordle says:

> My phone rang in the middle of the day, and I was getting divorced and there was a lot of crazy things going on, and I was playing six and seven nights a week and when I answered the phone, it was Ricky and he said, "Man, I'm going to be in Lexington on Saturday. Is there any way you could loan me fifty bucks?" He's calling me from somewhere in the Northeast and they're in a van pulling a trailer and they've had two or three hits, but they're just working their rear ends off, and I said, "Ricky, I guess. If I can pull it together." I had forty bucks and I got ten dollars off of somebody, and so I took him the money.

Skaggs took the cash and then handed him a cassette tape containing a rough cut of Cordle's "Highway 40 Blues," which Skaggs had earmarked for his next album. "He gave me a little tape recorder," recalls Cordle, "and said, 'I want you to write me some more songs. You ain't got no more excuses not to write songs and send them to me.'" Skaggs signed Cordle to a publishing company he had started, and he included one of his friend's numbers on every album he released in the 1980s.*

Slotting Cordle's song as the third single from his next album, *Highways and Heartaches* (1982), he watched it top the charts while receiving nearly unanimous credit for a whole new strain of country music people were beginning to call "new traditionalism." While introducing young listeners to great songs of yore—such as Bill Monroe's "Can't You Hear Me Callin'"—he showcased them in a polished musical framework built on familiar country music instruments, energized at times by western swing and rockabilly tempos and, always, electric guitar and drums. It was a new dimension in country music, as revolutionary as producers Chet Atkins's and Owen Bradley's country-politan arrangements in the 1950s and 1960s, and Waylon's and Willie's outlaw country of the 1970s.

Applying the new-traditionalist formula, Skaggs's interpretation of singer-songwriter Guy Clark's "Heartbroke"—recorded with little fanfare in the late 1970s by Rodney Crowell and by Clark himself in 1981—flew to number one when Epic released it from *Highways and Heartaches.* Famously replacing the word "bitch" in one of Clark's verses with the less-offensive "rich," Skaggs more significantly fueled the song with "drive," one of the time-honored traits of bluegrass music. "That thing just blazed," says Skaggs.

> And "I Wouldn't Change You If I Could" [credited to Jim Eanes but actually composed by Arthur Q. Smith] had triple fiddles and vocals and steel guitar. It was just such a really good clean, pure sound. And then I remember sitting down with Joe Casey—the radio guy [for CBS Nashville]—and he really liked "Highway 40 Blues." It really had "hit" stuck on it. But he wanted me to reedit it and cut out a bunch of the

---

*Many of the Cordle songs Skaggs later recorded originally showed up on recordings made by Cordle, with Skaggs producing, for an album that was never completed.

solos. He said, "You can't have forty-five or fifty seconds of solos . . . four solos back to back." I said, "They're half solos, so it's really only two verses or like a verse and a chorus." He didn't see how we were going to get away with that, and I said, "I don't want to mess with the integrity of the record. It's just going to chop it all up. We do it live and people love it and they're the ones buying the records, not us." And so he let me have my way. So here again history is the best teacher because it was a big number-one record.

"Highway 40 Blues" captivated young mandolinist Ronnie McCoury, some thirteen years Skaggs's junior, who had begun traveling in his father's band. Resting at a truck stop near Harper's Ferry, West Virginia, he popped a quarter in the jukebox to hear Skaggs's new single, accented with the mandolin, and then listened again and again, staring through the glass as the record spun. He could not fathom so heavy a mandolin presence on a mainstream country music record in 1982. "It was very soulful stuff," says McCoury, "and hearing it on the radio makes you want to emulate it."

AS HE PROMOTED his new brand of country music, Skaggs also took advantage of his prominence to share his Christian values, offering testimony onstage and in interviews with the news media. In later years, his label protested, but in the 1980s it seemed to be characteristic of the sweeping presence of evangelicalism in the culture, and promotion executives gave it little thought. "This was a time in the early '80s when, Monday morning, you ran down the roster to see who was in jail or laid up at the hospital," says former CBS product manager Jim Kemp. "But Ricky didn't drink. He didn't do drugs. There wasn't constant issues with marriages and things like that. I mean Ricky was a worker. That's one of his strengths. He worked at it, and that's what he enjoyed doing."

The message Kemp and others delivered to audiences and deejays was clear: Skaggs was reviving the taproot spirit and sound of country music in a modest 1980s fashion that could appeal to most anybody. "I think country fans were hungry for something different that had a little bit more country vibe to it," says Kemp. "And Ricky hit that vein."

The music press picked up the line word for word. Terms such as "tradition," "roots," "old-time," "home," "the past," and "basics" appeared in almost every headline, as music journalists across the nation hailed him as the leader of new traditionalism, a somewhat self-contradictory term. Can somebody or something be new and traditional at the same time? Well, Epic thought as much. The company had come upon a new vessel to carry elements of the old sound that research claimed the people wanted. "Skaggs was doing Bill Monroe," says Rick Blackburn. "But the persona of Skaggs would drive it forward. Damnedest thing."

No less than Ed Ward, prominent among rock music critics in the nation, proposed Skaggs was rejuvenating the lives of old songs, beginning with the first album, *Waitin' for the Sun to Shine*.

I like the odd way Flatt and Scruggs shaped the melody of "Don't Get Above Your Raising," and I'm indebted to Skaggs for emphasizing that better than Flatt and Scruggs did. I like the silly old-timey sentimentalism of "Lost to A Stranger," in which a guy sees his world crumble as his darlin' waltzes with another guy. I like the four-square Appalachian turnarounds in "You May See Me Walkin'." As for the title tune, I thought it was an undiscovered Neil Young gem until I saw it was by Nashville master Sonny Throckmorton, whose '78 Mercury album *Last Cheater's Waltz* belongs in the library of any unreconstructed, regressive country fan. I love its simplicity, and the way it tempts you to add strings toward the end, a temptation that probably never occurred to Skaggs.

THE INEVITABILITY AROUND Skaggs resounded. Richard Harrington of the *Washington Post*, Jack Hurst of the *Chicago Tribune*, and other prominent critics echoed Ward's sentiments. Longtime observers of the new star's Stanley-to-Harris genealogy, they understood his potential as well as the power of a major-label marketing campaign. Indeed, the trend Skaggs initiated was mighty and quick in developing.

Just as country music seemed poised to mortgage itself to the *Urban Cowboy* aesthetic, the new-traditionalist era signaled a mood shift in the industry, holding up the soul of country music as a guiding idea. Male and female artists entered through the door, carrying their own connections to various aspects of the tradition. George Strait and Reba McEntire brought Texas dance-hall vibes, while Dwight Yoakam, a Kentuckian, channeled the Bakersfield Sound. The Judds and Patty Loveless, Kentuckians also, worked their roots in Appalachian mountain music, and Randy Travis, radiating matinee-idol appeal, invoked George Jones and the neon-drenched honky-tonk vein in his new-tradition story.

Keith Whitley followed, too. He might have come sooner, perhaps arriving in Nashville at the same time as Ricky Skaggs, had he accepted his old pal's invitations to form bands during the 1970s. Instead, as previously noted, Whitley had rejoined Ralph Stanley in 1974 and then hopped to J. D. Crowe's band where he reunited with his former Country Store bandmate Jimmy Gaudreau, who had recruited him into the New South. "He was attracted to the steel player in the band and hoped Crowe would do some country music," says Gaudreau.

Over the years, Whitley had fashioned a yearning vocal style that called to mind Lefty Frizzell, and to which bandmates were treated in hotel rooms after the show when he uncapped his flask and sang himself to sleep.

"Keith wanted to do straight country," recalls Crowe, "and I knew he could do it." So just as the banjoist had thrown away pickups to accommodate Skaggs a few years earlier, he conceded to Whitley's taste. What followed was the album titled *My Home Ain't in the Hall of Fame,* an ironic gibe at mainstream country just as Crowe's band was heading full bore into it. Released in 1979 on Rounder, the performance was another demonstration of Crowe's versatility, deploying drums, electric instruments, covers of the Flying Burrito Brothers and Jimmy Buffett, and stellar lead vocals by Whitley like Tony Rice used to give him.

But Whitley's personal life was failing because of alcoholism. Bandmate Gaudreau had witnessed it as far back as their days together in Country Store, and rumors Crowe himself had heard were soon confirmed. "I had a lot of problems with him," he says, "and I knew that going in. But since he wanted to come into the band, I thought we could help him in some way, straighten him out a little bit. He and I had a lot of talks about his problem, and I just straight out told him, 'If you keep doing what you're doing, you won't live to be forty.'" Despite tensions over drinking, Whitley attacked the New South's next album, *Somewhere Between* (1982), with a heartbreaking tremolo worthy of Merle Haggard. "What an incredible singer," remarks Steve Bryant, the Boone Creek alumnus who joined Whitley in the New South. "I knew that guy was going to do something, and so did a lot of people in the bluegrass world. It might have taken a little longer than they thought, but Keith was really growing through Crowe. We played shows, and Keith just had those people in the palm of his hand."

The album title track, written by Haggard, mourned an unshakable barrier between two people, but it also spoke directly to where Whitley and the band found themselves at that very moment: somewhere between bluegrass and mainstream country. But there was little ambiguity over Whitley's direction, according to Crowe. In effect, he says, the album was a demo for his lead singer to use in shopping for a Nashville record deal. "I only used the banjo on two cuts on it, and I played rhythm guitar. But that's how he got his country contract, because of that *Somewhere Between* album. That album right there to me is the true Keith Whitley. That's country, and that's what he wanted to do."

Although the album fulfilled Whitley's dreams, it could not stanch his thirst for booze, jeopardizing the New South's reputation on the bread-and-butter southeastern circuit. "At one time he almost caused me to lose a ten- to fifteen-day tour on account of his drinking," says Crowe. "No matter how good a guy is, you can't do that and keep a band. So I said, 'That's it. You need to go do your own thing. I've done all I can for you . . .' I hated it worse than he did, really."

In 1984 RCA signed Whitley but promptly buried him in light rock embellishments from beyond the new-traditionalist movement. "When he got to Nashville they wanted him to do them 'bubblegum'-type things, and I hated them," grumbles Crowe. "I knew that's what they tried to do. He called me after he did [his first release, *A Hard Act to Follow*], and he said, 'You know, that ain't really what I wanted to do, but it's what I had to do.' And I knew that would happen. And I told him, 'If they're putting money into you, you kind of have to do what they want you to do if you're going to be a success. That's just the way it is, and once you get established, then you can kind of call your own shots.'"

In 1988, after Whitley's old partner in the Clinch Mountain Boys had posted ten number-one hits, Whitley's *Don't Close Your Eyes* catapulted him to the forefront of the new traditionalists. "For the first time since his early 1980s albums with J. D. Crowe," wrote frontline critic Bob Allen, "his subtle and unmistakable powers as a singer come through on vinyl." The title track and other cuts from the album, such as "I'm No Stranger to the Rain," distilled his honky-tonk dream. Four number-one songs followed over the next two years, but, sadly, he was found dead in his home of alcohol poisoning on May 9, 1989.

Skaggs had just finished up some family business back home in eastern Kentucky and decided to stop to see Whitley's mother in Sandy Hook on his way back to Nashville. As he approached the house, he guessed she was hosting company as several cars crowded the road in front, so he pushed on home, only to receive

a call from his wife, Sharon, shortly before he crossed the border into Tennessee letting him know his old friend had passed.
Teenage memories of two boys taping their radio show in Keith's
garage and stifling grins at Ralph Stanley's mountain philosophy
must have raced through his mind. They had never formed that
much-discussed musical partnership, but in bluegrass memory
Skaggs and Whitley would always be together.

ALTHOUGH MARTY STUART missed Reagan's visit to Neshoba
County, he was present in Nashville at the very moment country
music was looking for youthful artists with traditional pedigrees.
But it was almost as if Flatt's death had caught him off guard.
The twenty-one-year-old had no backup plan. He checked in with
prominent bands on the southeastern circuit, but nobody needed
a guitar or mandolin player, and his solo album of 1978 had not
attracted follow-up offers from viable record companies. "I was
glad that none of the traditional bluegrass people needed me
because I had this thing burning inside of me that I wanted to
explore and go beyond playing what I'd been playing for seven
years. . . . I wanted to become a better musician. I wanted to learn
how to write songs and sing. I knew I was still a musician in somebody's band, but I wanted to grow beyond that."

Vassar Clements hired the young man to play electric guitar.
But although Stuart was keen to pick up the guitar again after so
many years primarily playing the mandolin, he stumbled in Clements' hillbilly-jazz environment, and left after a few months. He
flew up to Michigan and jammed with blues-rock guitar legend
Lonnie Mack, and he tried to stay in touch with Bob Dylan, whom
he thought might be the answer but wasn't. The missed chance
with Glen Campbell loomed, but before regret consumed him,
he jammed with Doc and Merle Watson and their accompanist,
T. Michael Coleman. "It was like Sullivan Family fun and it clicked,"
says Stuart. "And Merle said, 'You know, if you want to run with us

for the rest of the summer, do it.' But I was reaching and knowing all the while that Doc and Merle's tour was fast going to come to an end."

In his season of discernment, Stuart was in the middle of producing what he calls a "ghost-band album" with other former members of the Nashville Grass for CMH Records, when he visited Nashville friend and master luthier Danny Ferrington at the Old Time Pickin' Parlor, who had set out on his work bench a glossy black guitar made for Johnny Cash, emblazoned with the image of an eagle, as if it were the sarcophagus of an Egyptian king. The moment tripped Stuart's well-oiled opportunity switch, and he asked to go along when Ferrington delivered the instrument to producer "Cowboy" Jack Clement's studio where Cash often recorded.

Some months later, the two men arrived at the studio greeted by Clement, who was dancing with a martini glass on his head while Cash accompanied him on rhythm guitar. Happily, Stuart spent the rest of the day picking with Cash and Clement. Then he found himself in Clement's car the next evening heading to Cash's lakeside home in Hendersonville, just around a bend in the shoreline from Flatt's old home, where there was more picking and hanging out and, in Stuart's head, a notion that the Man in Black might contribute to his ghost-band record.

As the sessions approached—it was early November 1979—Stuart went seeking Cash's phone number from Clement, who stammered and, finally, declined. But an address book was open on the producer's desk. "I just happened to look down," says Stuart, "and there was John's number and I went, 'I can't do this,' while I copied it down and became a pest at 822-5615."

Cash agreed to join the album, and after he finished his vocals on two cuts, he asked about Stuart's dizzying string of freelance gigs since Flatt's death, and then he went home. "And, so, weeks go by and I was in Cedar Rapids, Iowa, with Doc Watson, and it was the last show. The tour was over. I was going to have to come back to Nashville and figure my way from there. And my mom called me after the matinee show and she said, 'Bob Wootton is looking for you.'"

Wootton was Cash's lead guitarist, and he invited Stuart to join the show the next night in nearby Des Moines. Not surprisingly, Stuart seized the overture, and when the familiar bass-baritone voice bellowed, 'Hello, I'm Johnny Cash,' Stuart stood behind him on guitar, a member of the Great Eighties Eight, the singer's new-look band for what would turn out to be a frustrating new decade.

> I lay in bed that night after doing the show and meeting all the people thinking, "This really is more about the soap opera and the legend these days than it is about 'Folsom Prison' and recording music like that and *Ballads of the True West*." . . . Out on the road I felt I was unnecessary in that band, and I really was. I felt like where we made our best music was in the studio. But while I was there, whether it was as a band member or a friend, I experienced and saw just about every type of human behavior and I experienced about every emotion a human being could have. To hang out with that show and him and June and the whole size of that machine, it was worldwide. It was huge. And it was a great eye-opener for a twenty-two-year-old kid.

IN A SENSE, Stuart's entrance into Cash's world arrested his musical development. He had hoped to parlay his status as a former member of the Nashville Grass to burnish his songwriting skills and improve his vocal performance on the way to a solo career in the mold of Ricky Skaggs. But although plenty of people around Cash in the late 1970s and early 1980s were establishing recording and touring careers—Rosanne Cash, Carlene Carter, and Rodney Crowell, most prominently—the Cash band was never a pipeline to solo prosperity for aspirants who weren't in his family. So, as in the days of Flatt, Stuart himself would have to groom influences outside of his employer's immediate world—many of them now more accessible because of his association with Cash—in order to evolve.

The road was Stuart's initiation to the band, an arena of scenes comically surreal and deeply heart-wrenching that collectively told the Cash story. For example, a five-year-old Oklahoma kid named Chris who used to live next door to Hilda and John Stuart in Nashville demanded, via his parents, a meeting with the legend. "I brought him up there," relates Stuart, "and the matter that Chris needed to talk to Cash about was he had a tooth that he needed pulled and he wanted Johnny Cash to pull it out. And John got real nervous and started sweating, and he said, 'Son, I can't do that. It'll hurt you.' He says, 'No, you have to.' And he almost started crying. I sat there and witnessed it, and he pulled Chris's tooth and that was great."

On the same tour, the band played the Louisiana State Penitentiary, simply known in the dark chapters of southern lore by its location: "Angola." As they arrived in a prison van that picked them up at a nearby airport, the sight of armed guards on horses overseeing prisoners working the fields rattled them. Inside, Charles Colson, Nixon hatchet man turned prison evangelist, opened the show. "They treated us great, but the warden was a typical Boss Hogg, kind of southern, short, stubby cigar, potbelly, khaki-wearing, plaid shirt, little, rolled-up-Stetson kind of guy, truly a southern image," recounts Stuart.

> And I remember when you turn off the main road headed to Angola, it dead-ends in Angola and after Angola there ain't nothing but swamps and alligators that will kill your ass. . . . And we were walking out of the gate [after the show] to get on the van and there was a prisoner's mother whose son was on death row. She got down on her hands and knees and

wrapped her arms around Johnny Cash's legs and begged him to speak with the governor to get her son off death row.

That was the alpha and omega on that trip: to see the kind of presence that he had on people, and the power that God gave him to speak out on behalf of people, whether it was a little boy needing his tooth pulled or a mama needing to save her boy.

10

Hillbilly Rock

JOHNNY CASH INITIALLY brought Stuart into his band as a multi-instrumentalist, the kid's bottomless steamer trunk containing fiddle, mandolin, and myriad guitars impossible to ignore. But Cash had recently run though a string of bassists, so he redirected Stuart to the rhythm section. But music was rarely the primary concern. The new hire learned before his first tour ended that traveling with Cash mostly involved a type of weather forecasting, anticipating each day how his moods, addiction, or spats with wife June Carter might dictate the currents of the show. The legend appeared barely coherent in one town and, in the next, drained from moderating disputes among his considerable entourage. "I could take one look at him and tell where he was at," says Stuart, "if it was going to be a fast show, slow show, mad show, long show, a walk-through show or a real show. . . . He would walk onstage and hit the 'Johnny Cash' button and somehow get it done."

But not always. The young man had cared for drunken bandmates on the bluegrass circuit and cozied to pot and pills himself while still in his teens, but nothing he had ever witnessed matched Cash's spells of confusion, whether it was falling ten beats behind on the familiar "Folsom Prison Blues" in concert or regaining his balance onstage after an unrehearsed pratfall. Though Stuart might have considered intervening, he rarely if ever did, leaving that task to doctors and family members. "I was fool enough to try to run alongside of him and keep up," says Stuart. "I was right there in the thick of it, so I couldn't intervene. I needed to be intervened upon myself at those times."

Stuart brought the same easy deference to Cash that he'd offered to elders on the bluegrass circuit. "Marty was there when I got there," says Jimmy Tittle, who played guitar in the band with Stuart and married Cash's daughter Kathy. "I had worked with Merle Haggard and a lot of big guys with a lot of charisma, the greatest, but I was a little intimidated by Cash. But Marty would talk to him just like he was some old guy he'd known forever and John loved that."

Squarely on board the Johnny Cash train, he also attempted to improve Johnny Cash's music, both onstage and in the studio. "Marty was something like the music director without saying so," adds Tittle.

> Bob Wootton [who replaced guitarist Luther Perkins when he died in 1968] would always say, "I'm the bandleader." That always came up. But Marty just went right over his head. He didn't care about any of that. Marty was a prodigy. He'd been a musician since he was a baby, and he knew where he stood with John and he'd do his thing. He did Carl Perkins' part; he did Luther Perkins' part. And he sang harmony with John. He made it fun for John. It went from being tired to fun, which is what you really need when you're out there on that road doing that. That's what I saw Marty doing. He was a real friend as well. They could talk about anything, and they spent a lot of time together.

But in the studio, a confusing place for Cash, Stuart deferred to bankable producers and big-time recording execs who tried to solve the problem of Cash's slumping record sales in the early 1980s. The promise of his *Silver* album of 1979—recorded with Brian Ahern in the producer's chair, Ricky Skaggs on fiddle, and

Rodney Crowell with new songs in hand—had collapsed, followed by a series of albums that tended to evaporate soon after release. Cash pianist and country-rock pioneer Earl Poole Ball produced the highly anticipated *Rockabilly Blues* (1980), but it was more rockabilly talk than walk, while Nashville Sound producer Billy Sherrill piloted *The Baron* (1981), a charming though spongy album. Says Stuart:

> From the day I got there, I wanted to see my old hero, and, at one point, I remember having to have a talk with myself, going, "You know what, you can't expect Babe Ruth thirty years later to stand up there and knock it across the bleachers the way he once did. That's unfair, so you have to meet somebody where they are at this time." But I did understand that there was a sound that he owned, and sometimes they would use session players [instead of the road band] who would get the essence of that sound. But it was so inauthentic. They were trying everything.

Still reaching, the record company paired him again with Ahern for the album *Johnny 99* (1983), Stuart's fourth major Columbia project as a member of Cash's troupe. It was on its face inspiring. Ahern introduced "Highway Patrolman" and "Johnny 99" from Bruce Springsteen's *Nebraska* album, wedding Cash to one of his musical heirs, and nominated Guy Clark's "New Cut Road" as well as cuts by Paul Kennerley, a young Briton who later figured in Stuart's solo career and married Emmylou after she and Ahern split in the early 1980s. The missing ingredient was Cash's focus that, if in the mix, might have helped him parlay his credible covers of the Springsteen songs into a career milestone. But he recorded the album in Los Angeles during breaks from filming the television movie *Murder in Coweta County*, sessions that were often paused to greet visiting celebrities hot to meet the Man in Black.

In the early going, Ahern joined Cash on the road to filter through possible songs, and then he lugged his leather cases bursting with lead sheets to Cash's home on a night that fore-told *Johnny 99*'s identity crisis. "We went with Brian to the Cash cabin," says Stuart, "the compound which later became a studio. All the ladies brought dinner over from the main house. We were sitting there and John was sweating and twitching, and Brian sat down, quiet and nervous. And John came out of nowhere with a bowie knife. And Brian was sitting there at the end of the table, and John just threw it right over his head and—bam!—it found its mark on the cabin wall and it threw Brian completely off, and I just kept eating. And I thought, 'That's pretty good shooting right there.'"

When albums such as *Johnny 99* stalled, producer Jack Clement faithfully waited with a cola and a candy bar. A sorcerer who infused Cash's smash hit "Ring of Fire" of 1963 with Latin spice and ran the board at Sun Records during the singer's heyday on Union Avenue in Memphis, Clement was a Memphis-born bon vivant proud of his feathery ballroom-dancing steps and the defin-ing hits he had produced for Charley Pride and Waylon Jennings in the 1970s in between multiday benders that were legendary. But the Cowboy Arms and Recording Spa, where Clement and Cash chased shadows of their former selves, was exactly the wrong place to find a new million seller. Hidden behind tall picket fences near Belmont Boulevard in Nashville, the studio spun like a carousel—recall the martini balanced on Clement's head when Stuart first met Cash. The producer smoked a lot of weed while barking instructions over an intercom from his office chair into his upstairs studio. "It was a lot of fun," says Jimmy Tittle. "He had a lot of great gear, great characters hanging around. He was great. You'd always go in and hug and kiss Jack, try not to get too high, and then go do your work. And he did some good things. But in the end it got weird."

In the eyes of Stuart, Tittle, and engineer David "Ferg" Fer-guson, unusual instrumentation and zealous reverb smothered the clean sound they thought best showcased the Man in Black. "We'd make very cool basic tracks," says Stuart, "and by the next day you might hear a kazoo or a gong on it." Cash might finish a vocal in the evening only to find it sweetened beyond recognition by morning, though Cash, busy herding chickens into Clement's yard as a practical joke, rarely protested.

From the very beginning, Stuart recoiled at the overproduction around Cash's performances onstage, which he believed denied the power of the pioneer's original Memphis sound. Despite a Tennessee Three interlude in most of his concerts, the Great Eighties Eight should have been cut in half, he surmised. "It didn't take me long to go up to him and say, 'Why don't we do this like you used to do?' He's like, 'What?' 'You had it right a long time ago, and it feels bloated to me now. You should fire me because I don't add anything. I just clutter it up, and "I Walk the Line" does not need honky-tonk piano on it.' He said, 'Well, there's a lot of people depending on me.' I said, 'Well, you should still fire me.' But he wouldn't do it, so I should have quit."

Instead, Stuart shifted his campaign to the studio. Out of sight of Clement, and with Tittle and Ferg as his conspirators, he snatched the star's recorded vocals and mixed them anew, the warm-yellow of the Sun Records label their guiding light.

> John would just wake up some mornings and drop [son] John Carter off at school and go to Cowboy's upstairs and get an engineer to hit the button and sing for twenty, thirty minutes and get up and walk out and leave the tapes. And Ferguson and I would listen and go, "Man, this is really Johnny Cash," and we would put upright bass and Fluke Holland drums and Luther Perkins guitar on them and a whole bunch of slap-back echo and we would turn them into Johnny Cash tapes. And then I'd play them for him, and he liked them.

Cash, though, remained a conspirator in the mostly soft contouring of his Clement-produced albums of the 1980s and 1990s, such as *The Adventures of Johnny Cash* (1982) and *The Mystery of Life* (1991). "He was receptive, he was totally receptive," says Stuart.

"But he was also respectful of his producer, and he and Cowboy were already on this other trail. But we kept making these pirate tapes, and I'd slide them to him or just play them. He couldn't help but listen because it was good. I just kept promoting the original vision of simplicity." He recalls:

> And so when we had a crack at the right kind of song—Bob Dylan and Johnny Cash's "Wanted Man"—I was all over this town trying to get the right amplifier. I knew the sound I was looking for—even though it's going to be a buried track on a buried record. But in case history ever did take a look at it, I wanted it right. And I was at a buddy of mine's house one day, and I was plugged into his amplifier and I said, "Can I borrow this for a minute?" And I called Ferg and said, "I found the amp for 'Wanted Man.'" He said, "Aww, Stuart. You're killin' me. You don't want to mess with that song. We're done." I said, "No we're not done." But Ferg would always go the extra mile with me.

NOT EXACTLY AN innocent at this stage of life, but ignoring obvious sign posts, Stuart married Cash's daughter Cindy, following Jimmy Tittle and Rodney Crowell into the tunnel of love on the shores of Old Hickory Lake. Now dramas on the road concerning father carried into Stuart's home life, while he braced for taunts of "nepotism" from corners of the country music business. "When Cindy and I first got married, he would introduce me as his son-in-law onstage, and it bugged me," he relates. "And I went to him one night and said, 'J. R. . . . I really need to talk to you. You have no idea of how proud I am to be on this bandstand in your world and to be your son-in-law. But would you please not introduce me as your son-in-law?' He got the weirdest look on his face while I said, 'I worked a long time to get my credibility by talent.' And he said, 'You're the first one who ever told me that.' It stung him, but he understood." Nonetheless, Marty and Cindy had divorced by the end of the decade.

At a loss to discern a true purpose, Stuart found solace in the ghosts he courted from country music's past: most prominently guitar hero Clarence White, whom he had worshipped in the aftermath of White's sudden death, he says, as a way of consoling his old friend Roland White. He acquired the former Byrd's famed 1954 Telecaster guitar outfitted with the StringBender innovation whose pedal-steel sound helped yoke West Coast country and rock in the 1960s. Shortly after joining Cash, Stuart had heard from White's widow, Susie, offering to sell several of the master guitarist's belongings. He says:

> So I put Roland's son Lawrence in my car and we drove up to Elkhorn City, Kentucky, and Susie showed me this guitar she had in mind to sell which was a 1954 Stratocaster, and then she said, "You really want to see the *Telecaster*, don't you?" And she showed it to me, and I couldn't believe what I was seeing. I went, "My God, there it is." It was missing a string on it, and I said, "Do you mind if I put a string on it?" There were strings in the case. And I played it and didn't even know how to hold it. And she said, "That's the one you really want to buy, isn't it?"

Stuart left Elkhorn City that day with the coveted guitar and additional Byrds paraphernalia, including White's stage costumes, the nucleus of what would become a mind-boggling collection of country music artifacts still growing in 2023. Back in Nashville, he took the guitar for servicing to the venerable Old Time Pickin' Parlor, where friends marveled while he unbuckled the case, plugged the guitar into the test amp beneath a work bench, and launched into the opening licks of "Muleskinner Blues," the way White had played them in 1973 in his band named Muleskinner.

"When the word first got out, I think there was a lot of Clarence fans and Byrds fans that were incensed that somebody like me had it. I agreed with them. I thought this should be in way more capable hands, but I was the one chosen to take it and care for it and hold onto it and further its legacy. I loved the style of playing, and I wanted to learn that style." In sporting a feathered hairdo, neck scarf, and swinging stovepipe pants embroidered with tasteful western accents, as he does to this day, Stuart keeps alive the regal visage of White, striding in the 1970s across the stages of concert halls and listening rooms of the East and West like a prince from another planet, guitar cradled in his right arm.

> Clarence just seemed like almost a North Star figure because he was a bluegrass guy that had pretty much been raised on the same stuff as me but somehow had made it beyond that and he became a rock star and played for big crowds and was on the cover of a Columbia record album. He dressed cool, and people from Jimi Hendrix to Jimmy Page knew Clarence, but at the same time so did Doc Watson. And that California vibe surrounded him, and he was the template on how to live a life and get beyond just playing at the *Grand Ole Opry* in Nashville for somebody else.

STUART'S RELATIONSHIP WITH Cash, which was strained after his breakup with Cindy, soon returned, and he continued to show up for most of his former father-in-law's recording sessions, each one less fruitful than the last. As Cash searched for grounding, according to Jimmy Tittle, he went as far as to seek a permanent residency on the *Grand Ole Opry*, to in effect take the place of the recently deceased Roy Acuff, as its living symbol. But Cash instead moved to Branson, Missouri, the pensioner's paradise, where audiences initially flocked to his theater. The residency cut down on travel but rattled Cash's outlook when the audiences quietly shrank to fewer than a hundred per show. It looked to be the last stop before oblivion.

But in 1993, as he was extracting himself from Branson to announce his partnership with a Long Island–born hip-hop producer named Rick Rubin, who had just recorded him alone with only a single acoustic guitar as accompaniment, he called Stuart into his office and sang him the entire *American Recordings* album. It tapped the darkness in his image and reconnected with the basic framework of his sound, resurrecting the legendary artist in the international music conversation. The ballyhooed recording inspired a follow-up with accompaniment by Tom Petty and the Heartbreakers and Marty Stuart.

> I was on the way to California to start a tour with my band, sitting in the front end of the airplane, and when I got on I didn't notice who else was on board. And when the flight landed in LA, I stood up and, well, there was J. R., and I said, "What are you doing?" He said, "What are *you* doing?" I said, "Sitting three seats away from you and not knowing you're there. You need to work on your charisma." And when we were at baggage claim, he said, "How long are you going to be out here? . . . I'm going to the studio with Rick Rubin and Tom Petty. Why don't you come play some guitar?" Whether it was up to me to be a leaning post or a guitar player or whatever . . . it was the right thing to do. I rearranged my schedule for a few days, and we did those recordings [that became 1996's *Unchained*]. And I had the feeling when we were doing "The One Rose" by Jimmie Rodgers that this was really, really resetting country music's clock: "This is big. This is good music. This is important music." And the same thing with "Rusty Cage" and "I Never Picked Cotton," all those songs. And what I felt more than anything else was, "This finally happened for J. R. Mission accomplished."

FROM *UNCHAINED* UNTIL Cash's death in 2003, while Stuart negotiated his own solo career, he dipped in and out of Rubin's adventurous sessions with Cash. He often helped work out arrangements, and he played on some final cuts. But as the old master's health declined, Stuart observed a certain schmaltz in covers like the Beatles' "In My Life" or Simon and Garfunkel's "Bridge Over Troubled Water," chosen, it seemed, to narrate Cash's demise. Stuart recalls the horror of somebody with pull suggesting "My Way," and then feeling pride that nobody on the session, including Cash, knew the chords or the lyrics. Tittle, who also remained on the scene, his marriage to Kathy Cash intact, mounted an intervention. "We did 'My Way' at Marty's house, and John Carter did the [scratch] vocals. The next day I went to John's house, and I said, 'John, I do not mean to step out of bounds, but please don't do "My Way." Please, God in heaven, don't do "My Way."' He started laughing, and he said, 'I ain't going to do that song.' I said, 'You are bigger than "My Way." Everybody knows that. Please don't do it.'"

In the penumbra of his final year, Cash had begun piecing together scenes described in scripture with others from what he could remember of dreams and old spirituals, to construct "The Man Comes Around," an uncompromising meditation on God's final judgment. It realized the marriage of his lifelong attraction to biblical themes and his strengths as a songwriter, then so rarely on display amid his nagging ailments and the rush of contemporary music he was asked to record. Indeed, like "I Walk the Line" or "Five Feet High and Rising," it was quintessential, acutely so when he tried it out for the first time with Stuart on guitar, David Roe on bass, and Cash himself also on guitar, with a sheet of paper threaded among the strings re-creating the percussive effect of his Sun-era recordings.

"I kept my eyes closed the whole time [we recorded it], and when the last note sounded, I looked at J. R. and said, 'That was wonderfully strange.' And I had a feeling when it went to Hollywood it would get worked on, so when I left that day, I put out my hand and told [the engineer], 'Give me a copy of it.' That's the one I cherish the most because that's the last sound—the sound I fell in love with—when the original vision of Johnny Cash and the Tennessee Two passed before a microphone."

Months later, Cash exited life cognizant of the clamorous reaction across audiences to his cover of Trent Reznor's "Hurt," which represented Rubin's formula at its best: the singer paired with thoughtful selections from modern rock and its offshoot styles. But among the posthumous tributes and recollections, "The Man Comes Around," which held up Cash's artistic essence one last time, was barely considered, nor has it been since.

A FULL DECADE and then some before Cash started working with Rubin, Stuart and Skaggs, bachelors still, lived in a small apartment building in Madison, an inner-ring suburb of Nashville known for cheap rents and a community of hillbilly musicians who were either on their way up or on their way out. "I lived in the apartment directly above Skaggs," says Stuart, "but we never really connected much. It was always distant." Perhaps generations-old animosity between the Ralph Stanley and Lester Flatt camps had settled in between them, but more likely Skaggs's focus on the next session or an upcoming flight to Coldwater Canyon left little time for his young neighbor who, anyway, was earning a reputation around town as a bit of a hell-raiser. In between their clipped greetings, Stuart saw a fellow runner from the bluegrass days bending country music toward the spirit of the southeastern circuit, and he wondered if he, too, would have a shot at molding—rather than merely working in—the artistic culture around him.

Still between bluegrass and country during his first years with Cash, Stuart took a page from Skaggs's career and made a solo album in 1982 for Sugar Hill Records titled *Busy Bee Cafe*, calling on influences and friends to fuse the rockabilly revival of the early 1980s with the bluegrass tones of his formative years. Inviting Johnny Cash, Earl Scruggs, Doc and Merle Watson, Jerry

Douglas, Carl Jackson, and T. Michael Coleman, Stuart revived
"Hey Porter" with Cash on lead vocals and "Down the Road" from
the Flatt and Scruggs catalog. It was like his very own *Will the Circle
Be Unbroken* album—a marriage of young and old artists.

Says Stuart:

> I think that I've always seen that country music had broad
> shoulders, especially when you hit it from the roots angle—
> which all goes back to the Byrds' *Sweetheart of the Rodeo* album
> for me—because "One More Ride" was on the first Johnny
> Cash record I had, and "Get in Line Brother" was a part of
> Lester's set, and then there was "Boogie for Clarence," and
> then I sang a song about a place in my hometown [the title
> track] that I used to go to during the civil rights days and
> they'd let me dance along. I think I was trying to figure out
> what my story was and tell my story, and as usual my phone
> book was stocked with pretty cool people and so my friends
> came by to help me. But I think I was just trying to figure
> me out.

ALTHOUGH BARRY POSS at Sugar Hill would have welcomed
another album, two years passed before Stuart gained the major-
label chance he craved. It appeared in 1984 after Cash and the
band returned to Nashville after taping a Christmas special with
Waylon Jennings, Kris Kristofferson, and Willie Nelson in Switzerland. During production, the musicians had filled their evenings
together in Johnny and June's suite. "There was real magic there
when the four of them ignited, or engaged," says Stuart, who took
notes for a magazine article and shot photos while woodshed-
ding with the legends. At the time, Nelson's hot streak in popular music showed no sign of cooling, emboldening his producer,
Chips Moman, to pitch a Cash-Nelson duet album to Rick Blackburn, who immediately consented in the undying hope of stirring
Cash's sluggish sales.

"We came home and started a John and Willie record," says Stuart. "But it was just another trail. And after about two days and two or three things, it was just laying there. The voices were too different to be doing duets."

Moman then looked to the magic of the Switzerland jam sessions, inviting Jennings and Kristofferson to join Cash and Nelson. Stuart remembered a Jimmy Webb composition, "Highwayman," that Carl Jackson had suggested would be perfect for Cash, although Glen Campbell had already recorded it. "And I kept thinking about John saying, 'There ain't nothing wrong with us that a hit wouldn't cure.'"

Stuart contacted his cousin Marty Gamblin from Campbell's publishing company.

> He pulled it out and there were four verses on it, and no harmony required on the song. And I took it to the studio and played it for John and Chips. I told John, "You should take the last verse, it's the cool one." I sang the scratch, and the band put the track down and Campbell . . . came by and put a real vocal on it to show everybody how to sing it. And, two or three days later, after everybody was coming and going to the microphone at different times, "Highwayman" occurred. I remember [Cash] played it over and over and over in the bus. He knew he had one. We all knew it. . . . It was like a little oasis in the desert.

Cash, Nelson, Kristofferson, and Jennings soared to number one in 1985, and although Cash himself failed to parlay their hit into better sales for his solo records, the song more than rewarded Stuart. Rick Blackburn and his colleague Bonnie Garner at CBS had visited the studio during the "Highwayman" session and asked who unearthed the song that was creating such a commotion.* The Man in Black pointed to Stuart, while Waylon warned he'd

---

*Garner later managed Stuart.

soon be snatched up by another label. Stuart, never at a loss, possessed demo recordings ready to share, and for insurance Cash lobbied deputy president Dick Asher, Blackburn's boss in New York. Before "Highwayman" faded from the charts, Columbia signed Stuart in a wave of youthful acquisitions that the company branded collectively as "Horizon '86," the core of Blackburn's next trend in country music: an assertive reprise of rock-and-roll attitude. "This is the type of music that will attract the masses and not be just categorized as country," said the executive in an interview, who was primed, it seemed, to move past new traditionalism. "It has a backbeat to it, that Memphis shuffle. It has a 1950s feel with 1980s technology. I think it's clearly the way to follow." Stuart was only too happy to fill Blackburn's mold—though a faint voice inside warned that new traditionalism might be a more honest home for his musical spirit.

IN PRESS INTERVIEWS to promote his first Columbia release, Stuart exuded a rambunctiousness to go with Blackburn's rock-country marketing efforts. In a magazine article, he was portrayed rear-ending a green Toyota on the way to a show in downtown St. Louis, while in another he suggested the mothballing of new traditionalism, a quote that may have been painful to see in print. "You have a real traditional line here in Nashville—Ricky Skaggs, Reba McEntire, that set of folks," he pronounced. "Then there is a group of young mavericks who have had a lot of stuff bottled up inside them for years. They are dying to turn it loose. I'm afraid I qualify for that group. I still love playing my mandolin, but I also like turning up my guitar real loud and playing that way, too."

Quietly covetous of Skaggs's direction, Stuart lagged behind the country artists with a Blackburn beat. Columbia's Sweethearts of the Rodeo and Shenandoah pierced the top ten in the mid-1980s, but Stuart's singles from his self-titled debut album, actually an extended-play limited to eight tracks, sputtered. Today he says he should have worked harder to find quality songs, but he also remembers hearing whispers around CBS to the effect that it didn't know how to market him.

Although the new-traditionalist movement endorsed country music's foundation, many so-called legacy artists landed on the CBS cutting block, including Ray Price, Johnny Paycheck, Lynn Anderson, and Johnny Cash, who in 1986, according to Blackburn, was asking for a hefty advance in negotiations to renew his contract. The executive said later that he was inclined to sign Cash, assuming he could figure out how to boost sales to justify the larger advance. "My plan," says Blackburn, "was to go out and sit at the lake [Cash's home] and say, 'Look, how do we make this work?' Those kind of conversations which John would have."

At the time, loyalty appeared not to figure in the calculus. The Man in Black received no credit for contributing mightily to Columbia's status in country and pop music, not to mention its bottom line. Nor did anybody consider the value of future sales Cash's catalog would generate, long after both he and Blackburn were dead and gone. Simply, corporate headquarters demanded immediate profits from its investment in artists, and Cash showed no sign of remaining apace. But while Blackburn worked the numbers, a competing offer from Polygram rang in at $1 million.

When the local press announced the end of the Cash-Columbia relationship in July 1986, Stuart exploded. "I walked in the office and told Blackburn what I thought, arrogant little punk that I was. I went downstairs to my buddy Joe Casey, who was the promotions guy, and he was on the phone. And he hung up the phone and said, 'Well, I don't know what you just did, but, congratulations, you just killed your career here.' And they pulled my [next] single." At the time, Stuart's next album, *Let There Be Country*, was cued up for release, but as Stuart's stock plunged, it was consigned to the vaults, where it languished for six years.

AFTER CLOSELY WATCHING Cash, whose every struggle found a companion revival story for public consumption, Stuart spun his own redemption narrative set in the late 1980s. In the spare times after his expulsion from Columbia, as he related to hungry journalists, his mother urged him to reflect on his roots and the harried years in Nashville, and in this period of discernment he was presented with a cleansing opportunity to travel with the father-and-daughter gospel entertainers Jerry and Tammy Sullivan, an offshoot of the Sullivan Family Gospel Singers whom Stuart ran with in 1972. So, like David who found strength in the wilderness, he pulled onto the southern backroads with the beloved gospel duo, his mandolin at his side. "I found the way flowers smelled down there back then," he explained to Patrick Carr, the prominent country music journalist. "I saw my old friends. I went to the woods where I used to walk with my grandpa, sat on his front porch. I know I didn't belong there anymore, but I just stopped and was still."

When Stuart reemerged, label executive Tony Brown, the pianist and gospel singer who had played in Elvis Presley's band in the 1970s, was waiting for him. Celebrated at the time for reinventing MCA Records' Nashville division with bold signings of Steve Earle, Lyle Lovett, Nanci Griffith, and Vince Gill in the 1980s, Brown was a friend going back to the 1970s. He tapped guitarist-producer Richard Bennett, long a member of Neil Diamond's band and, recently, an essential talent in the team behind Earle's *Guitar Town* and *Exit 0* albums, to join him as a coproducer on Stuart's recordings. Together, with the familiar Paul Kennerley providing songs, they helped Stuart refashion his unsuccessful rockabilly-revival approach of the mid-1980s into "hillbilly rock," based on the art and attitude proffered by prerock figures such as Hank Williams and the Maddox Brothers and Rose who jacked up the rhythm while projecting undeniable country music affiliations.*

Bennett, who played guitar on the three albums he coproduced for Stuart, bonded with Stuart over their shared love of 1950s honky-tonk. They alternated guitar parts depending on who was

---

* Dwight Yoakam also emerged in this mold in 1986 with Warner Bros.

better suited for a particular task, Bennett quoting from Gershwin's "Rhapsody in Blue" on Stuart's first MCA hit "Hillbilly Rock," for example, while Stuart popped like Luther Perkins on a hit cover of Cash's "Cry, Cry, Cry." Bennett observes Stuart lacked a strong vocal persona in the early going but worked until he accomplished one, and he grew into songwriting by composing with Kennerley. "Paul wrote perfect songs that were so simple it takes a genius to write them," says Bennett. "And they're irresistibly melodic. He just has a way of doing demos that on the surface are very simple yet irresistible. When that partnership happened with Marty and Paul, it's like they became each other. That connection really gave focus to the tunes that were on the *Hillbilly Rock* album." The Stuart-Kennerley collaborations—"Hillbilly Rock," "Western Girls," and "Easy to Love (Hard to Hold)"—defined Stuart's new lane in popular music. It may not have formed a new vein in country music, like new traditionalism, but the freewheeling sound energized the nation's line dancers and finally launched Stuart's solo career. "With this one shining effort," wrote Bob Allen in 1990, "the culmination of, among other things, three years spent between albums honing his songwriting talents, Stuart puts himself into the front ranks of modern country music, where he's belonged all along."

Bennett correctly champions Stuart's second album, *Tempted*, emphasizing its song mix that was rooted in the singer's own background and tastes. It kicked off with the Bill Monroe–Hank Williams cowrite, "I'm Blue, I'm Lonesome," whose royal pedigree Stuart must have found impossible to ignore. Bennett comments:

> He seriously brought his bluegrass thing to that, but we didn't do it as a bluegrass thing. But it was definitely informed by his bluegrass background. We also did Cash's "Blue Train" on that second album. We weren't particularly trying to pay homage to him or the Tennessee Three, but it snuck in there. It had more to do with [referencing] Bruce Springsteen than it had to do with John. And later we did "Doin' My Time," which was an old Jimmie Skinner tune, but John had a great

record of that. In fact, Cash came in and sang on it. I remember at some point when he was doing his vocal, Marty said to
him, "When we're going into the instrumental, can you say
'suey' in there?" Marty was the only person in the world who
could say that to him, and he did.

Endowed with a brash modern kick and the drama of a Roy
Orbison ballad, the title track of the second album gave Stuart a
top-five hit for the first time. Recollects Stuart, "When we hit with
'Tempted' in 1991, I said, 'Okay, this is more where I belong. I
love this.' It's still the only song from those days, sometimes, that
I do. There was something identifiable in that one that I could
build on."

The hillbilly-rock theme also highlighted his growing collection of country music artifacts. He brandished his guitars once
owned by Hank Williams, Lester Flatt, and, of course, Clarence
White and donned his collection of star-spangled Nudie suits
formerly worn by veteran country stars for the seductive country music videos in which he starred. Sounding curiously distant
from his cradle in bluegrass, he claimed to be an apostle of the
masters of hillbilly music, perhaps more an acolyte of Lefty Frizzell than Lester Flatt. "I feel obligated to carry some of the pure
things that they taught me into the 21st century," he wrote in the
liner notes of *Tempted*. "I mean hard rockin' hillbilly music, that's
what I feel. I don't know, maybe I'm a bridge between the past
and the future."

11

Who Will Sing for Me?

IN THE GATHERING heat of a late morning in Brushy Creek, young Ricky Skaggs toddled to the barn next door where he found his grandfather rounding up fishing gear for an afternoon by the lake. The boy squatted down next to the tackle box, mindlessly opening and closing the latch again and again until the old man, working a plug of chewing tobacco between his cheek and gum, could take it no longer. "Son," he began, "that tackle box has just got so many times to open and close until it's tore up. You sure are wasting a whole lot of the times." Skaggs mumbled an apology and never forgot the straight line of wisdom his papaw had cast.

By his thirty-second birthday in July 1986, Skaggs's modern traditionalism had cut a deep furrow in Nashville. He counted four number-one albums in four years and more than twice that number in chart-topping singles, including "Uncle Pen," a Bill Monroe standard he had resurrected for his *Don't Cheat in Our Hometown* album of 1983. It was the kind of song, noted a contemporary review, with "an innocent charm which is hard to ignore." At least a half-dozen other country artists had followed Skaggs into new traditionalism, a few of them on the verge of surpassing him, notably George Strait and Reba McEntire, though, in McEntire's case, it would take the overpowering pop sound she created to attract mass audiences. On the other hand, some artists whom he idolized lagged behind in the row their disciple had hoed: Ralph Stanley continued to beat the same circuit as he had for decades, while Bill Monroe, despite receiving honors at the White House in 1983, still traveled in a bus that, according to Blue Grass Boy Mark Hembree, smelled of "rotted, potted meats, body odor, mouth odor, diesel fumes, hot rubber and the variegated bouquet of the john."

After five years in Nashville, Skaggs had won the coveted Country Music Association (CMA) Entertainer of the Year Award and a pair of Grammys for instrumental performances. He proved transformational, one of the industry's few innovators, injecting the taproot sounds of Appalachia along with western swing and honky-tonk into the mainstream during a time when commercial demands had threatened to engulf those regional styles with a mishmash of sound that seemed to come from nowhere in particular. And, in the long run, he made space for future invocations of tradition in popular music such as the *O Brother, Where Art Thou?* phenomenon of 2000 and, further into the new century, the acoustic-charged singer-songwriter train ridden by artists such as Gillian Welch and Dave Rawlings, Chatham County Line, Watchhouse, Sierra Hull, and others who found a home in the broad marketing category known as "Americana."

But in 1986, the gods of CBS Records decided Skaggs had fiddled with the tackle box one too many times. It was time to shake up the formula, apply the wax, rock the beat in order to take Skaggs to the pop market. The memory of *Urban Cowboy's* massive sales persisted in their minds, and too many years had passed without a follow-up. All this he learned on a visit to Rick Blackburn's windowless office on Music Row, just as his new live album recorded in London with guest Elvis Costello clambered to number one on the country music charts.

Skaggs often stopped by unannounced to see the executive, who was now focused on forcing more rock-and-roll influence into country music. But this day Blackburn just happened to have Skaggs on his mind while listening to Walter Yetnikoff, the unhinged overlord of CBS Records in New York, demand bigger audiences for their country artists. Blackburn waved Skaggs in the door and invited him to join the conversation.

> He put me on the phone with Yetnikoff who said, "Ricky, my boy, you're really doing good, but you can do better. We want to cross you over into the pop field and get you really selling records. You can sing anything." I said, "Well, I probably could. But I don't know if I would." He said, "Oh no. Just a few things could change, and it would be great." And I said, "My whole theory is do music so well that we get people to cross over to us, not me crossing over and changing my music just to appease that audience." I think he realized I wasn't going to change with that.

However, the message from New York was clear, and Skaggs, still the producer of his own work, agreed to concessions on the album that became *Love's Gonna Get Ya!* (1986). The guest stars of previous albums such as Jerry Douglas and Buck White disappeared, while covers of old country songs from the Monroe and Stanley catalogs remained in the cupboard. Alternately, in deference to the label, he worked up two songs by John and Johanna Hall, formerly of the pop-rock band Orleans: "Artificial Heart" and "New Star Shining," the latter as a duet with James Taylor. A New York producer selected by CBS came to Nashville to help record "Artificial Heart," a song that represented another reluctant compromise. "I think they thought it was a cute title since Barney Clark had just had the artificial heart transplant in Louisville," says Skaggs.

> So I thought if I'm going to cut this thing, maybe I can get [John Hall and Orleans bandmate Larry Hoppen] to sing harmony, and they did and they were happy to do it. I loved their harmony singing. I didn't feel like I was selling out or anything. I was always open to new songs, and if it brought

a little different sound, that's fine. I'd been with Emmylou long enough singing different songs to let people know I can do more than just bluegrass and country. . . . But I never did it for the sake of trying to get more airplay or get more record sales. I just never bent the knee to that. I thought more about my music and thought more about my integrity than that.

Longtime fans surely puzzled over Skaggs's chest-bearing shirt and gleaming cowboy boots on the album cover and expressed surprise at his unusually exuberant vocals and the occasional musical ambiguities, common in those modern country moments when it's hard to discern which instruments—if any—are actually at work. But there were plenty of familiar markings, too: a cut by the always reliable Larry Cordle, "Don't Stop Gypsy"; Skaggs's bold mandolin on the gospel favorite "Walkin' in Jerusalem"; and, in "Raisin' the Dickens," the always welcome revival of hillbilly jazz, present on his albums dating back to *That's It*—the very first.

Finally, he and his wife, Sharon, won a Country Music Association award for the duet "Love Can't Ever Get Better Than This," and the album climbed high in the country charts. But neither the album nor its single releases crossed over to the pop side or the European market, as the label had wished, and, what was worse in Skaggs's mind, there was the possibility he had alienated long-standing fans who may have resented his foxy dress on the cover and those songs devoid of obvious country flavor. "I will say that some of what you hear on there is about as pop as anything you'll hear from Ricky Skaggs," he told an interviewer at the time. ". . . It's a matter of fighting this preconceived notion of what a country artist should be like. Like he should be sittin' on a bale of hay, or standin' on the fender of a truck, or with an old hound dog or something." The album failed to expand Skaggs's audience, but with the sparkling James Taylor duet and a few of the hottest instrumental licks Skaggs had ever put to wax, who could quarrel with it?

Still, when his next album hit the streets in 1988, the sepia-toned cover framed him in front of Nashville's old Romanesque

Revival Union Station clutching his guitar. Not exactly a bale of hay but a sure enough mea culpa for the benefit of disaffected fans who needed to know the old train had returned to the depot. *Comin' Home to Stay* staged a half reunion of the New South, with J. D. Crowe and Jerry Douglas guesting, and trusty covers from the set lists of legends returned to the dinner table, reviving the ghosts of Webb Pierce and Bob Wills, to name two. Fans could also find an apology in the liner notes, though Skaggs says today he's forgotten exactly to whom he was apologizing.

> I just felt there was some disgruntled fans out there. We artistic types get a little bit heady and we overthink so much about whether or not we've let somebody down or hurt somebody's feelings. I do that stuff. I guess I didn't mean it so much as "I'm sorry I disappointed you" . . . I don't know. Sometimes you just write stuff that's on your mind at the time and send it in and say, "Here you go." . . . Maybe I didn't hit the mark and maybe I was apologizing to the label for giving them something [*Love's Gonna Get Ya!*] they couldn't sell like *Highways and Heartaches* or *Country Boy*. Be that as it may, I'm proud of it.

SOMEHOW, SHOW BUSINESS occupied Skaggs differently than most other stars. Naturally controlling, as colleagues often noted, Skaggs was reluctant to let projects pass him by. He continued to produce his own recordings as well as those of the Whites and, in 1989, Dolly Parton's *White Limozeen* album. He vied for prominence on country music television, which cast him as an emcee, his awkward stage banter of the Boone Creek days mostly in the past, and he single-handedly energized the video genre in country music with "Country Boy," a vignette featuring Bill Monroe buck dancing on a New York subway train as he chastised Skaggs, who played a harried business executive, for getting above his raising.

The video allegory hit close to home. Skaggs, far removed from his Kentucky birthplace, hovered over publishing interests, touring details, marketing plans, and various side projects, such as a bluegrass tribute for a Country Music Association awards show, Dan Fogelberg's *High Country Snows* album (1985), a derailed film score, and a duets album with legends such as Bill Monroe and Earl Scruggs that was never finished.

"It was just too much," he said of his frenzied pursuits in an interview from that era. "Way too much. I couldn't go on doing myself and my family like that. I mean, I put my poor pregnant wife through hell. . . . My cholesterol level had gotten to 301 at the end of all that. My triglycerides were up to 265. I weighed 211 pounds. So, basically, I was a heart attack looking for a place to happen. I realized that, and said 'That's it. I can't keep doing this to my body.'"

In frequent conversations with reporters about his Christianity—for his testimony had become central to most encounters with the public—he admitted his topsy-turvy life seemed antithetical to his faith. "It seems like the Lord always gets what's left of my time, and that's not the way it's supposed to be," he told Jack Hurst. "I carry that guilt around all the time. I used to think my kids had to take last place as far as my time goes, but now, I spend more time with my kids than on things I'd like to do spiritually. That's what comes last and that really makes you feel bad when you're tryin' to do better all the time."

Every new triumph met a corresponding trial, some personal and others tied directly to his work. In 1986, a French radio station owner lurked near the stage of an outdoor Skaggs concert in Nashville with a loaded .357-caliber Magnum pistol stuffed into his trousers, as if mimicking a crucial scene from Robert Altman's allegorical *Nashville* film of 1975, although the man never brandished his weapon. Claiming his diet of violent American television moved him to pack a gun for his trip to Tennessee, he had approached the stage wearing a "red winter jacket"—despite June temperatures well in the nineties—when a fan alerted a police officer. Before Skaggs even noticed the drama, the Frenchman was hustled off to a nearby police station. "This kinda shakes me up," said Skaggs in a later interview. "You never know what kind of sick people are around. I feel sorry for the guy."

Skaggs never learned the outcome of the man's arrest, but with increasing celebrity, the risks stacked up. "We had some threats a few times," he says.

> [Somebody would say] that the next time I came to a certain place, they were going to kill me. And so I would just walk out onstage and do a song or two and say, "Hey, I understand there's somebody here who said they're going to kill me, shoot me. So, all you all, just look at the person sitting next to you, and if they got something in their pocket, just shout it out. Y'all got more eyes than I got." That just flushed it out right there on the spot. We never had no more trouble with it.

Later in 1986, the bad dream of the gun-toting Frenchman was followed by the nightmare of a drug-addled trucker shooting Skaggs's seven-year-old son, Andrew, in the head on I-81 near Fincastle, Virginia. Andrew's mother, Brenda, had pulled past the erratic long hauler, who objected to her maneuver by firing his gun into her car. The boy was directly in his line of sight.

The bullet pierced Andrew's lip and jawbone, just missing the jugular vein, before it lodged in the back of his neck. As Brenda watched him slump across her lap, she sped to the nearest weighing station for help. Skaggs flew to the hospital in Roanoke as his son endured numerous surgeries to repair the damage. While he marveled at both his son's and his former wife's bravery, the tragedy moved him to reflect on the career pressures he was placing on himself. "I tried to be more involved in my family's life," he says today. "We were working a lot. So I would take the kids on the road with me more in the summer when they were out of school, although they both lived in Kentucky with their mom. . . . I definitely had some struggles trying to balance my kids, who were growing up, and Sharon and I had two kids here in Nashville."

While Skaggs's work schedule returned to earlier levels and Andrew recuperated, the trucker, who was also charged with possession of meth, cocaine, and pot in addition to assault, got a forty-year prison sentence, and both he and his employer were ordered to make monthly financial payments to Andrew for the rest of his life. "It will never really be over," said Skaggs at the time. "But my son is out of the hospital, and he's back in school doing good. And, boy, he's a miracle to see."

THE COMMERCIAL ENTITY Skaggs had become was beginning to falter. Duties that came with representing country music and attempting to broaden his own reach scrambled his focus. *Country Music* magazine's Bob Allen found Skaggs crisscrossing Nashville in 1987 to meet with disc jockeys and business associates and explaining why MCA had just booted him from the producer's chair of the Whites' albums. "All is not right in Ricky-land," commented the reporter.

In the midst of recasting himself for a bigger audience, he and his management were also trying to understand the music fan's view of him. "I . . . have these little cards, little questionnaires that I send out to everybody at our shows," he told Allen. "It's more or less a customer survey, like the Cracker Barrel restaurant chain or Hilton does. I ask everybody in the audience what their favorite Ricky Skaggs song is, their favorite album. I ask 'em what they liked about the show, what they didn't like. I even ask 'em if they had just one piece of advice they'd give Ricky Skaggs, what would it be. I even let them rate my show, on a scale of one to five." More sophisticated market research was telling Epic that Randy Travis and George Strait, who had joined Skaggs in the vanguard of new traditionalism, were now outselling their guy.

"I think part of it is that the newness, the mystique . . . has worn off," he continued with Allen. "I mean, I *ain't* the new kid on the block anymore. And, you know, man, once they've handed you that big gold ring—the CMA's Entertainer of the Year trophy—it's like, 'Okay, you've had your shot.' And I think there's a lot of people right now who are saying, 'Skaggs just ain't as hot as he once was' . . . And maybe I ain't. So, I guess we'll have to make some adjustments. I guess we'll just have to put some more water in the soup."

Why not "more gas in the tank" or "more muscle in the swing"? Despite the unfortunate metaphor, he valiantly tried to thicken the stew, but the loss of momentum he sensed in his interview with Allen proved accurate. Epic paired him with another producer for the first time, which launched the hard-driving number-one hit "Lovin' Only Me" (1989), but he was off the label five years later. Skaggs followed Rick Blackburn to Atlantic Records in 1995, where his sales tanked despite the continued high quality of his productions. The taste for fireside themes that defined so much of Skaggs's repertoire was overwhelmed by hillbilly rock and the unrelenting popularity of "hat acts" Garth Brooks and Clint Black who bowed to the honky-tonk tradition and, at least in Brooks's case, Top 40 pop. Mountain influence, which Skaggs had spear-headed in modern country music, vanished back into the Appalachian mist where it hovered until *O Brother, Where Art Thou?* and the Americana movement, both standing on a foundation reinforced by Skaggs, pulled it back into view.*

He says today:

> I was just trying to balance so many things, trying to be a bet-ter dad, a better band leader, a better musician, better song producer, trying to find good songs. You get finished with one record and you start listening to new songs or going through old songs that you passed on at the time. I never really was a songwriter who would sit down and write a whole record like

---

* Skaggs's wife, Sharon, with the Whites, appeared in the *O Brother, Where Are Thou?* film and on the soundtrack album.

Rodney Crowell does or some of the other great songwriters here in town would do. But I had guys who wanted to send me songs all the time because of my past record sales. Songwriters loved the style of music we were doing, and it gave them something fresh to try to write for. But there was a lot of pressure. I remember having three albums I was producing all at the same time: *White Limozeen, Comin' Home to Stay,* and the Whites' gospel record *Doin' It By the Book.* I wasn't trying to be [Nashville producer] Jimmy Bowen because he had six or eight records going at the time, but he had lots of people working for him and I didn't. I just cared too much about what my name came out on, the music that I put out. I was too consumed with my legacy. I just wanted to have good quality of music. . . . So much I tried to do.

A few Skaggs watchers blamed his slide on the Christian witness and conservative political declarations he shared with his live audiences, as natural to him as exchanging news of the day around the woodstove in Brushy Creek but offensive to many who came to see him play. In an interview, he was philosophical about it. "Being outspoken about my beliefs has put me at odds with my record labels at Epic and Atlantic," he told music writer Geoffrey Himes. "The only regret I have is I didn't have the wisdom to know when to speak out and went to shut up. The Scripture says faith builds the house and wisdom fills it. I've built a big house but it hasn't always been full. I realize when people pay $25 to hear me sing and play music, they haven't come out to hear a sermon."

Skaggs's proselytizing of the 1980s and 1990s foreshadowed dubious statements that roughly paralleled the fall of Donald Trump's presidency years later. The house evidently still half full, his public denial of Trump's election defeat in 2020 and endorsement of troubling conspiracy theories disappointed and even outraged supporters of ethical discourse in America who also happened to love and value Skaggs's creative genius and contributions to popular music.

AS SKAGGS'S MAINSTREAM country music career faltered, he often heard the call of his old life in bluegrass. When he ran into old friends like Del McCoury and Ralph Stanley, he remembered the simplicity of walking from the van with mandolin or fiddle in hand to perform his songs in contrast to the Tenth Army logistics of a massive country music tour.

"After I left Emmylou and started my country band, I met Ray Charles," he says.

> When you'd meet Ray, he'd shake your hand and then he'd take your other hand and he'd rub up and down your arm. He'd rub all the way up and down your arm and he'd feel how big you were. That was his way of connection. And I remember him saying, "Oh, Ricky Skaggs. I love your music. I love what you're doing. I love that bluegrass." And I thought, "I'm not playing bluegrass." But he heard the roots of what I was doing even in country music. He was hearing the foundations of my life and the foundations of the music that I make. I never tried to correct him. I just said, "I love Bill Monroe."

In the corridors of the Opry House in suburban Nashville, which had replaced the Ryman Auditorium as home to the *Grand Ole Opry*, Skaggs might hear George Jones and Bill Monroe wailing a gospel duet or run into an old outlaw like Johnny Paycheck enthusing over the father of bluegrass music's high tenor. Chatting with Carl Perkins on a country music television show Skaggs hosted, the rockabilly legend allowed that he and the Memphis boys may have sniffed at the *Grand Ole Opry*, but they hushed up during Monroe's turn at the microphone. "It was because his music had the excitement, it had the fire in it," says Skaggs.

I felt like I was being drawn back to my roots, and my dad, every time I'd go home, he would say, "I wish, son, you'd just do you a good bluegrass record." And I said, "Dad, I can't just do a bluegrass record with the record label I'm on. It's in the contract that I have to record songs that can be singles for radio." And he said, "I'd get out of that outfit." He knew in his heart that I still had a lot of old traditional music to bless and get out to where the masses could hear it.

Occasional reunions with old bandmates also tethered Skaggs to the bluegrass tree. In 1991 he gathered with his contemporaries in J. D. Crowe and the New South for a highly anticipated series of shows where he enjoyed playing again with Jerry Douglas by his side and the instrumental sparring with Tony Rice.

It would stand to reason in the eyes of an outsider that Rice, such a powerful lead singer and guitarist with handsome features, would follow Skaggs into country music stardom. But through the 1980s and 1990s, back from California, he clung to the southeastern loop he'd known since the 1970s, showcasing next-generation players such as the young Alison Krauss, and indulged his experiments in jazz and folk. "It was fresh," says Jimmy Gaudreau, a member of the Tony Rice Unit in the 1980s. "It was 'Tony Rice is back and he's singing.' That was the battle cry going around the bluegrass circuit. 'And he's got a group that will absolutely send you over the top.' We toughed it out for a while, but once the word got around everybody wanted it. Tony was like singing with a vocal machine. He was just spot-on, always on pitch, never threw you any curves. It was always fastballs."

But Rice chose not to bend toward mainstream country music, leaving that spotlight for Skaggs to occupy. He preferred a more elusive lifestyle that allowed plenty of time at home in North Carolina to sleep in the day and wake toward night, regaining focus for the long drives to festivals in his Ford Mustang Cobra. "Tony wanted to live the life of a blues guy or a jazz dude," says Jerry Douglas. "He wanted to be particular. He wanted to be hard to deal with at points . . . be incapable of performing suddenly . . . just 'genius' stuff that just happened to be overwhelming."

Ironically, when Rice's singing voice began to fail him in the 1990s, the result of singing out of his natural range and other factors, he refused surgery that might have helped him and retreated from the main stage in phases. "When he had that guitar in his hand . . . that was his conduit," continues Douglas. "That was his real personality. Then he would go home and hide out until the next gig."

Rice passed on Christmas Day in 2020, having played his final show in 2013. But the flame he lit in music—drawing Skaggs into the New South, buttressing David Grisman's eclectic "Dawg music," pulling modern folk stylings and repertoire into mainstream bluegrass, and, finally, improving the abilities of anybody who had ever served in a band with him—remains his lasting legacy.

WHILE SKAGGS CONTEMPLATED the meaning of bluegrass music in his life, Marty Stuart rode the hillbilly-rock vehicle deep into the 1990s. He remained on the charts and launched a sort of antiestablishment franchise with Travis Tritt on MCA that rendered the Grammy-winning hit "The Whiskey Ain't Workin'" (1991). The duo's "No Hats" tour was a playful rejoinder to the gentleman-cowboy mantle of the day worn by George Strait, Clint Black, and Alan Jackson. But Stuart sensed the pull of his birthright handed down by the Lethal Jacksons, Enoch Sullivans, and Lester Flatts in his past. The hip-wiggling videos and orchestrated bravado of his act with Tritt created mainstream recognition and thus would be difficult to abandon, but he knew his recent approach to music making lacked the nuance of the bluegrass tradition in which he'd grown up, where an inspired mandolin solo or vocal harmony rated with a sweet glissando or a keen melodic phrase in jazz performance. In search of artistic credibility, he snatched up opportunities his celebrity and musicianship afforded him, highlighting his versatility and instrumental prowess on projects such as "the tribute album," its own line of country music merchandise in which legendary artists and even social causes were celebrated.

A reawakening of the spirit of the Nitty Gritty Dirt Band's seminal *Will the Circle Be Unbroken,* such recordings featured duets between honored legends and their progeny or, in the legend's absence, new interpretations of his or her songs.* Initially, Stuart was a supporting act among the cast of supplicants, checking in with background vocals, for example, when the Dirt Band recorded its second edition of *Will the Circle Be Unbroken* in 1989, while Skaggs and Jerry Douglas shared billing with Emmylou Harris and Rosanne Cash. But following the turn of the new decade, Stuart won a featured role on prominent collections such as *Red Hot + Country* (1994), an AIDS fund-raiser, and *Not Fade Away: Remembering Buddy Holly* (1997). *Rhythm Country and Blues* (1994), highlighting the often-ignored cross-pollination of Black and white musical styles, matched Stuart with the Staple Singers. "That's the good side," he says today of their pairing. "The bad side was they assigned us 'The Weight,' which was a suicide mission. That's like recording 'I Walk the Line' or something.** But the collaboration turned into a lifelong friendship." Soon, he shared equal credit with Skaggs and other country stars on the Grammy-nominated *Clinch Mountain Country* (1998) for Ralph Stanley, dueting with the old master on "She's More to Be Pitied," which the Stanley Brothers recorded on September 30, 1958—Stuart's date of birth.

In 1994 Skaggs and Stuart joined forces in the recording industry's tribute to country music great George Jones titled *The Bradley Barn Sessions* (1994), produced by Brian Ahern, on which the

---

* High-water marks during the heyday of this particular album genre include *Mama's Hungry Eyes* (1994), *Livin', Lovin', Losin': Songs of the Louvin Brothers* (2003), and *Beautiful Dreamer: The Songs of Stephen Foster* (2004).

** The Staple Singers first recorded "The Weight" for their *Soul Folk in Action* album of 1968.

guests—including guitarist Keith Richards of the Rolling Stones—
sang duets with the legendary "Possum." Skaggs marveled at Richards's early-morning boozing when the session got under way
outside Nashville, but Stuart, when he bounced in, looked past
Richards to the mystery of his and Skaggs's relationship. It had
always been on the cool side despite their shared history.

Outside the studio, a light snowfall churned into a blizzard,
and musicians were slow in arriving.

> We had nothing to do but sit around the studio and look at
> each other. And I thought, "This is what I want to do with my
> time," and I said, "Skaggs, you got a minute?" And we went
> inside the drum booth, and the gist of it is, I said, "I don't
> think we were ever that close, but I absolutely love you and
> I respect you so much and I think you're great and you just
> need to know that." And somehow we came out of that drum
> booth, and we were pals after the end of the conversation
> and we've been like brothers ever since.

They shared a heritage, two boys who became men in the bluegrass days, and, in later years, they found a common connection in
country music queen Connie Smith, a longtime friend in faith to
Ricky and Sharon whom Marty married in 1997. But their prized
bond was Bill Monroe, who had blessed both with his attention
early in their childhoods, handing a pick to Stuart in Alabama and
lending his mandolin to Skaggs in Kentucky. On their individual
paths, each grew up in Monroe's shadow, looking up in reverence
in the heat of community jams on bluegrass festival stages, sharing
bus rides, and—in the early days of their solo fame—appearing
with him on country music shows produced by the Nashville Network (TNN).

Monroe's fading health in the year prior to his death in 1996
had drawn bluegrass heirs who wished to savor his dimming
flame. Stuart hosted him on various scholarly stages around town
spotlighting his contribution to American music, and he drove to

his farm in Goodlettsville to photograph the bluegrass father—though he was feeling peaked that day—against the backdrop of his splintered chicken coop and barn, portraying the nobility he had brought to rural America through his music. When Monroe entered the hospital, Stuart visited him there, too, but Skaggs, who in recent years had redirected his lineage from Ralph Stanley to Monroe, was determined to hold his hand as long as he possibly could.

Skaggs says:

I think if Ralph lived here in Nashville, I would have spent a lot more time with him. But he was living in Virginia. And I think just seeing Mr. Monroe at the *Opry* all the time, particularly after they made me a member, and just the fact that there wouldn't have been a Stanley Brothers or Flatt and Scruggs, probably, if Bill hadn't made a perfect place for them to land and draw inspiration from, drew me to him. He created the sound, the mechanism, and the tools that those people needed in order to be the stars that they became. I think because of the years I was a student, fan, lover of his music, I was seeing such an openness in him to a relationship with someone who wasn't in his band and was kind of getting a name in country music and having a desire to record his music. . . . And he was realizing, whether he remembered it or not, that I got up onstage when I was six years old and played his mandolin because I know I played his mandolin that night when I didn't have one. I had left mine at home. . . . I think I saw an opportunity to get to know him better. Marty had certainly had a great relationship with Lester all those years and then with Johnny Cash. I didn't want to take Bill on as a project, but he was starting to come to church with us because he loved [my in-laws] Buck and Pat and loved the girls, and they had seen him and been around him since the '70s. There was a real openness there and an open door, and

I went through it and just had a great relationship with him that wasn't strained. I didn't feel like I had to do anything. I'd call him up and see if he wanted to go to lunch. And he'd say, "That'd be fine. I'll be standing at the gate down there."

But the day came when he could no longer reach the gate. On the Ides of March in 1996, he left the stage of the *Grand Ole Opry* more exhausted than usual, and a day later he entered the hospital, where doctors determined he had suffered multiple strokes. He never returned home nor to the *Opry* stage, and over the next six months old friends and enemies filed through the room to say good-bye. Stuart brought Monroe's Stetson hat to him and encouraged him to play "Wheel Hoss" on his mandolin while Skaggs, a frequent visitor, brought peace of mind.

I really think in a lot of ways those last few weeks that I got to spend with Mr. Monroe was really times of assurance for him that his music would never die, his story would never die, that I would tell his story. I would tell people about him, the person who started this music. But I also let him know, too: "Bill, this music is never going to die. Whenever God calls you home, your body's going to go, but the spirit that you put into this music and the creation of bluegrass is going to long outlive any of us. There'll be people playing this music a hundred years from now. So don't try to hold on to something that you can't hold on to. Just be assured. I promise you that I will do my part. Marty loves it. Vince Gill loves it. Alison Krauss loves it. We all have bigger names, we've got notoriety, we've got credibility." . . . I think he breathed a sigh of relief because it wasn't long after that he passed on.

Monroe passed on September 9, 1996, and the lanterns on the southeastern circuit dimmed. In Nashville they gathered two days later in the morning at the Ryman Auditorium where Skaggs hosted country music's farewell with luminaries such as Vince Gill, Patty Loveless, Connie Smith, and Emmylou Harris. Stuart, prominent among them, quietly contemplated the promises he knew Monroe had made to band members and *Opry* comrades to sing by their graveside when they died and the promises they'd made to return the favor. With the beauty of such loyalty in mind, he noted from backstage the air growing heavy out in the gallery and turned to Skaggs and Emmylou Harris and proposed they perform "Raw Hide," Monroe's signature barn burner that Stuart himself had often brandished as a youngster with Lester Flatt. Skaggs hesitated, but Harris egged him on. "So we went out there and played 'Raw Hide,'" says Stuart, "and it tore the place apart."

In the rhythmic drive, Skaggs sensed the gloom dissipate along with his own reluctance. "And I thought, 'Man, what a perfect tune to do. What better way to honor him than by doing one of his instrumentals,'" he recalls.

> Music is such a beautiful language, such a beautiful way of expression. It's the language of heaven, but not only the language of heaven. It certainly is a way that people can feel God's spirit in ways where you don't even have to say a word. You just play these songs and they have something in them that makes you happy. That makes you joyous, cheerful. I heard Mr. Monroe talk about WJKS in Hammond, Indiana, where he played as a young man. He said the call letters stood for "Where Joy Kills Sorrow." And I thought, "Man, that is right. Joy will kill sorrow."

While the mourners settled down again, Stuart thought about Monroe's old musician friends who hadn't survived to repay the debt of a song to him, the very point of the bluegrass chestnut "Who Will Sing for Me?" "And I remember just pointing down at the casket and saying, 'We did it for you, sir.' I thought that's what he wanted, and I remember when we walked offstage, Ricky [mentioned] it was eleven minutes after 11:00 on the clock back-stage. And Ricky called me a little later and quoted the book of Isaiah, 11:11 . . . and it speaks of a 'remnant.' And Ricky said, 'We are the remnant of that old man.'"

OVER THE MONTHS that followed, Skaggs pondered the spirit of Monroe he felt inside. His slipping record sales—he hadn't notched a top-ten record in seven years and had resorted to a cover of Harry Chapin's "Cats in the Cradle" for chart action—and the cumbersome logistics of big country music tours seemed to be a message. Then Hobert Skaggs died three months after Monroe, and his deceased father's admonitions about record-ing a bluegrass album now overwhelmed his thoughts.

"I really felt that call back to my roots. And people were say-ing—crazy, stupid people—'Oh, you're coming back into this music because you think you can take Bill Monroe's place now.' And, man, it was so unkind because that was the last thing in the world that I ever wanted to try to do. . . . There was only one Bill Monroe. He was the greatest of singers of this kind of music. I love Del McCoury and others who sing like that, but Mon was just a cut above everybody."

Skaggs's fusion of country music and bluegrass in the early 1980s had showcased the string-based style for the masses just as he had intended, and bluegrass, at least partially as a result, con-tinued to grow through the 1980s and 1990s, launching new tal-ents such as Rhonda Vincent and Nickel Creek—then Rounder and Sugar Hill artists, respectively. Now, in 1996, though still signed to Atlantic but with little prospects of reclaiming his sta-tus on the country charts, he dug back down to his roots. In point of fact, he and his band had never stopped picking in the traditional style on the bus and in hotel rooms, but when he brought a straight-ahead bluegrass show to the eclectic Merlefest in North Carolina, which was followed by two or three similar performances, he felt the wind shifting. He told bluegrass chronicler Jon Weisberger,

> After those first couple of bluegrass dates, we did a tour of New Zealand, where we pretty much opened for ourselves as a bluegrass band. Afterwards, I would go to a preset place on the stage and do some solo country or play some fiddle while the stage was reset, and then we'd do a country show. After that, in some cities, we'd open as a country band, then talk about the roots of country, and finish up playing bluegrass. We were getting some confidence, we were having fun, and people were telling me that there was an expression of joy on my face that I hadn't had on shows in a long time.

He negotiated permission from Atlantic to partner with Rounder on a revival album titled *Bluegrass Rules!* (1997). The set was both a tribute to his roots in bluegrass and a statement of his own towering presence, for few could dispute that much new bluegrass of the era, performed by a generation raised on Ricky Skaggs and the bands he played in, bore his imprint. Naturally, the new release traveled through the Stanley catalog and highlighted Earl Scruggs and Monroe, including the father's "Raw Hide."

"With *Bluegrass Rules*," commented the *Chicago Tribune*, "not even the cynics who thought Skaggs had sold his soul to Nashville can question his talents in this most demanding arena of popular music, for this is simply a stunning bluegrass recording of class material. . . . Skaggs is in peak form on mandolin and tenor vocals, and his septet, which includes fiddle legend Bobby Hicks, fuses razor sharp precision with feverish intensity, with their version of the instrumental 'Get Up John' even approaching Monroe's apocalyptic 1950s rendition."

The album captured a Grammy and eclipsed his concurrent country release for Atlantic, selling more than two hundred thousand copies in its first year, estimates Skaggs, and set him once and for all back down in bluegrass music, although his concerts then and in the future continued to make room for his considerable hits of the 1980s and experiments in western swing, rock, gospel, and world music. He had expressed his sense of duty in the early 1980s after leaving Emmylou Harris to bring bluegrass music back into the country mainstream, and now the task was similar: to be a tradition-bearer, returning the very soul of the bluegrass tradition, elusive now in Bill Monroe's absence, to the country music tent.

"If it hadn't have been lucrative for us to do something like that, it might have been harder to do," he says today.

> But it was an easier thing to do, and all the guys in the band . . . all of our hearts were just overflowing with joy to play these songs every night, to work up a bluegrass set and see people respond to it at festivals or performing arts centers or places like that. So we were getting to bring traditional mountain music and bluegrass to the New York audience in some of the jazz clubs and the Beacon Theater and Lincoln Center—and just lighting it up. I feel like the Lord was opening doors for that. Plus, we were able to share the gospel a bit. In my country days, it was always much harder to do with those audiences. Not that it's easy now, but it's certainly easier to do it now. That was the thing I liked about it, too, that there was almost a ministry birthed in it as well—not just to promote the music—but to promote the God of the music, the one who gave us the music. I can't say there was a moment I woke up in bed and just raised up and said, "This is the time." It was just one of those things that one day we had a tour together, and we haven't stopped and haven't looked back. It's just been the way we do things now musically.

After Skaggs's transition back to the heart of bluegrass, Hobert returned, as if to bless his son's new direction. Skaggs says:

> He would come to me in dreams, and one time he said, "Son, I really love it up here in heaven. They're treating me

so nice." It was just him talking, and then one time he came to me and said, "I've been playing Bible trivia. I'm learning so much. I know more than you do." And then he came to me again, and I cried when I saw him. I just missed him so much, and he reached down and got me by the side of the face and pulled me up and kissed me on the mouth, and I don't know if my dad ever kissed me on the mouth. It was like he had a two- or three-day-old beard, I felt that prickly feeling on his face. It was just so real, like he was here.

With his father's ethereal endorsement and the adventurism of the New South–Boone Creek era as guiding lights in the decades after the new-traditionalism period, Skaggs has recorded with electric guitars, keyboards, bodhrans, harps, uilleann pipes, the bouzouki, and other instruments generally unknown in the bluegrass realm. He's also partnered with the pianist and late-century hit maker Bruce Hornsby on two albums that highlight Skaggs's eclecticism as clearly as any project he's ever undertaken. But like a faithful lover he comes home at night to bluegrass, abiding by his vow—rooted in the sandy soil back on Brushy Creek—to propagate the spirit and tones of the forefathers on award-winning albums such as *Ricky Skaggs and Friends Sing the Songs of Bill Monroe* (2002) and *Honoring the Fathers of Bluegrass* (2008). "He got out there and made it known he was no longer a country music guy, but a bluegrass guy," says Jerry Douglas, still a regular guest on his friend's recordings. "He pledged his allegiance, and he's sticking to it. He's going to coast out on that one, I'm sure, and he should. It was always the best thing he did."

12

Which Side Are You On?

THE "BOY WONDER" on guitar and mandolin in Philadelphia, Mississippi, often stretched to find stages beyond John and Hilda Stuart's living room or his friends' birthday parties, pestering booking agents for the Neshoba County Fair, and the Colonial House Motel where local bands appeared. What was immediately accessible often seemed less than ideal. Why settle for bluegrass man Carl Sauceman or the Lewis Family on television when John or Hilda could drive him to their live shows? He resolved to have his picture made with Connie Smith at the Choctaw Indian Fair in 1970 rather than merely watch her croon her 1964 smash hit, "Once a Day," from the splintered benches in the back. And long after he left home, in the wake of Flatt's death, he could have continued serving the pure country music he knew by sticking with Doc Watson, the patron saint of clear waters. But he courted Johnny Cash instead, who offered an apple in the shape of the world. "I have never seen anybody that determined to be a star," says Little Roy Lewis.

When moved by the death of Bill Monroe to tally up his own payments to the soul of country music from the previous ten years, Stuart counted not one, complaining—as he has many times since—that he couldn't bear to listen to anything he had recorded during that time span. It was an undeservedly harsh assessment of his hillbilly-rock era, and, besides, he could have offered his role in Rick Rubin's recalibration of Johnny Cash's career as payment to tradition or his roots-minded *Busy Bee Cafe* album on Sugar Hill. But the forty-one-year-old Mississippian yearned to make a grand statement from the producer's chair. So he shut down the boot-scooting phase of his career, which was cooling off like new traditionalism anyway, and reached to produce *The Pilgrim* album (1999), an earnest, ambitious mapping of country music's genetic code that in its own way forecasted the *O Brother, Where Art Thou?* film and its million-selling soundtrack. It also recalled the swaggering mini-dramas he'd written and recorded earlier for MCA: "Me and Hank and Jumpin' Jack Flash" (1992) and "The Mississippi Mudcat and Sister Sheryl Crow" (1996).

Like Stuart's first album effort for Ridge Runner in 1978, and virtually every solo session that followed, he herded his community to *The Pilgrim*: George Jones, Emmylou Harris, Pam Tillis, and, from his Flatt era, Uncle Josh Graves, Earl Scruggs, and Ralph Stanley. Fiddler Stuart Duncan—another young pledge in bluegrass during the 1970s—joined in, too, linking Stuart's album-length reset to Skaggs's similarly inspired *Bluegrass Rules!* of 1997, on which Duncan contributed to three tracks. Assembled like the ruddy cast on the cover of *Sgt. Pepper's Lonely Hearts Club Band*, Stuart's troupe performed in three acts the story of a lonesome wanderer, vaguely reminiscent of Bill Monroe, who was the abandoned, cross-eyed child with nowhere to go but the next town. "Gone is the party-hearty country-rock of Stuart's previous records," wrote Bill Friskics-Warren in a *Washington Post* review. "In its place is a tapestry that stretches across a century's worth of Americana, from old-time music and bluegrass to blues and honky-tonk."

What's more, the heart of the album's repertoire emerged from Stuart's own pen. Cowriting over the years with Paul Kennerley and absorbing the structure and devices of Johnny Cash and then Harlan Howard, with whom he had collaborated on previous albums, had helped him produce taut, poignant verse in cuts such as "Reasons," "Goin' Nowhere Fast," and "The Observations of a Crow." Plenty of other song nuggets protruded from the sterling production, which was carried by Stuart's most seasoned vocals to date.

Nashville-based critic and author Craig Havighurst suggested *The Pilgrim* was country music's *Quadrophenia*, and others declared Stuart keeper of tradition's flame. But the appetite for experimentation in Nashville that served up so many great albums in the 1970s as well as Steve Earle's, Nanci Griffith's and Lyle Lovett's albums in the 1980s had all but disappeared. The mass market in country music's corner of the world that had lifted Stuart and Skaggs to the charts in the 1980s and 1990s wasn't interested in attending to big statements.

In fairness, Stuart had arguably reached too far this time, loading *The Pilgrim* with concept-album devices, such as a towering benediction by Johnny Cash, still living in 1999. Ironically, aspects of the album achieved an artistic standard so high that his guiding concept was obscured in its shadow. A mass market now used to seeing country music served to them in gingham halter tops and cutoff shorts—one by-product of the party-boat ethos of hillbilly rock—was frankly in no mood to hear from Stuart about what was or wasn't country music. MCA, his label for ten years, dropped the experimentalist as *The Pilgrim* tanked, and he released nothing under his name for five years.

Bruised but unbowed, and still in a thorny relationship with alcohol and prescription drugs, he discarded his jumpin'-jack-flash persona and retreated this time not into the piney woods of Mississippi but to his new wife, Connie Smith, thirty years down the road from their Choctaw Indian Fair meeting. Later, his former father-in-law, who identified with misbegotten concept albums, advised him to embrace his artistic impulses despite the hollow ring of the cash register. "And he was right," says Stuart today.

The Pilgrim was the line in the dirt for that, and, in my mind, restored all the credibility I had squandered along the way.

I took time off and scored a movie or two, and just wrote
songs and produced—anything except get on a bus and go
on tour.* But one day I woke up and said, "I want to do this
again." And I started looking around and I said, "It's time
to go back to work." And I listened to what was going on in
country music. That was when I started my quest into the
unknown. And I had a great time with it, but it was work. I
mean work.

STUART SEARCHED FOR embers of country music brilliance still
in Nashville, some of it rooted in the southeastern circuit. Skaggs's
return to bluegrass had turned heads, and Jerry Douglas, his
expressive performances the very definition of the Dobro sound,
had driven influential projects such as the Grammy-winning *Great
Dobro Sessions* of 1994, the aforementioned *O Brother, Where Art
Thou?* soundtrack, and Alison Krauss's popular recordings as a
member of her Union Station band.

Remnants of the "Great Credibility Scare in Nashville" of the
late 1980s, a phrase coined for the brief but spectacular singer-
songwriter emphasis of the era, came into Stuart's focus, too, as
Rosanne Cash, Rodney Crowell, Nanci Griffith, Jim Lauderdale,
and others approached the new millennium with sterling albums,
and Steve Earle, rugged darling of the Credibility Scare, sidled
up to bluegrass on *The Mountain* album, recorded with the Del
McCoury Band in 1999.

Somewhere in the midst of the creativity thriving outside the
world of major labels and hot country radio airplay, Stuart saw a
place for himself. While producing an album for Billy Bob Thornton and compiling a retrospective of his photography for a small
Nashville press, he tapped into cash saved up from collaborations
with Travis Tritt and built a new band around Harry Stinson,

All the Pretty Horses (2000) and *Daddy and Them* (2001), both directed by
Billy Bob Thornton.

drummer and high harmony singer for Earle's Dukes in the 1980s and, more recently, a principal in the risk-taking Dead Reckoning Records. Stinson was also a songwriter—"Let It Be You" recorded by Skaggs in 1989 among his credits—and busy session artist whose work ran from Emmylou Harris to Vince Gill and back to *Hillbilly Rock*, Stuart's first album for MCA.

Stuart then hired the rangy guitarist Kenny Vaughan, whom he had seen playing in Lucinda Williams's band on the *Austin City Limits* television show. Growing up in Denver, Vaughan studied jazz guitar and, brandishing a fake ID, traveled through bands whose interests ranged from Chicago blues to West Coast honky-tonk before making his way to Nashville in the 1980s. "They were all putting out these records with real good lyrics," recalls Vaughan. "They were interesting and well done and they weren't cheesy. They were like records you'd actually want to buy and play at home, which hadn't happened in a while. But it turned out to be the tail end of it. Dwight Yoakam was the last guy who had any credibility at all. It was over when Garth Brooks came in and wiped everything out."

When Stuart finally tracked down the versatile guitarist, they spent hours expressing mutual affection for Merle Haggard and Bob Dylan records and the classic steel-guitar playing of Jimmy Day, Ralph Mooney, and other wizards who worked their magic in the 1950s and 1960s. It was all the courtship they required. Stuart hired Vaughan, who then brought in bassist Brian Glenn, a Ricky Skaggs disciple. The youngest in the band that Stuart dubbed "the Fabulous Superlatives," Glenn also preferred Garth Brooks's country to the Bakersfield Sound, but his strong vocals forgave all that.

The band's diverse musical knowledge and sharp delivery, on display in Nashville gigs here and there, got Stuart a single album deal with Columbia. Simply titled *Country Music*, it aimed for the country charts with its smattering of strutting, radio-friendly cuts reminiscent of the MCA releases. But Stuart also meant to deliver the full breadth of the genre for which he'd named his album.

A guest appearance by Merle Haggard on "Farmer's Blues"—a Stuart cowrite—and visits from Earl Scruggs and Uncle Josh Graves combined with a cover of Johnny Cash's "Walls of a Prison," channeled the still-beating heart of *The Pilgrim.*

Communicating to Music Row that he was feeling okay despite the rejection of his concept album, he opened the set with "A Satisfied Mind," the big hit for Porter Wagoner in 1955. But his critique of his adopted hometown became one of the collection's shining efforts, "Sundown in Nashville," still a favorite of Kenny Vaughan's:

> It's a monster, a really good band and vocal performance and a good mix and a good arrangement. And [studio musician] Robby Turner played his ass off on the steel, and Marty was a big part of that. He sat down face-to-face with Robby and battled it out for about three hours to get that steel part down, one line at a time. Marty's really a steel-guitar nut. Usually, when he works with a steel player, he sits right in front of them, face-to-face with his acoustic guitar, and he orchestrates every move of the steel guitar. He's like a frustrated steel player, so basically when he hires a steel player, he's going to play what Marty would play if he could play.

Vaughan's exuberance has not translated to Stuart's current assessment of the album, despite its rosy sales. "It's a pretty good record, but it's a double-minded record," cautions Stuart.

> I listened back to it at the time and said, "It's either going to be [defined by] 'Farmer's Blues' and 'Walls of a Prison' and 'Satisfied Mind' or the radio-friendly things like 'If There Ain't There Oughta Be,'" which was one of those kind of songs. They would take me to radio stations, and the phones would blow up. People would want to talk. "Glad to see you're back," the program directors said. "Never has anything happened around here like this." And I'd walk out and not get

any [plays] on the station. The visits meant nothing. So at the end of that promotional exercise, I went back to the old Hazel Dickens song and asked myself, "'Which Side Are You On?' You learned your lesson with *The Pilgrim*. You've tried it again here. It seems like you're at a fork in the road. You've got to be wise about this." And that's when the Superlatives said that "Walls of a Prison" and "Farmer's Blues" and "Satisfied Mind" was the way to go. "Let's take our case to the people. Go into the backwoods and bring the stories of the American people back with us. Don't pay any attention to charts." *The Pilgrim* was a line in the dirt. This was a line in the concrete. It was like, "All right. This is how we will live from this day forward."

The album, which had included in its circle Haggard and the spirit of Johnny Cash, was sitting on the country music album charts when Cash passed in September 2003. So it was only fitting when, a decade later, notes of both men found their way into Stuart's sleep while he traveled to the wedding ceremony of one of Haggard's daughters. Recounts Stuart of his dream:

The sun was shining and up walks J. R., and he was tanned and his hair was black and he looked like he did when he was really glowing around 1971, 1972. And I said, "J. R., you look so good." And he said, "I know I do. I haven't had a cigarette since I've been here, and I haven't wanted one." I said, "That's wonderful. You look so restful and peaceful." And he said, "Do you know what else I can do, if I want to?" And I went, "What?" "I can sing just like Merle Haggard." And he did. And we just stood there by a pond and laughed and laughed. And later that day when I saw Merle, I said, "Come here. I want to tell you about a dream I had last night." And I told him, and Merle said, "Was it in color?" I went, "Yes, it was." And he said, "Good. A dream like that deserves to be in color."

WHILE STUART PURSUED his "this day forward" in the early aughts, somebody near Meridian, Mississippi, shot a bullet into the gravestone of murdered civil rights activist James Chaney, defacing an embossed mingling of Black and white hands that appeared to cradle a photograph of the deceased—more evidence of hatred's grip on the state's pine belt. But a movement to address racial injustices of the past had gained traction in the region, inspired unexpectedly by the Hollywood feature film *Mississippi Burning* (1988) starring Gene Hackman, which was based on Philadelphia's conspiracy of silence in the face of the murders of Chaney, Schwerner, and Goodman. Caught up in a mood of hard reflection, Mississippi's secretary of state, Dick Molpus, publicly apologized to the families of the slain civil rights workers in 1989, an unthinkable gesture in the minds of anybody old enough to remember the state's ironclad opposition to courtroom justice for Black people—this while journalist Jerry Mitchell of the *Clarion-Ledger* in the state capital of Jackson had begun investigating unsolved civil rights–era murders, which would lead to convictions of several Klansmen in other parts of the state.

Not surprisingly, probing questions made their way to Philadelphia, giving rise to the Philadelphia Coalition, a diverse group of town citizens that included NAACP president Leroy Clemons; local historian Florence Mars, who had exposed the town's deeply rooted racism in her book *Witness in Philadelphia*; and Jim Prince III, the newly installed editor and publisher of the *Neshoba Democrat*, the same local paper that in the 1960s had called Chaney, Goodman, and Schwerner's disappearance a self-promoting hoax.

Stymied by internal debate as to how the city might pursue justice and reconciliation, the group nonetheless planned and staged memorial services on the fortieth anniversary of the killings, encouraging side discussions in the cafés and barbershops of the city. Then, in 2004, the coalition demanded that state and federal authorities reopen the investigation into the deaths of the activists and finally win a murder conviction, if not for the families then for the tattered honor of the state of Mississippi. In its formal plea for justice, the committee spelled out Philadelphia's complicity. "We state candidly and with deep regret that some of our own citizens, including local and state law enforcement officers, were involved in the planning and execution of these murders."

Indeed, Philadelphians in certain circles had whispered for years about fellow townspeople who had avoided prosecution, and they had heard others brag about their deeds in reference to both the doomed trio and the deaths of other local Black people. One of them was Edgar Ray Killen, a so-called kleagle, or recruiter, in the KKK, who operated a sawmill on the outskirts of town and had been acquitted of conspiracy after friendly witnesses refused to place him in a restaurant where he had laid out plans for the murders. During his trial in 1967, Killen drew the rebuke of the judge after he passed a note to his attorney requesting that he ask a prosecution witness if Schwerner had made Black men agree to rape one white woman per week during Freedom Summer. But at that time Killen seemed to be invulnerable. The jurors could not or would not reach a decision on his guilt or innocence, although they did convict seven others on conspiracy to commit murder.

THE PHILADELPHIA COALITION'S call to reopen investigations had at least caught the attention of Mississippi law enforcement at the state level. Drawing on earlier investigative interviews primarily with former Deputy Sheriff Cecil Price—a colleague of John Stuart's under Sheriff Hop Barnett who had described Killen's role in planning the killings for a previous investigation—state attorney general Jim Hood believed a modern jury free of the threat of Klan rule would vote to convict. The only problem was Price had died in 2001 after falling from a cherry picker in Philadelphia, not long after he had given Marty the Stetson hat he'd worn in countless photographs taken by photojournalists covering the FBI investigation in the 1960s. A tragic remnant of Philadelphia history, the hat sits today in a warehouse among

Stuart's collection of historical artifacts. Hood would have to rely on Price's transcribed testimony as well as recorded interrogations of other witnesses, now deceased, who had cooperated with the FBI.

On January 6, 2005, a grand jury indicted Killen on three counts of murder as if it were 1964 all over again. The decision immediately attracted reporters from around the globe, this time with live satellite trucks that had become ubiquitous props in other major legal dramas across the nation. It would be an international news story with a now familiar script: Mississippi community stained by race-based hatred during the civil rights movement seeks redemption in the conviction of a prime suspect who had hidden in plain sight for more than forty years.

In Nashville, Hilda and John Stuart peered at their television, hearing names that were as familiar to them as the rumble of the train that used to pass behind their home on Kosciusko Road. Their son caught bits of news during concert tours.

> The thing I remember most about it was sitting on our bus and listening to a correspondent on CNN who was probably twenty-three years old telling about everything that happened in my hometown in the '60s, and I went, "You really don't have a clue. You're just a talking head with some words in your mouth." I thought it was a pretty grand show. It felt like a chapter in a big, old mess. I think the lack of justice had to be addressed, but I feel like the spirit in which it was being done . . . there might have been a politician or two trying to make a name for themselves. I really just checked out, and I don't know enough about it to talk about it very well, but it just felt like another chapter of bad news

Stuart represented a camp in Philadelphia culture that, while condemning racism, believed after forty years the city deserved freedom from reminders of its sins in order to start anew. In this narrative, Philadelphia—which would soon elect an African

American mayor and see a local woman become chief of the Mississippi Band of Choctaws—became another victim.

The singer's impression of a circus growing around the trial was not far off the mark. In addition to the expanding press corps, Killen himself became more spectacle than defendant. While awaiting the opening of his April 2005 trial, his attorneys filed no fewer than four motions to either delay the start of the trial or have indictments canceled. But only one stuck. When a tree fell on Killen at home, breaking bones in both of his thighs, the judge delayed the trial until June 13. Then, arriving at the courthouse on June 16, the first day of scheduled witness testimony against him, his blood pressure rose above 210, and he informed his nurses of a "smothering sensation," presumably in his chest. That was enough to send him to the hospital, and the judge recessed the trial until the next day. Back in the courtroom, he stared down members of the press, and by closing arguments, June 20, the so-called country preacher was mouthing expletives in the direction of the attorney general as the official told the men and women in the jury box Killen was as evil as "venom."

The next day, the jury found Edgar Ray Killen guilty of manslaughter in the deaths of Chaney, Goodman, and Schwerner, convinced he had influenced those who kidnapped and murdered the victims. It was the first time anybody had been convicted of charges more serious than conspiracy in the killing of the young men.

Voices from around the world applauded justice in Philadelphia, some suggesting the verdict atoned for the death of hundreds of other Black residents in the state. But nobody sounded more hopeful about the conviction's resonance than the editors of the *Neshoba Democrat.* "The world has seen the better side of our community, our true moral character, for the first time in 40 years. We must not fall into division that seems to come naturally and allow this opportunity to pass. . . . Significant challenges lie ahead in education, the eradication of poverty and illiteracy that will require the utmost in patience and forbearance in us all. It's a new day in Philadelphia and Neshoba County, Mississippi, because we have been freed."

MINDFUL OF JOHN Stuart's proximity to Lawrence Rainey, Hop Barnett, and Cecil Price in the Neshoba County Sheriff's Department during a tragic era, Marty has pursued racial reconciliation within the boundaries of his music. Ingrained with the Black gospel and blues of Philadelphia and his mother's teachings on Christian love, Stuart had not permitted hatred in Philadelphia to prevent his public relationships with Black people. Remember Earl Peaks playing bass on his first album and his collaboration with the Staple Singers on the *Rhythm Country and Blues* album of 1994, the path to friendship with Pops Staples, the family patriarch, and daughter Mavis Staples. Pops and Marty connected over their shared Mississippi roots, and, like the boy who would not let Roland White forget his name, Stuart remained in touch. "I tell you, hanging out with Pops Staples was like hanging out with Moses," says Stuart. "He became like extended family, and one of the greatest moments of my life, my take-to-heaven moment, was when the state of Mississippi honored Pops and me with an arts award [in 1999]. We were standing on the floor of the senate that morning, and Pops made everybody hold hands and he started crying a little bit and he said, 'I never dreamed as a little boy that I'd be standing here or see a man of color in this room,' and he made everybody in the room stand and sing 'Will the Circle Be Unbroken.'" Stuart chimed in on guitar as the gospel legend harked back to the original Carter Family, who had popularized the song in the 1920s and 1930s after borrowing a tune familiar in Black gospel music in their interpretation. "That was profound, and I said to myself, 'These are deep waters.' These kind of things are hooked up down in Mississippi that are beyond comprehension."

That moment with the gospel legend from Winona, Mississippi, opened a direct line to 2005—the year of the Killen trial—when Stuart and the Fabulous Superlatives released *Souls' Chapel,* a collection of southern gospel songs, a few based squarely on the Staple Singers sound. For the first time since his *Busy Bee Cafe* album, he ignored what he perceived as the recording industry's expectations of country music, channeling his influences—not the least of which was his Southern Baptist upbringing—into a startling blend of elements from southern sacred music, including white quartets who blanketed the South and the sanctified jubilates from the Black gospel tradition. "It was a fun record to make because we recorded it live," says Kenny Vaughan. "We didn't build a house on every song and have overdubs after overdubs and all that bullshit. It was just live performance, really vibrant. You can hear the interaction a little more than what you hear on our other records. It sounds lively and spontaneous because it was."

The album tapped Stuart's summer on the Pentecostal stages with the Sullivan Family, the Sabbath-morning television shows, featuring soul-stirring quartets and trios, and the ubiquitous Black spirituals on Philadelphia radio, revealing a raw influence that not even Elvis Presley—to name another Saturday night–Sunday morning star from Mississippi—had exhibited in performance. Diving into the soul of the music, and well beyond the conventions of country music, he played Pops Staples's electric guitar, a gift from his family, and hired organist Barry Beckett of the swampy Muscle Shoals Rhythm Section. The set gained traction with "Come into the House of the Lord," a churning quartet showcase led by Harry Stinson, and took flight when Mavis Staples appeared on the Pops Staples original "Move Along Train."

"Whether it's Native American people or Black people, music has been the thing that pulled all that together. And if I had to stand on one song it would be 'Uncloudy Day' by the Staple Singers," he explains.

Back in the summer of 1964, you could hear that song coming out of people's houses. You could hear it on the radio. It's a lot like "We Shall Overcome," but it was a different level. When I heard that coming out of Jimmie Richmond's house—Jimmie was the lady who took care of us, who was like our family—it was like ghosts singing in the cotton field, hearing it come through that screen door. But that's why it was important to me to befriend Pops Staples, and we hit it off immediately. That's why it was important to me to take Pops' guitar and record that song with Mavis because that song obliterates 1964 to me. It puts a divine canopy over it for some reason. You have to address it. But I think the way to address it more than anything is to open the doors and say, "We have broad shoulders. Everybody is welcome."

Stuart hesitates to submit *Souls' Chapel* as atonement for the sins of his hometown. But he and his band released a companion album in 2005 that raged against the nation's other original sin: the conquest and ultimate marginalization of Native people in the United States. His eyes locked on the Pine Ridge Reservation of South Dakota, the album titled *Badlands: Ballads of the Lakota* proved to be in substance and execution the most searing social commentary to come from country music since Johnny Cash's *At Folsom Prison* album of 1968.

Again, as on *Souls' Chapel*, Stuart turned in a performance with few obvious country music markings. Only the artist's own associations with country music—with Flatt, Cash, and hillbilly rock—made it country. And if the point of *Souls' Chapel* was to fulfill his relationship with Pops Staples, who had died in 2000, then *Badlands* allowed him to work in Johnny Cash's spirit two years after the Man in Black's death, recalling his *Bitter Tears: Ballads of the American Indian* of 1964.

Although Stuart had grown up in the shadow of the Choctaw Reservation in Neshoba County, where he observed Native American women submissively walking behind men on the country roads into town and danced with tribespeople at their annual fair, it was through Cash and Cash's friend and discographer John L. Smith, a historian of the Lakota people, that Stuart developed concern and understanding of the original Americans. On his very first show with Cash in Des Moines back in 1980, Stuart eyed a wondrously crafted bag inspired by Lakota designs Smith had made and given to Cash, and soon after he rode with both of them to the reservation. "On the bus we kept riding and riding and I asked him, 'Why are we here?'" Stuart recalls Cash's scolding tone in his reply:

> "Because it's the poorest county in the United States and these people need our love and our support and our help and we're here to encourage them." And I went, "Got it."
>
> I had a big red suitcase, and pretty much everything I owned that was worth anything was in that suitcase. I had just moved out of my apartment in Nashville, and it was filled. I kept it under the bus when we traveled, and that night at the end of the show we did "As Long as the Grass Shall Grow" [the Peter LaFarge ballad from *Bitter Tears*], which is one of the only times I remember J. R. doing it. And towards the end of the song this elder came from the back of the auditorium toward the stage and, John being John, could see something happening and he just let the music ride and didn't stay a word and stood there very reverently. And when the old man got down there, he just raised his fist and stood while John sang the last verse. And it tore my heart out. And the people stood up and started hollering and cheering, and after that moment, I was in.
>
> I walked out of the auditorium that evening. I remember there being a bunch of kids, and I said, "Follow me." And I just took that red suitcase from under the bus and dumped it onto the ground and walked off. That's how it was. I left there with nothing, and years later—this goes back to the very early days of the Superlatives when we were working anywhere we could work—we played this awful little casino in Valentine, Nebraska. There were security guards around me, and I was on my way to the bus and this big Native American man came and had a knife in his hand. And security was going to take

this guy down and I said, "Hold it." I recognized the knife. It was one of my bowie knives that I had in the red suitcase. I walked up to the guy and I shook his hand, and he said, "Do you remember this knife?" And I said, "I do." He said, "I got it that night when you dumped everything on the ground. I'm a doctor now, and I just want to thank you guys for coming up here back then. Thank Johnny Cash for me." I went, "You got it."

Stuart made friends among the Lakota, performed benefits, married Connie Smith on the reservation, and was adopted into the tribe. But the impulse to apply his creativity to the Native story that had unfolded in front of him over the years came only after Cash's death in 2003. It was a way to deal with the loss of his mentor, he says. "The framework and canvas of Pine Ridge was about the only place I could think of that was big enough to hold all my pain and deal with it, and I knew on the back side of the *Badlands* project I'd feel better."

He brought in John Carter Cash, still grieving himself over the loss of his parents, who offered production expertise and the use of the Cash cabin studio at an affordable rate, for by then Stuart was mostly self-financing his records. He also leaned heavily on John L. Smith, who shared stories Stuart could fashion into song lyrics and checked facts when the historical record eluded him. "Marty was tied to that guy," says Kenny Vaughan.

In search of inspiration and in the midst of finally wrestling down his chemical addictions, he sifted through albums by Buffy St. Marie and Peter LaFarge and reviewed Cash's *Bitter Tears* groove by groove. Then he traveled to the reservation with John L. Smith, contemplating the mingling of history and nature and the people drawing the lifeblood of both despite their considerable burdens. They peered over the tragic valley of the so-called last Indian battle, Wounded Knee, where women, men, and children were mowed down by US cavalry, and he walked with elders who traced legends and stories along the contours of the buttes and bluffs. "I would take trips out there just to play the songs inside the land to know if I got it right. And I'd find old-timers I could play them for, and if they shook their head I knew I'd got it. It was worked on. The record was worked on."

The path led back to the Cash Cabin studio outside Nashville, where Stuart characteristically created a parallel world for the final recording sessions of an album attempting to capture the spirit and history of a people. Lakota elders Marvin and Everette Helper and others came from South Dakota for the sessions, says Kenny Vaughan. "They were doing some of their ceremonies and had their drums. They're cool cats. Some of them brought their kids with them."

Everette Helper's chants over distant thunder heralds the Lakota story that Stuart tells on the album, giving way to the slicing guitar of the title track. What follows are heated indictments and grim recitations of injustices past and present surging toward "Three Chiefs," a nine-minute climax, in which Red Cloud, Sitting Bull, and Crazy Horse, each having passed from life, express to God the redeeming example of Native people. Stuart's cover of Cash's "Big Foot" propels the rising action, a prelude to a pair of Stuart-penned protest songs in succession: "Broken Promised Land" and "Casino," the former an indictment of Bill Clinton's late-term gestures toward the Lakota in the 1990s: "It's not an area that I do so well in," says Stuart of the protest canon.

> But you have to understand at the end of the day we're still white kids and they're still Indians, and there's a difference in how things work, and I understand that, and a lot of times things implode on the reservation before [cries of help] ever make it off the res. So it makes it impossible for anybody to help fix some things. But politicians, when it's time to be reelected president . . . , it's real great to go out there and get it in your heart and see nineteen people living in a trailer and get your picture made and make a bunch of promises and then go back to Washington and forget about it because it's a

hard place to get to, and you can't do much with it once you get to it. I get that. That's what I was speaking to: "Yet another great white father that makes some promises that didn't quite come to pass." Nothing new there.

Six years after *The Pilgrim*, he had produced the quintessential concept album: focused and meaningful, sonically consistent, carried by a vision that he was more than capable of articulating. "The cumulative effect is a stirring reminder of a strain of American history and culture that is too often set aside," wrote critic Geoffrey Himes in the *Washington Post*. Like Skaggs's return to bluegrass, *Badlands* bravely hailed the impulse to communicate in the spirit of truth, and once again endorsed bluegrass music's emphasis on virtuosity that had molded Stuart to begin with. And should the son of Mississippi ever directly consider the darkness of Philadelphia through his art, then *Badlands* will credibly stand in until such time might come.

EPILOGUE

THERE'S A STAGE out on the old southeastern circuit drooping in the dense overgrowth of what used to be the grounds of a bluegrass festival. Thick moss burdens the roof of the wooden structure, and floor planks that once supported the waltz-time shuffling of countless traveling musicians are splintered and soft with age. Soon the structure will collapse into the sticky soil, the last fragment of a time at this spot when bluegrass music shook the trees and freed the fans from their worldly cares.

Stuart and Skaggs transitioned from such venues after service in the Flatt and Stanley bands, respectively, and though they carried with them the seeds of traditional country music to disseminate in future decades and new settings, they were young and bold, insisting that various traditions—bluegrass, jazz, mountain, gospel, rock—deserved a place, if not prominence, in country music. In return, they have been inducted into the Country Music Hall of Fame in Nashville: Skaggs in 2018 and Stuart in 2021. And while their bronze plaques hang on dark, imposing walls, their gifts remain alive and on display in those they've influenced and the music they continue to perform around the world.

They live barely two miles apart outside Nashville and occasionally partner on the stage of the *Grand Ole Opry*, a familiar hearth in one way or another since their childhoods, when Skaggs bobbed up backstage at the Ryman Auditorium in his father's hopes of a

235

break for his son and when Stuart took his Nashville baby steps on the other side of the curtain a few years later. Together they have come to represent tradition on the face of commercial country music. The two musicians seem to delight in that role, but it belies their experimentalism, apparent in Stuart's recent country-rock collaborations with Chris Hillman and Roger McGuinn of the Byrds, and Skaggs's buoyant team-ups with Ray Charles and Bruce Hornsby and his trippy sacred album _Mosaic._ An even better example of their fearlessness appears in a clip from Skaggs's _Monday Night Sessions_ on cable television, originally broadcast in 1997, in which he and Stuart, electric guitars strapped on tight, joined forces with rockabilly great Brian Setzer in a burning-house performance of "Rock This Town" that briefly reorders country music consciousness.

But when the two men, together, return to the simple virtue of picking the strings of their acoustic instruments, there is nothing more engaging in Nashville.

"I'll never forget one night we were playing the _Opry_, and Ricky and Marty went out there unrehearsed," tells Kenny Vaughan of the Fabulous Superlatives. "They spontaneously did a duet with the mandolin and the guitar, and it was so good. It was an old gospel tune, and they went out there and sang it together, harmonized, played. And it was a moment. Everybody stopped and watched, backstage and in the audience. It's one of those excellent moments when the song is the centerpiece of the whole entire evening. It was just Ricky and Marty. It had nothing to do with anything but their gospel influences. They just went out there and did it, and it was like all the way back to their childhood. It was just so great. One of the best things I ever saw at the _Grand Ole Opry_, easily."

ACKNOWLEDGMENTS

I'M THINKING ABOUT Mary Chapin Carpenter's "The Way I Feel," the closing track on her *Age of Miracles* album (2010). She's driving down I-81 South, contemplating friends in Nashville. And I'm in sync with her mood, on the trail of another book about country music, the most recent one ten years and a pandemic ago. Merging onto a narrative thread running from eastern Kentucky to central Mississippi, I, like Carpenter, have friends and allies along the way for whom I'm grateful.

There are in Tennessee Ryan C. Bernard, education and outreach archivist, Archives of Appalachia, East Tennessee State University; Kathleen Campbell, Brenda Colladay, Michael Gray, Ben Hall, Adam Iddings, and Michael McCall of the Country Music Hall of Fame and Museum in Nashville; Tammy Carver of Skaggs Family Records; Richard Bennett; Steve Bryant; Larry Cordle; Rodney Crowell; Jerry Douglas; Carl Jackson; Lanny LeRoy; Haskel McCormick; Del McCoury; Ronnie McCoury; Maria-Elena Orbea; Tamara Saviano; Hilda Stuart; Jennifer Stuart; Jimmy Tittle; Kenny Vaughan; Roland White; and Michael Woods and Miriam Perkins. And others elsewhere: Tim Binkley, Special Collections and Archives, Berea College; Kate Campbell, Special Collections and Archives, University of Maryland Libraries; Bestor Cram; Caleb Farley and the staff of the Lawrence County Public Library in Louisa, Kentucky; Carly Smith and Matthew Hill at the Bluegrass

Music Hall of Fame and Museum in Owensboro, Kentucky; Mike Allard and the staff of the William F. Winter Archives, Mississippi Department of Archives and History in Jackson; Butch Hodgins and Lucy Baxstrom in Philadelphia, Mississippi; Wayne Stevens and Michelle Heintz of the Inter Library Loan Office, Le Moyne College; Eddie Adcock; Steve Andreassi at the IUP Lodge and Convocation Center in Hoboken, New Jersey; Terry Baucom; Harry and Ann Bickel; Carolyn Brown; Victor Camp; Rosanne Cash; J. D. Crowe; Joe Davoli; Brian Downes; Dayton Duncan; Chris Harris; Jess Kelleher who achieved elegance in transcribing; Joe Kelly and Melissa Short; Jim Kemp; Doyle Lawson; Little Roy Lewis; Laurie Matheson; Maureen and Ozzie Mocete; Alanna Nash; Barry Poss; Roy Roberts; Adam Stubbs; David Stubbs; Mark Stubbs; Philip Stubbs; Ron Thomason; and Johnny Warren.

And, oh, do the voices in my birthplace of Washington, DC, still speak out on music: Johnny Castle, T. Michael Coleman, Eddie Dean, Linda McCawley Dillon, Bill Emerson, Billy Emerson III, Jimmy Gaudreau, Richard Harrington, Joan Kornblith, Joe Lee, Akira Otsuka, John Sprague, David and Valerie Streissguth, and Karl and Phil Streissguth.

Record stores always provide the critical tools and a feeling of home, and I anticipated visits to each of them: Joe's Record Paradise in Silver Spring, Maryland; Rock & Roll Graveyard and the Record Exchange in Frederick, Maryland; David Wiggins's record shop in Galax, Virginia; County Sales in Floyd, Virginia; the Sound Garden, Books and Melodies, and Syracuse Vintage Vinyl in Syracuse, New York; Angry Mom Records in Ithaca; Academy Records in New York City; Amoeba Records and Record Surplus in Los Angeles; McKay's and the Great Escape in Nashville; McKay's in Winston-Salem and Greensboro, North Carolina; and Mr. K's in Johnson City, Tennessee.

Special props are due the readers who helped ensure a more readable and accurate text: Fred Bartenstein (who also recommended texts and lines of inquiry), Edward Brown, John Cadley, Eric Gibson, Travis Kitchens, and Leslie Bailey Streissguth. And to the photographers: Mike Clark, Doc Hamilton, Ron Petronko, Phil Primack, Fred Robbins, and Hilda Stuart.

It's been fun working again with Ben Schafer, executive editor at Hachette. His love and knowledge of popular music run deep, surfacing again and again in the guidance and encouragement he offered during the span of this project. Thanks also to Hachette's Amber Morris, senior production editor.

And always there "when the light is changing," again, is my wife and first editor, Leslie Bailey Streissguth. And Emily Streissguth, Cate Streissguth, and Will Streissguth.

Finally, I wanted to write a book that tracked Ricky Skaggs and Marty Stuart from their childhood in the shadows of bluegrass giants all the way to country music fame in Nashville in the 1980s and thereafter, knowing their stories promised to reveal untold tales, insights into their influence as musicians, perspectives on difficult social realities, and portraits of seductive minstrels and impresarios who surrounded them. And I hoped to prominently employ their voices. Fortunately, they agreed to cooperate with me. Both spent countless hours retracing miles on their southeastern circuits and beyond, journeys that reveal commitment to the soul of country music, and I am indebted to them.

SELECTED DISCOGRAPHY

Boone Creek. *One Way Track.* Sugar Hill Records, 1978.

The Country Gentlemen. *The Complete Vanguard Recordings.* Vanguard Records, 2002.

Crowe, J. D., and the New South. *J. D. Crowe and the New South.* Rounder Records, 1975.

The Earls of Leicester. *Live at the CMA Theater in the Country Music Hall of Fame.* Rounder Records, 2018.

Flatt, Lester, with Bill Monroe. *Live Bluegrass Festival.* RCA, 1974.

Flatt, Lester, Earl Scruggs, and the Foggy Mountain Boys. *The Complete Mercury Sessions.* Mercury Records, 1992.

Flatt and Scruggs. *The Essential Flatt and Scruggs.* Columbia Records, 1997.

Fogelberg, Dan. *High Country Snows.* Epic, 1985.

Harris, Emmylou. *Roses in the Snow.* Warner Bros. Records, 1980.

Harris, Emmylou, with Ricky Skaggs. *Hickory Wind.* Zip City, 2005.

Monroe, Bill. *Bean Blossom.* MCA Records, 1973.

——. *The Music of Bill Monroe, 1936–1994.* MCA Records, 1994.

Rice, Tony. *California Autumn.* Rebel Records, 1975.

The Tony Rice Unit. *Manzanita.* Rounder Records, 1979.

Skaggs, Ricky. *Bluegrass Rules!* Rounder Records and Skaggs Family Records, 1997.

——. *Don't Cheat in Our Hometown.* Epic and Sugar Hill Records, 1983.

——. *Highways and Heartaches.* Epic, 1982.

——. *Sweet Temptation.* Sugar Hill Records, 1979.

——. *That's It!* Rebel Records, 1975.

Skaggs, Ricky, and Tony Rice. *Skaggs and Rice.* Sugar Hill Records, 1980.

Stanley, Ralph, and the Clinch Mountain Boys. *Cry from the Cross.* Rebel Records, 1971.

Stanley, Ralph, and Friends. *Clinch Mountain Country.* Rebel Records, 1998.

The Stanley Brothers. *Earliest Recordings.* Rich-R-Tone Records/ Revenant, 1997.

Stuart, Marty. *Badlands: Ballads of the Lakota.* Universal South Records, 2005.

———. *Busy Bee Cafe.* Sugar Hill Records, 1982.

———. *Country Music.* Columbia Records, 2003.

———. *The Pilgrim.* MCA Records, 1999.

———. *Souls' Chapel.* Universal South Records, 2005.

———. *This One's Gonna Hurt You.* MCA Records, 1992.

Various Artists. *The Great Dobro Sessions.* Sugar Hill Records, 1994.

Various Artists. *O Brother, Where Art Thou?* (soundtrack). Mercury Records, 2000.

Whitley, Keith and Ricky Skaggs. *2nd Generation Bluegrass.* Rebel Records, 1971.

NOTE ON SOURCES

IN MY DISCUSSION of the 1964 murders of James Chaney, Andrew Goodman, and Mickey Schwerner as well as subsequent investigations and trials, I was highly reliant on a number of printed works: Seth Cagin and Philip Dray's *We Are Not Afraid: The Story of Goodman, Schwerner, and Chaney and the Civil Rights Campaign for Mississippi*, Howard Ball's *Justice in Mississippi: The Murder Trial of Edgar Ray Killen*, William Bradford Huie's *Three Lives for Mississippi*, and Florence Mars's *Witness in Philadelphia*. Mars was a native of Philadelphia, Mississippi, with deep roots in the area. A white woman, she wrote about the murders and the city's subsequent silence at some risk to her personal safety.

Periodicals such as *Bluegrass Unlimited, Country Music*, and the *Journal of Country Music* have kept a running record of country music through the decades and remain indispensable to me and others. *Country Music* and *JCM* are out of print as of this writing but still very much alive as sources in the ever-expanding country music literature.

Both Marty Stuart and Ricky Skaggs have told parts of their stories in book form. I often consulted Skaggs's *Kentucky Traveler: My Life in Music*, written with Eddie Dean, and Stuart's *Pilgrims: Sinners, Saints and Prophets: A Book of Words and Photographs* and his recent *The World of Marty Stuart*, edited by Robin C. Dietrick. Stuart's mother, Hilda, the original artistic eye in the family, has published her photography in a collection titled *Choctaw Gardens*. The vivid images she captured helped me illustrate life around the Stuart family in the 1950s and 1960s.

Finally, quotes from interviews I conducted use present-tense attribution ("she says," for example). Attributions in past tense accompany quotes from interviews previously published by other writers.

BIBLIOGRAPHY

References

Bogdanov, Vladimir, Chris Woodstra, and Stephen Thomas Erlewine. *All Music Guide to Country: The Definitive Guide to Country Music.* San Francisco: Backbeat Books, 2003.

Bufwack, Mary A., and Robert K. Oermann. *Finding Her Voice: Women in Country, 1800–2000.* Nashville: Country Music Foundation Press and Vanderbilt University Press, 2003.

Cantwell, David, and Bill Friskics-Warren. *Heartaches by the Number: Country Music's 500 Greatest Singles.* Nashville: Vanderbilt University Press and Country Music Foundation Press, 2003.

Cusic, Don. *The Sound of Light: A History of Gospel and Christian Music.* Milwaukee: Hal Leonard, 2002.

Federal Writers Project of the Works Progress Administration. *The WPA Guide to the Magnolia State.* New York: Viking Press, 1938.

Kingsbury, Paul, ed. *The Encyclopedia of Country Music.* New York: Oxford University Press, 1998.

———. *The "Grand Ole Opry" History of Country Music.* New York: Villard Books, 1995.

Kingsbury, Paul, and Alanna Nash, eds. *Will the Circle Be Unbroken: Country Music in America.* London and New York: Dorling Kindersley, 2006.

Lomax, John A., and Alan Lomax. *American Ballads and Folk Songs.* New York: Dover, 1994.

Malone, Bill, and Tracey E. W. Laird. *Country Music USA.* 50th anniversary ed. Austin: University of Texas Press, 2018.

McCloud, Barry. *Definitive Country: The Ultimate Encyclopedia of Country Music and Its Performers.* New York: Perigree, 1995.

Meade, Guthrie T., Jr., with Dick Spottswood and Douglas S. Meade. *Country Music Sources: A Biblio-Discography of Commercially Recorded Traditional Music.* Chapel Hill: University of North Carolina Press, 2002.

Rosenberg, Neil V. *Bluegrass: A History.* Urbana: University of Illinois Press, 1993.

Smith, John L. *The Johnny Cash Discography.* Westport, CT: Greenwood Press, 1985.

———. *The Johnny Cash Discography, 1984–1993.* Westport, CT: Greenwood Press, 1994.

Smith, Richard D. *Bluegrass: An Informal Guide.* Chicago: A Cappella Books, 1995.

Tindall, George Brown. *America: A Narrative History.* Vols. 1–2. New York: W. W. Norton, 1984.

Whitburn, Joel. *Top Country Albums, 1964–1997.* Menomonee Falls, WI: Record Research, 1997.

———. *Top Country Singles, 1944–2001.* 5th ed. Menomonee Falls, WI: Record Research, 2002.

———. *Top Pop Singles, 1955–1993.* Menomonee Falls, WI: Record Research, 1994.

Willis, Barry R. *America's Music: Bluegrass.* Franktown, CO: Pine Valley Music, 1998.

General

Adler, Thomas A. *Bean Blossom: The Brown County Jamboree and Bill Monroe's Bluegrass Festivals.* Urbana: University of Illinois Press, 2011.

Ball, Howard. *Justice in Mississippi: The Murder Trial of Edgar Ray Killen.* Lawrence: University Press of Kansas, 2006.

Bartenstein, Fred, ed. *Roots Music in America: Collected Writings of Joe Wilson.* Knoxville: University of Tennessee Press, 2017.

Bartenstein, Fred, and Curtis W. Ellison, eds. *Industrial Strength Bluegrass: Southwestern Ohio's Musical Legacy.* Urbana: University of Illinois Press, 2021.

Black, Bob. *Come Hither to Go Yonder: Playing Bluegrass with Bill Monroe.* Urbana: University of Illinois Press, 2005.

Cagin, Seth, and Philip Dray. *We Are Not Afraid: The Story of Goodman, Schwerner, and Chaney and the Civil Rights Campaign for Mississippi.* New York: Macmillan, 1988.

Campbell, James T., and Elaine Owens. *Mississippi Witness: The Photographs of Florence Mars.* Jackson: University Press of Mississippi, 2019.

Cantwell, Robert. *Bluegrass Breakdown: The Making of the Old Southern Sound.* Urbana: University of Illinois Press, 1984.

Caudill, Harry M. *Night Comes to the Cumberlands: A Biography of a Depressed Area.* Boston: Little, Brown, 1963.

Cobb, James C. *Industrialization and Southern Society, 1877–1984.* Lexington: University Press of Kentucky, 1984.

———. *The Selling of the South: The Southern Crusade for Industrial Development, 1936–1990.* Urbana: University of Illinois Press, 1993.

Cohen, John. *Speed Bumps on a Dirt Road: When Old Time Music Met Bluegrass.* New York: Powerhouse Books, 2019.

Delmez, Kathryn, ed. *American Ballads: The Photographs of Marty Stuart.* Nashville: Frist Center for the Visual Arts and Vanderbilt University Press, 2014.

Dent, Tom. *Southern Journey: A Return to the Civil Rights Movement.* New York: William Morrow, 1997.

Dietrick, Robin C., ed. *The World of Marty Stuart.* Jackson: University Press of Mississippi, 2022.

Doggett, Peter. *Are You Ready for the Country: Elvis, Dylan, Parsons and the Roots of Country Rock.* New York: Penguin Books, 2001.

Du Mez, Kristin Kobes. *Jesus and John Wayne: How White Evangelicals Corrupted a Faith and Fractured a Nation.* New York: Liverlight, 2020.

Ewing, Tom. *Bill Monroe: The Life and Music of the Blue Grass Man.* Urbana: University of Illinois Press, 2018.

Fleischhauer, Carl, and Neil V. Rosenberg. *Bluegrass Odyssey: A Documentary in Pictures and Words, 1966–86.* Urbana: University of Illinois Press, 2001.

Freese, Barbara. *Coal: A Human History.* New York: Penguin Books, 2003.

Godbey, Marty. *Crowe on the Banjo: The Music Life of J. D. Crowe.* Urbana: University of Illinois Press, 2011.

Goldfield, David R. *Promised Land: The South Since 1945.* Arlington Heights, IL: Harlan Davidson, 1987.

Goldsmith, Thomas, ed. *The Bluegrass Reader.* Urbana: University of Illinois Press, 2006.

———. *Earl Scruggs and "Foggy Mountain Breakdown": The Making of an American Classic.* Urbana: University of Illinois Press, 2019.

Graves, Josh. *Bluegrass Bluesman: A Memoir.* Edited by Fred Bartenstein. Urbana: University of Illinois Press, 2012.

Guralick, Peter. *Looking to Get Lost: Adventures in Music and Writing.* Boston: Back Bay Books, 2020.

Harris, Craig. *Bluegrass, Newgrass, Old-Time, and Americana Music*. Gretna, LA: Pelican, 2018.

Hembree, Mark. *On the Bus with Bill Monroe: My Five-Year Ride with the Father of Blue Grass*. Urbana: University of Illinois Press, 2022.

Hoskyns, Barney. *Hotel California: The True Life Adventures of Crosby, Stills, Nash, Young, Mitchell, Taylor, Browne, Ronstadt, Geffen, the Eagles, and Their Many Friends*. Hoboken, NJ: Wiley, 2006.

Huie, William Bradford. *Three Lives for Mississippi*. Jackson: University Press of Mississippi, 2000.

Johnson, David W. *Lonesome Melodies: The Lives and Music of the Stanley Brothers*. Jackson: University Press of Mississippi, 2013.

Kagarise, Leon. *Pure Country: The Leon Kagarise Archives, 1961–1971*. Port Townsend, WA: Process Books, 2008.

Klotter, James C., and Craig Thompson Friend. *A New History of Kentucky*. 2nd ed. Lexington: University Press of Kentucky, 2018.

La Chapelle, Peter. *I'd Fight the World: A Political History of Old-Time, Hillbilly, and Country Music*. Chicago: University of Chicago Press, 2019.

Lambert, Jake, with Curly Seckler. *The Biography of Lester Flatt: The Good Things Outweigh the Bad*. Hendersonville, TN: Jay-Lyn, 1982.

Lornell, Kip. *Capital Bluegrass: Hillbilly Music Meets Washington, DC*. Oxford: Oxford University Press, 2020.

Mars, Florence. *Witness in Philadelphia*. Baton Rouge: Louisiana State University Press, 1977.

McCord, William. *Mississippi: The Long, Hot Summer*. Jackson: University Press of Mississippi, 2016.

Menconi, David. *Step It Up and Go: The Story of North Carolina Popular Music from Blind Boy Fuller and Doc Watson to Nina Simone and Superchunk*. Chapel Hill: University of North Carolina Press, 2020.

Meyer, David N. *Twenty Thousand Roads: The Ballad of Gram Parsons and His Cosmic American Music*. New York: Villard Books, 2008.

Murphy, Reg, and Hal Gulliver. *The Southern Strategy*. New York: Charles Scribner's Sons, 1971.

Nash, Alanna. *Behind Closed Doors: Talking with the Legends of Country Music*. New York: Alfred A. Knopf, 1988.

Parsons, Penny. *Foggy Mountain Troubadour: The Life and Music of Curly Seckler*. Urbana: University of Illinois Press, 2016.

Portelli, Alessandro. *They Say in Harlan County: An Oral History*. New York: Oxford University Press, 2011.

Robins, Butch. *What I Know 'bout What I Know: The Musical Life of an Itinerant Banjo Player*. Bloomington, IN: First Books, 2003.

Roland, Charles P. *The Improbable Era: The South Since World War II.* Lexington: University Press of Kentucky, 1975.

Ronstadt, Linda. *Simple Dreams: A Musical Memoir.* New York: Simon and Schuster, 2013.

Rosenberg, Neil V. *Bluegrass Generation: A Memoir.* Urbana: University of Illinois Press, 2018.

Schulman, Bruce J.: *The Seventies: The Great Shift in American Culture, Society, and Politics.* New York: Da Capo Press, 2001.

Skaggs, Ricky, with Eddie Dean. *Kentucky Traveler: My Life in Music.* New York: It Books, 2013.

Smith, Richard D. *Can't You Hear Me Callin': The Life of Bill Monroe, the Father of Bluegrass.* Boston: Little, Brown, 2000.

Stafford, Tim, and Caroline Wright. *Still Inside: The Tony Rice Story.* Kingsport, TN: Word of Mouth Press, 2010.

Stanley, Dr. Ralph, with Eddie Dean. *Man of Constant Sorrow: My Life and Times.* New York: Gotham Books, 2009.

Stuart, Hilda. *Choctaw Gardens.* Taylor, MS: Nautilus, 2012.

Stuart, Marty. *Country Music: The Masters.* Nashville: Superlatone, 2007.

———. *The Pilgrim: A Wall-to-Wall Odyssey.* Nashville: BMG, 2019.

———. *Pilgrims: Sinners, Saints and Prophets: A Book of Words and Photographs.* Nashville: Rutledge Hill Press, 1999.

Sullivan, Enoch, and Margie Sullivan. *The Sullivan Family: Fifty Years in Bluegrass Gospel Music.* Many, LA: Sweet Dreams, 1999.

Twain, Mark. *Life on the Mississippi.* 1883. Reprint, New York: Viking Penguin, 1984.

Unterberger, Richie. *Eight Miles High: Folk-Rock's Flight from Haight Ashbury to Woodstock.* San Francisco: Backbeat Books, 2003.

Weller, Jack E. *Yesterday's People: Life in Contemporary Appalachia.* Lexington: University of Kentucky Press, 1965.

Whisnant, David E. *All That Is Native and Fine: The Politics of Culture in an American Region.* Chapel Hill: University of North Carolina Press, 1983.

Wolfe, Charles. *Kentucky Country.* Lexington: University Press of Kentucky, 1996.

Wright, Gavin. *Old South, New South: Revolutions in the Southern Economy Since the Civil War.* New York: Basic Books, 1986.

Wright, John. *Traveling the High Way Home: Ralph Stanley and the World of Traditional Bluegrass Music.* Urbana: University of Illinois Press, 1995.

Zwonitzer, Mark, and Charles Hirshberg. *Will You Miss Me When I'm Gone? The Carter Family and Their Legacy in American Music.* New York: Simon and Schuster, 2002.

Websites

digi.countrymusichalloffame.org
Discogs.com
Encyclopediaofalabama.org
Frobbi.org
Martystuart.com
mdah.ms.gov
Rickyskaggs.com
Sweetwater.com

Films

Bluegrass Country Soul. Directed by Albert Ihde. Washington Film Group, 1972.

Bluegrass Roots. Directed by David Hoffman, 1965.

Bonnie and Clyde. Directed by Arthur Penn. Warner Bros.–Seven Arts, 1967.

Country Music. Directed by Ken Burns. Florentine Films, 2019.

Deliverance. Directed by John Boorman. Warner Bros., 1972.

Harlan County U.S.A. Directed by Barbara Kopple. Cabin Creek Films, 1976.

High Lonesome: The Story of Bluegrass. Directed by Rachel Liebling. Northside Films, 1991.

The High Lonesome Sound: Kentucky Mountain Music. Directed by John Cohen. Brandon Films, 1963.

New River: A Family Musical Tour. Directed by Tom Sims. Above the Line Films, 2017.

O Brother, Where Art Thou? Directed by Ethan Coen and Joel Coen. Buena Vista Pictures, 2000.

The Sound of the Mountains. WYMT-TV, 1992.

Urban Cowboy. Directed by James Bridges. Paramount Pictures, 1980.

NOTES

Prologue

It was late spring: Historian Neil V. Rosenberg referred to the early 1950s as the "golden era" in bluegrass. Similarly, his fellow historian Bill C. Malone called those years the "classic period." Neil V. Rosenberg, "They Started Calling It Bluegrass," *Journal of Country Music* 10, no. 3 (1985); Bill C. Malone, "From Bluegrass to Newgrass," *Journal of Country Music* 10, no. 2 (1985).

"If the audience seemed": Thomas A. Adler, *Bean Blossom: The Brown County Jamboree and Bill Monroe's Bluegrass Festivals* (Urbana: University of Illinois Press, 2011), 119.

"When one of the horses": Author interview with Ron Thomason, 2019.

"In 1958, I went": Author interview with Eddie Adcock, 2019.

Flatt performed with his: Richard D. Smith, *Can't You Hear Me Callin': The Life of Bill Monroe, the Father of Bluegrass* (Boston: Little, Brown, 2000), 220; Adler, *Bean Blossom*, 122.

At home in Philadelphia: Smith, *Can't You Hear Me Callin'*, 91.

"I wanted to know": Author interview with Marty Stuart, 2021.

"You could have filled": Author interview with Stuart, 2020.

"I would go to their house": Author interview with Stuart, 2020.

"The first two people": Author interview with Stuart, 2019.

Chapter One: Get the Music Out

Musicians from as far away: "The Historically Famous Neshoba County Fair Opens Monday, July 27," *Neshoba Democrat* (Philadelphia, MS), July 23, 1959.

"Either you believe in states' rights": Joseph A. Loftus, "Mississippi Foes Assail Kennedys," *New York Times,* August 4, 1963.

Stuart's father had found: "U.S. Electrical Motors Observe First Anniversary in New Philadelphia Plant," *Neshoba Democrat* (Philadelphia, MS), December 5, 1963.

"I think Mama was my ally": Author interview with Marty Stuart, 2021.

"I remember Daddy coming in": Author interview with Stuart, 2021.

"We would get together": Author interview with Butch Hodgins, 2020.

While coffee and cake: Author interview with Stuart, 2022.

Still marveling at the: Author interview with Hilda Stuart, 2020.

"We'd be looking in": Author interview with Jennifer Stuart, 2020.

Now brandishing a Fender: Author interview with Marty Stuart, 2020.

"Marty and I were also": Author interview with Jennifer Stuart.

"We thought we were": Author interview with Hodgins.

And there were very: Author interview with Marty Stuart, 2020.

For no apparent reason: Seth Cagin and Philip Dray, *We Are Not Afraid: The Story of Goodman, Schwerner, and Chaney and the Civil Rights Campaign for Mississippi* (New York: Macmillan, 1988), 253–254; Florence Mars, *Witness in Philadelphia* (Baton Rouge: Louisiana State University Press, 1977), 78.

"In spirit, everyone belonged": Cagin and Dray, *We Are Not Afraid,* 373.

Members of the Mount Zion: Cagin and Dray, *We Are Not Afraid,* 271.

"With low wages": Harry M. Caudill, *Night Comes to the Cumberlands: A Biography of a Depressed Area* (Boston: Little, Brown, 1963), 329.

More than 20 percent: "Library Releases Illiteracy Statistics Change, Arduous Task," *Big Sandy News* (Louisa, KY), April 1, 1965.

"We never really saw": Author interview with Ricky Skaggs, 2022.

"The reason they did that": Alessandro Portelli, *They Say in Harlan County: An Oral History* (New York: Oxford University Press, 2011), 284.

"He just didn't like": Author interview with Skaggs, 2021.

Some ballad collectors: Jack Tottle, "Ricky Skaggs: Clinch Mountain to Boone Creek," *Bluegrass Unlimited,* January 1977.

"They'd buy transfers": Author interview with Larry Cordle, 2021.

"People would start gathering": Author interview with Cordle.

"People would come": Author interview with Skaggs, 2022.

"Euless could have been": Author interview with Skaggs, 2022.

"They'd get in the living": Author interview with Cordle.

"I remember Mr. Monroe": Author interview with Cordle.

"I wanted to be in": Steve Price, "Ricky Skaggs: Portrait of a Young Bluegrass Musician," *Pickin',* February 1974.

"Sometimes we would only": Author interview with Skaggs, 2021.

Chapter Two: Old Southern Leanings

"I remember waking up": Author interview with Marty Stuart, 2021.

One woman told local: Florence Mars, *Witness in Philadelphia* (Baton Rouge: Louisiana State University Press, 1977), 207.

"This is a terrible town": Seth Cagin and Philip Dray, *We Are Not Afraid: The Story of Goodman, Schwerner, and Chaney and the Civil Rights Campaign for Mississippi* (New York: Macmillan, 1988), 382.

"I remember Daddy saying": Author interview with Stuart, 2020.

Invited to join the force: Price admitted in questioning by FBI agents that Hop Barnett had recruited him into the KKK. Though he said he had joined shortly after the civil rights murders, the interviewer suspected he was lying. Interrogation transcript in Mississippi Department of Archives and History, Series 2870: Mississippi Burning Civil Rights Cases, box 34564, Cecil Ray Price Proffer.

"I think Daddy had old": Author interview with Stuart, 2022.

Though John's immediate family: Cagin and Dray, *We Are Not Afraid*, 272.

"Some of the people": Author interview with Hilda Stuart, 2020.

"Cecil's wife, Connor": Author interview with Marty Stuart, 2021.

"It was not going": Author interview with Marty Stuart, 2022.

"I would get up every day": Author interview with Marty Stuart, 2021.

Lewis recalled Stuart: Author interview with Little Roy Lewis, 2020.

"The first day of school": Author interview with Marty Stuart, 2021.

"If I knew a gospel group": Author interview with Marty Stuart, 2021.

When Stuart learned: Author interview with Marty Stuart, 2021.

"My dad spent countless": Author interview with Carl Jackson, 2020.

"The Sullivans had a": Author interview with Hilda Stuart.

"It still stands out": Author interview with Marty Stuart, 2021.

"In most of those old": Author interview with Marty Stuart, 2021.

Their rousing arrangements: Author interview with Marty Stuart, 2022.

"I can remember we'd": Author interview with Jackson.

He can't remember: Author interview with Marty Stuart, 2022.

"Enoch Sullivan was one": Author interview with Marty Stuart, 2021.

"I was really more interested": Author interview with Marty Stuart, 2021.

"They'd find the worst-looking": Author interview with Larry Cordle, 2021.

As Cordle's complaint suggests: Robert Coles, "What Appalachia Needs," *Appalachian Journal* 5, no. 2 (1978).

"If you were from": Author interview with Cordle.

Naturally, Appalachian migrants: This crossroads is discussed by Larry Nager in his essay "Sing Me Back Home: Early Bluegrass Venues in Southwestern Ohio," in *Industrial Strength Bluegrass: Southwestern Ohio's Musical Legacy*, eds. Fred Bartenstein and Curtis W. Ellison (Urbana: University of Illinois Press, 2021).

"I went ahead into": Bob Cantwell, "The Lonesome Sound of Carter Stanley," *Bluegrass Unlimited*, June 1976.

"He had everybody": Author interview with Eddie Adcock, 2019.

During the Skaggs family's residency: Ricky Skaggs with Eddie Dean, *Kentucky Traveler: My Life in Music* (New York: It Books, 2013), 73.

But not surprisingly: Jim Lantz, "Meaning, 'Nerves,' and the Urban-Appalachian Family," *Journal of Religion and Health* 3, no. 2 (1992).

"I had a very strong": Author interview with Ricky Skaggs, 2021.

"We would tape": Author interview with Skaggs, 2021.

"It put chills on": Author interview with Doyle Lawson, 2020.

Ralph Stanley lived: Author interview with Skaggs, 2019.

"We got there and": John Wright, *Traveling the High Way Home: Ralph Stanley and the World of Traditional Bluegrass Music* (Urbana: University of Illinois Press, 1995), 63.

"Ricky sounded good": Author interview with Terry Baucom, 2019.

"Ralph really wanted": Author interview with Skaggs, 2021.

"We just kind of": Author interview with Skaggs, 2021.

"After that," says Skaggs: Author interview with Skaggs, 2019.

Chapter Three: Down the Road

He asked if Skaggs: Author interview with Ricky Skaggs, 2022.

"plunged like fate into the lone Atlantic": Herman Melville, *Moby Dick* (1851; reprint, New York: Barnes and Noble Classics, 2003), 139.

"The only thing I": Jack Hurst, "Ricky Skaggs: Nashville's Next Superstar," *Chicago Tribune*, July 25, 1982.

"On some songs we": Dr. Ralph Stanley with Eddie Dean, *Man of Constant Sorrow: My Life and Times* (New York: Gotham Books, 2009), 283.

"The bluegrass festival is": Albert Ihde, dir., *Bluegrass Country Soul*, 1972.

"I got to where": Author interview with Doyle Lawson, 2020.

The corpulent promoter: Author interview with Fred Bartenstein, 2019.

"When I put on a show": John Pugh, "The P. T. Barnum of Country and Western Music," *Hustler*, November 1977.

"In an earlier stint": Author interview with Lawson, 2020.

"I had no idea it": Author interview with Bill Emerson, 2020.

"When you sit down": Interview with Carlton Haney, May 27, 2006, by Fred Bartenstein, Louie B. Nunn Center for Oral History, https://kentuckyoralhistory.org/ark:/16417/xt7qbz618g3x.

"Summertime stuff is the": "Ricky Skaggs: Boon(e) Creek to the Hot Band," *Omaha Rainbow* 17 (1978).

"I mean I could see": Author interview with Jerry Douglas, 2021.

"But Ralph never took": Author interview with Skaggs, 2019.

"I knew after a while": Author interview with Ron Thomason, 2019.

"I loved being where": Author interview with Thomason.

"The overall effect": "Record Reviews," *Bluegrass Unlimited*, May 1971.

Annotator Gary Reid: Gary B. Reid, liner notes, *Cry from the Cross*, Ralph Stanley and the Clinch Mountain Boys (Rebel Records, 2001).

"We all knew a lot": Steve Price, "Ricky Skaggs: Portrait of a Young Bluegrass Musician," *Pickin'*, February 1974.

He hustled over: Marty Stuart, *Pilgrims: Sinners, Saints and Prophets: A Book of Words and Photographs* (Nashville: Rutledge Hill Press, 1999), 17.

"He was just really": Author interview with Marty Stuart, 2021.

Sister Jennifer fluttered: Author interview with Jennifer Stuart, 2020.

"He's thinking ahead": Author interview with Hilda Stuart, 2020.

"But the first time": Author interview with Marty Stuart, 2020.

"We were in that park": Author interview with Marty Stuart, 2019.

"We didn't push him": Author interview with Hilda Stuart.

"The day we went over": Author interview with Hilda Stuart.

"After the first show": Author interview with Marty Stuart, 2021.

"My parents had to": Author interview with Marty Stuart, 2019.

"I felt like my": Author interview with Jennifer Stuart.

But in the spirit: Mark Twain, *Life on the Mississippi* (1883; reprint, New York: Viking Penguin, 1984), 68.

A fellow employee: Author interview with Hilda Stuart.

"Earl was the best": Author interview with Terry Baucom, 2019.

"Every Wednesday morning": Author interview with Little Roy Lewis, 2020.

"I don't think Earl": Author interview with Skaggs, 2019.

On the other side: Author interview with Thomason.

Along those lines: Author interview with Skaggs, 2019.

Scruggs embraced the duo's new direction: Author interview with Lanny LeRoy, 2021.

"I never will forget": Author interview with Lewis.

Chapter Four: The Soul of Bluegrass

Unlike the Nitty Gritty: Robert Cantwell, "Believing in Bluegrass," *Atlantic Monthly*, March 1972.

Bassist Johnny Castle: Author interview with Johnny Castle, 2022.

"I felt that there": Author interview with Ricky Skaggs, 2021.

"It was a big old": Author interview with Skaggs, 2021.

Larry Cordle, Skaggs's friend: Author interview with Larry Cordle, 2021.

"I was just fried": Alanna Nash, *Behind Closed Doors: Talking with the Legends of Country Music* (New York: Alfred A. Knopf, 1988), 466–467.

"They were a unique": Author interview with Bill Emerson, 2020.

"I'm sitting up there": Author interview with Skaggs, 2019.

"And that eventually led": Author interview with Emerson.

"Me and Doyle Lawson": Author interview with Emerson.

"You're up there": Author interview with Emerson.

When Emerson broached: Author interview with Skaggs, 2019.

"This quartet from": John S. Wilson, "Bluegrass Music a Bit Different," *New York Times*, May 16, 1972.

"He had been with": Author interview with Emerson.

And when the band: John S. Wilson, "New Bluegrass," *New York Times*, May 2, 1973.

"The show we did": Steve Price, "Ricky Skaggs: Portrait of a Young Bluegrass Musician," *Pickin'*, February 1974.

Skaggs's tenor vocals: Bill C. Malone, "From Bluegrass to Newgrass," *Journal of Country Music* 10, no. 2 (1985).

"He took us in a": Author interview with Emerson.

"He brought the soul": Author interview with Doyle Lawson, 2020.

"He was like sixteen": Author interview with Skaggs, 2019.

"He was really hot": Author interview with Marty Stuart, 2021.

"Some of my favorite": Author interview with Stuart, 2020.

The latest enlistee: Author interview with Haskel McCormick, 2019.

"They were monumental": Author interview with Stuart, 2019.

"You generally have": Don Rhodes, "Lester Flatt," *Bluegrass Unlimited*, October 1974.

"I don't know where": Author interview with Stuart, 2019.

"It was a salaried gig": Author interview with Stuart, 2020.

"There was a tiny": Author interview with Stuart, 2020.

"The other thing": Author interview with Stuart, 2020.

"But Lester would not": Author interview with Stuart, 2020.

"About once a year": Author interview with Stuart, 2020.

"I used to hear Marty": Author interview with Jerry Douglas, 2021.

"We played that song": Author interview with Stuart, 2017.

"This show changed": Robin C. Dietrick, ed., *The World of Marty Stuart* (Jackson: University Press of Mississippi, 2022), 64.

Apparently, the sons: Author interview with Lanny LeRoy, 2021.

Within Stuart's first three months: Author interview with Stuart, 2019.

A local newspaper's account: "Flatt to Appear Here for GOP Candidate Today," *Beckley (WV) Register Post-Herald*, November 6, 1972.

In that, Flatt: Live recording of Flatt and Scruggs show, Houston, 1966, https://frobbi.org/doch/FS66/03%20Band%20intro.mp3.

Chapter Five: Peace, Love, and Country

"Just playing with": Barney Hoskyns, *Hotel California: The True Life Adventures of Crosby, Stills, Nash, Young, Mitchell, Taylor, Browne, Ronstadt, Geffen, the Eagles, and Their Many Friends* (Hoboken, NJ: Wiley, 2006), 86.

"I tended to look": Author interview with Marty Stuart, 2019.

"So we go to this": Author interview with Stuart, 2020.

"I saw such pain": Author interview with Stuart, 2020.

"Curly became 'the guy'": Author interview with Stuart, 2020.

Banjoist Haskel McCormick: Author interview with Haskel McCormick, 2019.

"And I would ask Monroe": Author interview with Stuart, 2021.

To experience teenage Stuart's ease ff.: Carl Fleischhauer and Neil V. Rosenberg, *Bluegrass Odyssey: A Documentary in Pictures and Words, 1966–86* (Urbana: University of Illinois Press, 2001), 38–39.

"If there was a downside": Author interview with Carl Jackson, 2020.

"I was supposed to have": Author interview with Stuart, 2020.

But when the older boy: Author interview with Ronnie McCoury, 2020.

"We always, always": Author interview with Jennifer Stuart, 2020.

"My mom's father": Author interview with Jennifer Stuart.

"We had to get here": Author interview with Jennifer Stuart.

The town had hosted: John T. Toler, "The National Championship Country Music Contest," *Warrenton (VA) Lifestyle Magazine*, September 2012.

"There's going to be": Author interview with Fred Bartenstein, 2019.

"In his own way": Author interview with Richard Harrington, 2021.

According to bluegrass historian: Neil V. Rosenberg, *Bluegrass: A History* (Urbana: University of Illinois Press, 1993), 296.

"The stage was at": Author interview with Jerry Douglas, 2022.

"It was just wild": Author interview with Ricky Skaggs, 2022.

"And I walked behind": Author interview with Douglas.

When the last attendee: Toler, "National Championship Country Music Contest."

"The *Bluegrass Unlimited* crowd": Author interview with Bartenstein.

"It was a gargantuan": Author interview with Marty Stuart, 2020.

"They had piercings": Author interview with Linda McCawley Dillon, 2021.

Chapter Six: New South

"You'd see Linda Ronstadt": Author interview with Doyle Lawson, 2020.

"He'd call me": Author interview with Ricky Skaggs, 2019.

"Clearly, something unusual": Linda Ronstadt, *Simple Dreams: A Musical Memoir* (New York: Simon and Schuster, 2013), 79.

"I'm sitting here": Author interview with Jerry Douglas, 2021.

"But the difference": Daniel Cooper, "Out of the Past," *Journal of Country Music* 18, no. 2 (1996).

"Emmy was playing": Author interview with Rodney Crowell, 2021.

"I was always sort of": Author interview with Crowell.

"He certainly understood": Author interview with Crowell.

"If there wasn't a real session": Author interview with Crowell.

"That was the first time": Author interview with Skaggs, 2019.

"Ricky is everywhere": Jack Tottle, "Ricky Skaggs: Clinch Mountain to Boone Creek," *Bluegrass Unlimited,* January 1977.

"The group was kind of": Author interview with Douglas.

But in May 1974: Kenneth D. Tunnell, "The Death of Roy Lee Centers," *Bluegrass Unlimited,* July 2003.

"What happened there": Author interview with Skaggs, 2019.

Briefly stunned at: Author interview with Larry Cordle, 2021.

"He had a real certainty": Author interview with Steve Bryant, 2019.

"It's hard to mix": Author interview with J. D. Crowe, 2019.

"You couldn't get in": Author interview with Crowe, 2020.

"One night we": Author interview with Crowe, 2019.

"They advertised in newspapers": Author interview with Crowe, 2019.

"People would have killed": Author interview with Crowe, 2019.

When Lawson left Crowe: Marty Godbey, *Crowe on the Banjo: The Music Life of J. D. Crowe* (Urbana: University of Illinois Press, 2011), 108.

He suggested the young man: Author interview with Crowe, 2020.

"I called them 'grassholes'": Author interview with Crowe, 2019.

"I did not want": Author interview with Crowe, 2019.

"Of course, Ricky knew us": Author interview with Crowe, 2019.

"Ricky was sitting": Author interview with Douglas, 2022.

"Every time that I": Author interview with Skaggs, 2021.

"I had heard Jerry": Author interview with Crowe, 2019.

"Jerry's very humble": "Sweetwater Interview: Ricky Skaggs," https://www.youtube.com/watch?v=0wx9X1sVKaU&t=779s.

"I get down there": Author interview with Douglas, 2021.

"You know, I might": Author interview with Douglas, 2021.

"You don't talk": Author interview with Douglas, 2021.

Skaggs proposed stacking: Author interview with Skaggs, 2022.

"I saw Tony take": Author interview with Douglas, 2021.

In a review of the album: "Record Reviews," *Bluegrass Unlimited*, November 1975.

"I think [listeners]": Author interview with Douglas, 2021.

"When Ricky joined": Author interview with Crowe, 2020.

Chapter Seven: Close to the Fire

"We eased off": Author interview with Jerry Douglas, 2021.

"My dad had said": Author interview with Ricky Skaggs, 2019.

Guitarist and lead singer: Author interview with Wes Golding, 2021.

"I'd always heard": Author interview with Golding.

"I've got a God-given talent": "Ricky Skaggs: A Boon[e] to the Hot Band," *Omaha Rainbow* 17 (1978).

"I consider myself": "Ricky Skaggs: A Boon[e] to the Hot Band."

"Ricky always made me": Author interview with Golding.

Although the bass's propulsive rhythm: Author interview with Douglas.

"We didn't realize how": Author interview with Douglas.

"I don't remember us": Author interview with Steve Bryant, 2019.

"It is all over the": "Boone Creek" (record review), *Bluegrass Unlimited*, February 1978.

"Ricky is one of these": Author interview with Barry Poss, 2020.

"I had some very sweet offers": Author interview with Poss.

"The park's success": James C. Cobb, *The Selling of the South: The Southern Crusade for Industrial Development, 1936–1990* (Urbana: University of Illinois Press, 1993), 175.

The number of southern: Charles P. Roland, *The Improbable Era: The South Since World War II* (Lexington: University Press of Kentucky, 1975), 107–108.

"I made a statement": Author interview with Poss.

"I don't know when": "One Way Track" (record review), *Bluegrass Unlimited*, July 1979.

"It was that mountain sound": Author interview with Golding.

"One time we toured": Author interview with Bryant.

During a Boone Creek set: Author interview with Skaggs, 2022.

"It was her and a couple of guys": Author interview with Douglas.

"We fronted for her": Author interview with Terry Baucom, 2019.

It was directly: Author interview with Douglas.

"We were a band": Author interview with Douglas.

Stuart ran across: Author interview with Marty Stuart, 2021.

"Grandpa was just blazing hot": Author interview with Stuart, 2021.

"When Lester got that bus": Author interview with Stuart, 2020.

Little more than a year later: Don Rhodes, "Talking with a Bluegrass Giant," *Pickin'*, February 1979.

"I learned the effects": Don Rhodes, "Marty Stuart and Lester Flatt," *Bluegrass Unlimited*, September 1978.

"There were prescriptions": Author interview with Stuart, 2017.

"When I got to the *Grand Ole Opry*": Author interview with Stuart, 2021.

"I knew what the standards were": Author interview with Stuart, 2021.

Chapter Eight: Roses in the Snow

"They'd been playing": Author interview with Jerry Douglas, 2021.

"And it was more money": Author interview with Marty Stuart, 2019.

"He was just one of those kids": Author interview with Stuart, 2021.

"It was a long drawn": Don Rhodes, "Arthur Smith: A Wide and Varied Career," *Bluegrass Unlimited*, July 1977.

"He had a big recording": Author interview with Roy Roberts, 2021.

"One day I woke up": Author interview with Stuart, 2019.

"We played some": Author interview with Stuart, 2019.

"The Foggy Mountain Boys": Author interview with Stuart, 2021.

Whether he mulled over: Author interview with Stuart, 2022.

"Brian just made": Author interview with Douglas.

"That's in the nature": Author interview with Barry Poss, 2020.

"Ricky was a utility guy": Author interview with Douglas.

As one writer commented: Robert Kyle, "Ricky Skaggs: Moving Beyond Bluegrass," *Pickin'*, February 1979.

"Emmylou saw the gold mine": Author interview with Douglas.

"It was magic": Author interview with Douglas.

"Getting the divorce": Ricky Skaggs with Eddie Dean, *Kentucky Traveler: My Life in Music* (New York: It Books, 2013), 206.

"We called it the": Author interview with Douglas.

Harris reflected on her reaction: Patrick Carr, "Emmylou Harris: Vision and Heart," *Country Music*, January–February 1989.

As she told Patrick Carr: Carr, "Emmylou Harris."

And, says Skaggs: Author interview with Ricky Skaggs, 2019.

"Brian let me produce": Author interview with Skaggs, 2022.

"That was as much": Author interview with Douglas.

"My point being": Author interview with Rodney Crowell, 2021.

"Piles of cocaine": Author interview with Crowell.

"I knew I didn't want": Author interview with Skaggs, 2022.

"We were much more": Author interview with Poss.

"I remember the endless discussion": Author interview with Poss.

"If I could sell": Kyle, "Ricky Skaggs: Moving Beyond Bluegrass."

"If we had to do it": Author interview with Poss.

"We knew that was": Author interview with Poss.

"I didn't want to": Author interview with Poss.

On a plane bound: "Sweetwater Interview: Ricky Skaggs," https://www
.youtube.com/watch?v=0wx9X1sVKaU&t=779s.

"It's real stuff": "Sweetwater Interview: Ricky Skaggs."

"They wanted a traditional sound": Paul Kingsbury, "The Hard Realities of Hard Country: Conversations with Nashville Label Heads," *Journal of Country Music* 11, no. 2 (1986).

"And certainly for": Author interview with Poss.

"Ricky would get the major-label push": Author interview with Poss.

Breaking away from some: Bill C. Malone, "CMA Awards: Winds of Change," *Journal of Country Music* 11, no. 1 (1986).

"At times it's hard": Rich Kienzle, "Record Reviews," *Country Music*, October 1980.

Chapter Nine: New Traditionalists

"I believe in people": "Ronald Reagan's 1980 Neshoba County Speech," *Neshoba Democrat* (Philadelphia, MS), https://www.neshobademocrat
.com/stories/ronald-reagans-1980-neshoba-county-fair-speech,49123.

But come 1980: For more on the interplay between Reagan and evangelicals, consult Kristin Kobes Du Mez's *Jesus and John Wayne: How White Evangelicals Corrupted a Faith and Fractured a Nation* (New York: Liverlight, 2020).

In the 1980 campaign: Bruce J. Schulman, *The Seventies: The Great Shift in American Culture, Society, and Politics* (New York: Da Capo Press, 2001), 216.

Rosanne Cash, newly signed: Paul Kingsbury and Alanna Nash, eds., *Will the Circle Be Unbroken: Country Music in America* (London and New York: Dorling Kindersley, 2006), 336.

"The same ten or twelve guys": Author interview with Larry Cordle, 2021.

"He had come a long way": Author interview with Cordle.

"I want to give these old songs": Jack Hurst, "Racing Across the Bluegrass Field," *Chicago Tribune,* June 7, 1981.

About a year into: Jack Hurst, "Ricky Skaggs: Nashville's Next Superstar," *Chicago Tribune,* July 25, 1982.

"I was feeling": Author interview with Ricky Skaggs, 2019.

"The quality of the instrumentation": Author interview with Skaggs, 2022.

Observing that modern country music: Author interview with Skaggs, 2022.

"A lot of your bluegrass fans": Hurst, "Racing Across the Bluegrass Field."

"A lot of bluegrass people": Hurst, "Racing Across the Bluegrass Field."

"My phone rang": Author interview with Cordle.

"That thing just blazed": Author interview with Skaggs, 2022.

"It was very soulful": Author interview with Ronnie McCoury, 2020.

"This was a time": Author interview with Jim Kemp, 2021.

"Skaggs was doing Bill Monroe": Author interview with Rick Blackburn, 2005.

"I like the odd way": Ed Ward, "Ricky Skaggs Is Too Damn Country," *Village Voice,* June 17–23, 1981.

"He was attracted": Author interview with Jimmy Gaudreau, 2020.

"Keith wanted to do": Author interview with J. D. Crowe, 2019.

"I had a lot of problems with him": Author interview with Crowe.

"What an incredible singer": Author interview with Steve Bryant, 2019.

"I only used the banjo": Author interview with Crowe.

"At one time": Author interview with Crowe.

"When he got to Nashville": Author interview with Crowe.

"For the first time": Bob Allen, "Keith Whitley, New Kid in Town Finally Makes Good," *Country Music,* July–August 1988.

Skaggs had just finished up: Ricky Skaggs with Eddie Dean, *Kentucky Traveler: My Life in Music* (New York: It Books, 2013), 273.

"I was glad that": Author interview with Stuart, 2021.

"It was like Sullivan Family fun": Author interview with Stuart, 2021.

"I just happened to look down": Author interview with Stuart, 2021.

"And, so, weeks go by": Author interview with Stuart, 2004.

"I lay in bed": Author interview with Stuart, 2004.

The road was Stuart's: Author interview with Stuart, 2003.

Chapter Ten: Hillbilly Rock

"I could take one look": Author interview with Marty Stuart, 2022.

"I was fool enough": Author interview with Stuart, 2017.

"Marty was there": Author interview with Jimmy Tittle, 2022.

"Marty was something": Author interview with Tittle.

"From the day I got there": Author interview with Stuart, 2021.

"We went with Brian": Author interview with Stuart, 2004.

"It was a lot of fun": Author interview with Tittle.

"We'd make very cool basic tracks": Author interview with Stuart, 2004.

"It didn't take me long": Author interview with Stuart, 2021.

"John would just wake": Author interview with Stuart, 2021.

"But he was also respectful": Author interview with Stuart, 2006.

"And so when": Author interview with Stuart, 2004.

"When Cindy and I first": Author interview with Stuart, 2022.

"So I put Roland's son": Author interview with Stuart, 2021.

Back in Nashville: Author interview with Victor Camp, 2022.

"When the word first got out": Author interview with Stuart, 2021.

"Clarence just seemed": Author interview with Stuart, 2021.

As Cash searched: Author interview with Tittle.

But in 1993: Author interview with Stuart, 2004.

"I was on the way": Author interview with Stuart, 2004.

"We did 'My Way' at Marty's": Author interview with Tittle, 2004.

"I kept my eyes closed": Author interviews with Stuart, 2022, 2006.

"There was real magic": Author interview with Stuart, 2004.

"This is the type of music": James Dickerson, "Nashville's New Wave," *Commercial Appeal Mid South Magazine*, February 23, 1986.

"You have a real traditional": Dickerson, "Nashville's New Wave."

Although the new-traditionalist movement: Author interview with Rick Blackburn, 2005.

"I walked in the office": Author interview with Stuart, 2004.

"I found the way": Patrick Carr, "Marty Stuart: Country's Biggest Fan," *Country Music*, May–June 1991.

"Paul wrote perfect songs": Author interview with Richard Bennett, 2022.

"With this one shining effort": Bob Allen, "Record Reviews," *Country Music*, January–February 1990.

"He seriously brought": Author interview with Bennett.

Recollects Stuart: Author interview with Stuart, 2021.

"I feel obligated": *Tempted* (album liner notes), MCAD-10106, 1990, 1991.

Chapter Eleven: Who Will Sing for Me?

In the gathering heat: Author interview with Ricky Skaggs, 2022.

It was the kind of song: Bob Allen, "Record Reviews," *Country Music*, March–April 1984.

On the other hand, some artists: Mark Hembree, *On the Bus with Bill Monroe: My Five-Year Ride with the Father of Blue Grass* (Urbana: University of Illinois Press, 2022), 51–52.

"He put me on the phone": Author interview with Skaggs, 2022.

"I think they thought": Author interview with Skaggs, 2022.

"I will say that": Bob Allen, "Ricky Skaggs: That's Just the Way It Is," *Country Music*, May–June 1987.

"I just felt there": Author interview with Skaggs, 2022.

"It was just too much": Patrick Carr, "Ricky Skaggs: High Energy Meets Moderation," *Country Music*, November–December 1989.

"It seems like the Lord": Jack Hurst, "'Renko' Needed Music: Skaggs Got the Call," *Chicago Tribune*, November 25, 1984.

Every new triumph: Robert K. Oermann, Alan Bostick, and Rob Bingham, "Armed Man Caught at Skaggs Concert," *Tennessean*, June 12, 1986.

"We had some threats": Author interview with Skaggs, 2022.

"I tried to be more involved": Author interview with Skaggs, 2022.

"It will never really be over": Allen, "Ricky Skaggs: That's Just the Way It Is."

"All is not right": Allen, "Ricky Skaggs: That's Just the Way It Is."

"I . . . have these": Allen, "Ricky Skaggs: That's Just the Way It Is."

"I think part of it": Allen, "Ricky Skaggs: That's Just the Way It Is."

"I was just trying to balance": Author interview with Skaggs, 2022.

"Being outspoken about my beliefs": Geoffrey Himes, "Roots and Wings," *Country Music*, June–July 1999.

"After I left Emmylou": Author interview with Skaggs, 2019.

"It was because his music": Author interview with Skaggs, 2022.

"I felt like I was": Author interview with Skaggs, 2022.

"It was fresh": Author interview with Jimmy Gaudreau, 2020.

"Tony wanted to live the life": Author interview with Jerry Douglas, 2022.

"When he had that guitar": Author interview with Douglas.

"That's the good side": Author interview with Marty Stuart, 2021.

Outside the studio: Author interview with Stuart, 2019.

"I think if Ralph": Author interview with Skaggs, 2022.

"I really think in a lot of ways": Author interview with Skaggs, 2019.

With the beauty of such loyalty: Author interview with Stuart, 2022.

"And I thought": Author interview with Skaggs, 2022.

"And I remember just": Author interview with Stuart, 2022.

"I really felt that call": Author interview with Skaggs, 2022.

"After those first couple": Jon Weisberger, "Ricky Skaggs Rediscovers the Rules of Bluegrass," *No Depression*, November–December 1997.

"With *Bluegrass Rules*": David Duckman, "Ricky Skaggs: Bluegrass Rules" (album review), *Chicago Tribune*, October 26, 1997.

"If it hadn't have been lucrative": Author interview with Skaggs, 2022.

After Skaggs's transition: Author interview with Skaggs, 2022.

"He got out there": Author interview with Douglas.

Chapter Twelve: Which Side Are You On?

"I have never seen anybody": Author interview with Little Roy Lewis, 2020.

"Gone is the party-hearty": Bill Friskics-Warren, "'The Pilgrim' Progressing," *Washington Post*, August 11, 1999.

Nashville-based critic: Craig Havighurst, *The Pilgrim* (album review), *Country Music*, August–September 1999.

"*The Pilgrim* was the line": Author interview with Marty Stuart, 2021.

"I took time off": Author interview with Stuart, 2004.

"They were all": Author interview with Kenny Vaughan, 2021.

"It's a monster": Author interview with Vaughan.

"It's a pretty good record": Author interview with Stuart, 2004.

While Stuart pursued: Tom Dent, *Southern Journey: A Return to the Civil Rights Movement* (New York: William Morrow, 1997), 359.

"We state candidly": Howard Ball, *Justice in Mississippi: The Murder Trial of Edgar Ray Killen* (Lawrence: University Press of Kansas, 2006), 84.

"The thing I remember most": Author interview with Stuart, 2021.

"The world has seen": "Closure, yet a Beginning," *Neshoba Democrat* (Philadelphia, MS), June 29, 2005.

"That was profound": "Closure, yet a Beginning."

"It was a fun record": Author interview with Vaughan.

"Whether it's Native American people": Author interview with Stuart, 2021.

"On the bus we kept riding": Author interview with Stuart, 2022.

"I would take trips": Author interview with Stuart, 2022.

"They were doing some": Author interview with Vaughan.

"It's not an area": Author interview with Stuart, 2022.

"The cumulative effect": Geoffrey Himes, "Marty Stuart Souls Chapel, Badlands," *Washington Post*, January 20, 2006.

Epilogue

"Ricky and Marty": Author interview with Kenny Vaughan, 2021.

INDEX